The Death and Resurrection of Jesus

A THEOLOGY OF JESUS
Volume 2

The Death and Resurrection of Jesus

Donald Goergen, O.P.

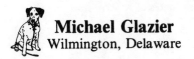
Michael Glazier
Wilmington, Delaware

First published in 1988 by Michael Glazier, Inc. 1935 West Fourth Street, Wilmington, Delaware, 19805. ©1988 by Michael Glazier, Inc. All rights reserved.

Library of Congress Catalog Card Number: 87-82343

International Standard Book Number: 0-89453-602-8

DEATH AND RESURRECTION OF JESUS: 0-89453-604-4

Typography by Laura Burke, Angela Meades.

Printed in the United States of America.

Table of Contents

To My Dominican Brothers and Sisters

PREFACE

In Volume One of this series I outlined four methodological steps that I would follow: (1) Jesus research, (2) historical retrieval, (3) hermeneutical re-construction, and (4) socioethical evaluation. With this second volume we have now completed the first of these four "moments" in the formulation of a christology: an interpretation of the earthly Jesus as prophetic preacher, teacher of wisdom, servant-victim, and as raised from the dead by the power of God.

In modern times, a false distinction can often be made between theology and spirituality. Theology must be academically credible and rational, and yet there is much more to theology than rational critical respectability alone, lest theology become "scholastic," a school's theology separated from faith and life.

As I mentioned in Volume One, theology must be professionally, confessionally, and socially responsible. Theology must also be grounded in the life of the Spirit. Theology is both scientific and contemplative. Theology and prayer are distinguishable but not separable human acts.

In Eastern Orthodoxy, the distinction between theology and spirituality is not so easily made. The articulation of faith would never be severed from the practice of the faith. Liberation theology's emphasis on praxis as a starting point in theology could only have developed as a result of Western theology. In the East theology could not be conceived as severed from life and particularly life in the Spirit. Theology is talking about God and is less credible if it does not follow from having talked to God.

In the previous volume I indicated that theology is both science and art. It involves all the critical, exegetical, hermeneutical, historical, philosophical, social, and analytical skills previously referred to. But it also involves prayer. Both theology and hermeneutics involve one's experience, but that experience includes one's experience of God in prayer.

As always, there are too many to whom I owe thanks. I shall limit myself to naming Stan Drongowski, Jerome Murphy-O'Connor, Mary Margaret Pazdan, Diana Culbertson, Priscilla Wood, Mary Fitzgerald, Ruth Mary Gendrich, Frances Plass, John Gerlach, Jim Marchionda, Dennis Zusy, Tom McGonigle, Ed Ruane, Brian Bricker, Michael Mascari, Michael Monshau, Patrick Norris, Richard Peddicord, the monks at Christ in the Desert, the staff of Parable, and my two sisters, Janet and Judy.

With respect to inclusive language, I continue to find help in *The Handbook of Nonsexist Writing* by Casey Miller and Kate Swift (New York: Harper and Row, 1980); and in Gail Ramshaw Schmidt's "De Divinis Nominibus: The Gender of God," *Worship* 56 (1982), 117-31, as well as her *Christ in Sacred Speech* (Philadelphia: Fortress Press, 1986); and also Elizabeth A. Johnson's "The Incomprehensibility of God and the Image of God Male and Female," *Theological Studies* 45 (1984), 441-65. Biblical quotations are taken from the Revised Standard Version, unless otherwise indicated, and sometimes adjusted in favor of inclusive language as justified by the Greek text.

Part One

The Death of Jesus

1

Jesus Is Crucified

Jesus still has meaning for us today, but he speaks to us out of his Galilean, Palestinian, Jewish context. He cannot be separated from the people of whom he was a part and who were a part of him. Jesus conveys to us the challenge of a prophetic religious spirit, and his teaching continues to challenge and to console. As a man of faith and prayer, in solidarity with God, Jesus was also in solidarity with the people. For it is of the essence of Jesus' God to be with the people. God belongs to the people.

Jesus' world was both Jewish and yet hellenized, which created tension both within Judaism and between Judaism and non-Jews. Judaism in the time of Jesus was pluralistic and sectarian: Sadducees, Pharisees, Essenes, as well as varied baptizing, messianic, and resistance movements—varied programs competing for the liberation, renewal, or survival of Judaism. There was a difference between life and religion in rural Galilee and in Jerusalem-dominated Judea. In both there was a gap between the rich and the poor. The presence of the Roman occupying forces was more strongly felt and apparent in Judea.

Within strict limits, Judaism was allowed self-governance. Its leadership, officially the Sanhedrin, comprised an aristocratic elite: the chief priests, elders, and scribes. The chief priests and elders were predominately Sadducean; the scribes represented both Sadducean and Pharisee interests. The reigning high priest presided over the Sanhedrin. The Jerusalem high priestly families who rose quickly to power during the Roman period exercised much power and influence. The two most powerful families in this priestly aristocracy were those of Boethus and Annas. Joseph Caiaphas, the son-in-law of Annas, was high priest from 18 to 36 C.E. The houses of Boethus and Annas could both boast eight high priests each.

The lay aristocratic membership on the Sanhedrin comprised large landowning, prominent Jerusalem-based Jewish families. The Sanhedrin was predominantly Sadducean in spite of the rise of the Pharisees after 76 B.C.E. and their membership on the Sanhedrin as well. But the priestly and lay aristocracy remained Sadducean, and the Sadducees were an economic elite and political power as well as an identifiable religious group.

Taxes were excessively burdensome, especially for the farmers, and agriculture was the most important occupation in Galilee. The abuses of taxation were complicated by the method of collecting taxes as well as by two sets of obligations—the taxes required of Jews by their Law and the taxes imposed by Rome. The foreign occupation was the dominant political fact. The wealth of most Sadducean families induced them to be politically favorable to the *status quo*. They were not suffering economically under the occupation, and peaceful co-existence was to their advantage. The Sadducees were religiously conservative as well; the basis of their doctrine was strictly the five books of Moses, the Law. The Sadducees did not believe in resurrection. The justice of God that the doctrine of resurrection had come to undergird was not their primary concern; they need not be concerned with heavenly rewards. The Pharisees by contrast were a predominantly lay movement, more popular with the people, theologically or religiously open, with a basis for their beliefs in the oral Law or Tradition; nevertheless, strictly observant, sectarian, and conscious of legal and racial purity. Although never involving a majority of the people, the Pharisees provided a program for the renewal of Judaism that contrasted with those of the Essenes and some of the baptizing sects. The Pharisees as a whole were well intentioned, faithful, practicing, zealous Jews—the future of Judaism after 70 C.E. lay with their program for renewal and reconstruction.

It is highly questionable whether there was anything like a "Zealot party" at the time of Jesus, but there was resistance to Rome, sporadic and varied uprisings, and resistance fighters. Open rebellion was always a threat, and often associated with messianic hopes for the people and the nation.

The far majority of the people were neither Sadducee nor Pharisee nor Essene, whose programs hardly reached out to their lives; they were simply the people, with diverse needs and interests, *am ha - aretz* (people of the land) who fell short of the canons of someone else's more strict observance of the Law, or were ignorant of the Law, those judged by the more righteous to be outside the Law and the pale of salvation, those without status or learning or wealth. These are the ones to whom Jesus of Nazareth had great appeal.

From among these, the crowds and multitudes who sought after Jesus for healing, for hope, for his teachings, for wonders, there emerged disciples more consciously committed to Jesus' program for the renewal of Judaism. These were among those he more regularly taught. He was their Teacher. To others he was their prophet. And to some the awaited Messiah. Not even all his disciples grasped all he had to say. Some disciples preached in association with his name; some he sent out on a mission like his own; some confused his message as much as they proclaimed it. These Galileans were inspired by him and put their hope in him. He also had his "disciples" or "friends" in Judea as well; we think of the Bethany stories in particular.

Jesus, a practicing and devout Jew himself, observant of the Law as he so keenly understood it, someone who so loved the people, and so completely loved his darling God with all his strength, this Jesus had made frequent visits to Jerusalem during the course of his life, for the great Jewish festivals. There his preaching and teaching, his prophetic spirit and actions, his reputation and following did not go unnoticed—by the people, by the chief priests, by the elders, by scribes, by resistance fighters, by the Romans. In Judea as in Galilee, the charismatic and enigmatic Jesus attracted crowds as well as friends and disciples. But the friends of Jesus were not the whole picture. In Jerusalem he surfaced an opposition as well, which was to prove to be more serious than the kind of repartee in which he engaged the Pharisees in Galilee.

The opposition to Jesus cannot be identified with Judaism as a whole, nor with the majority of Jews, nor with the more popular Pharisee party. Jesus was recognized as a prophet and sage by a vast number of Palestinian Jews. Yet it was Jesus' "fate" that his mission, ministry, message, and style would bring him into his greatest conflict with the Jerusalem aristocracy—although even here there were among the leaders those who defended him and may have been in some sense his disciples, particularly Pharisees like Nicodemus and Joseph of Arimathea. Jesus' final pilgrimage to Jerusalem was an occassion for a clash with the Sadducean leadership and with Rome. The Synoptic Gospels themselves attribute little that is negative to the Pharisees in the "trial" of Jesus.

Jesus' uncompromising integrity, radical opposition to religious hypocrisy, prophetic solidarity with the poor and social outcasts, freedom to challenge, sense of authority with respect to the Law, all contributed to an inevitable tension between his charismatic sense of mission and the more or less "legitimated" roles of the Jerusalem elite and Roman procurator. At this point it would be enviable to be a combination of economist, social scientist, cultural anthropologist, and ancient historian to be able to convey more effectively the dynamics of a society quite different from our own. We know today that there can be no quest for a historical Jesus apart from the quest to understand better from the inside that Judaism which was a part of Jesus and of which he was a part as well.[1] If Jesus was anything, he was a Jew par excellence.

---

[1]See the bibliography in Volume One of this series. One might mention in particular J. Duncan M. Derrett, *Jesus's Audience, the Social and Psychological*

We have seen Jesus in the first volume of this series as a public figure, praying, preaching, healing, teaching, attracting disciples, provoking opposition. His ministry lasted for approximately two years and was located primarily in Galilee; it ended abruptly and tragically in Jerusalem. The story of his death is one of the earliest elements of the Jesus material which we have. Yet, historiographically, it is even more difficult to assess the events of Jesus' last days than it is other points in his ministry. The individual passion narratives in many aspects confirm each other. In other aspects they make the search for history exceedingly difficult. Can all the related events be fit into the amount of time allotted? Do we know whether the Sanhedrin in fact passed the death sentence and what the precise role of the Roman procurator was? Any effort to reconstruct the final days of Jesus will remain a hypothesis. Although some hypotheses are better grounded, such efforts remain hypothetical, tentative, speculative, and most likely will continue to remain that way. This is so, given the nature of the materials at our disposal—four very convergent and yet highly individual narratives.

At one time consensus favored the existence of a very early, pre-Marcan, passion narrative. In fact, it was almost axiomatic that Mark was that passion narrative with an extended introduction. But such can no longer be assumed. There may not have been such a well organized narrative behind Mark who played an active editorial role in the construction of what appears to be his very own passion narrative.[2] Mark's narrative is the major source for

Environment in Which He Worked (London: Darton, Longman and Todd, 1973), an introductory work with an excellent annotated bibliography; and Emil Schürer, *The History of the Jewish People in the Age of Jesus Christ,* (175 B.C.-A.D. 135), 3 vols., revised and edited by Geza Vermes, Fergus Millar, Matthew Black, and Pamela Vermes (Edinburgh: T. and T. Clark, 1973).

[2]See Gerard S. Sloyan, *Jesus on Trial, the Development of the Passion Narratives and Their Historical and Ecumenical Implications* (Philadelphia: Fortress Press, 1973), an introduction to the sources, issues, and bibliography. The movement away from the existence of a pre-Marcan passion narrative and toward an emphasis on Marcan composition and redaction can be seen in H.C. Kee's *Community of the New Age: Studies in Mark's Gospel* (Philadelphia: Westminster Press, 1977), 30-32; also in the collection of essays, *The Passion in Mark,* ed.

Matthew.[3] Yet the Matthean narrative is distinctively Matthean, as well as being heavily dependent upon the Marcan narrative. With respect to Luke and John, however, the same cannot be said.[4] In these cases it appears as if we have another source or tradition and not simply Mark. Thus we can speak of three primary sources (the Marcan-Matthean, Lucan, and Johannine) for understanding Jesus' final days on earth. At the center of these sources is one central indisputable fact: Jesus of Nazareth was put to death by crucifixion outside Jerusalem while Pontius Pilate was the Roman procurator of this occupied territory. The year was probably 30 C.E.

Jesus and the Temple

There is no reason to conclude (despite the impression one can get from the Synoptic Gospels) that Jesus only went to Jerusalem once during the time of his public ministry as a preacher. As a religious, practicing, and prayerful Jew, he probably went to Jerusalem often, perhaps even annually, after the age of twelve. There was no reason for him to refrain from going to celebrate the great feasts after his baptism. Thus it is very probable that he would have gone to

Werner H. Kelber (Philadelphia: Fortress Press, 1976), esp. 8-16, 153-59, 176-80. For an introductory discussion of the Marcan passion narrative, see Donald Senior, *The Passion of Jesus in the Gospel of Mark* (Wilmington, Del.: Michael Glazier, 1984), vol. 2 in a series of four.

[3]See Donald Senior, *The Passion Narrative According to Matthew, A Redactional Study* (Louvain: Leuven University Press, 1975), esp. 1-8, 335-41. For a more introductory discussion of the Matthean passion narrative, see Donald Senior, *The Passion of Jesus in the Gospel of Matthew* (Wilmington, Del.: Michael Glazier, 1985), vol. 1 in a series of four.

[4]See Joseph Fitzmyer, *The Gospel According to Luke, X-XXIV,* Anchor Bible, vol. 28A (Garden City, N.Y.: Doubleday and Co., 1985) 1359-1531. Harold Hoehner, *Herod Antipas* (Cambridge: University Press, 1972), 224-50. A.M. Perry, *The Sources of Luke's Passion Narrative* (Chicago: University of Chicago, 1920). On the Fourth Gospel, see Raymond Brown, *The Gospel According to John, XIII-XXI,* Anchor Bible, vol. 29 A (Garden City, N.Y.: Doubleday and Co., 1970), 787-91. Note that Brown seems to favor the existence of a pre-Marcan narrative, 7887-89, a point questioned by others. See n. 2 of this chapter.

Jerusalem at least twice during the course of his ministry. And there was sufficient reason for him to carry on his mission there. Although Galilee was home base, Jesus does not seem to have limited himself to bringing the message to the Galileans. The Gospels give evidence that Jesus had close friends in Bethany. These relationships did not simply develop during the Passover week of Jesus' last days. He had been to Jerusalem, had preached and taught there, before the final visit during which he was put to death. When Jesus came to Jerusalem that last time, he was already known there.

It appears as if Jesus set forth quite resolutely on the occasion of what would be his last visit to Jerusalem. He was not unaware that danger was involved. Had he been there on a previous occasion, perhaps the year before, when he had already made enemies and created a disturbance? Was it after the opposition he had evoked on an earlier occasion that he became more and more conscious of a prophet's death? Had he become so determined to speak the truth that he knew it was unlikely that he would return alive from this visit? Yet Jesus set his face towards Jerusalem one more time, aware of danger. The disciples were perhaps more naive.

On varied occasions Jesus seems to have taught in the Temple and its vicinity. There are frequent references to his presence there (Mk 14:49//Mt 26:63; Lk 19:47; 21:37-8; 22:53; Jn 8:2; 18:20). Jesus visited the Temple, and respected its role in Jewish life. The prophet from Galilee would have been known in Jerusalem and the surrounding area. On one such occasion, after teaching in the Temple, Jesus predicted its destruction (Mk 13:1-28//Mt 24:1-2; Lk 21:5-6). In itself, this displayed no lack of respect. At the same time Jesus seemed able to envision a Judaism without the Temple. He did not seem alarmed by such a possibility. Although he did not speak of himself as destroying the Temple, his words may have reflected a callousness with respect to Temple and Jewish traditions. Did Jesus not see the Temple as essential to his faith, to Jewish faith? Whatever Jesus may have thought, the news of such a prediction would have gotten

around. The prophet from Nazareth predicted the destruction of the Temple! How would such teaching have affected
the priests? The scribes? What about the danger of such a
teaching to the people?

There is little reason to doubt that Jesus made such a
prediction. This is only one way in which the Galilean was
like the prophets of old. Jeremiah too had foretold the end
of the First Temple (Jer 7 and 26) and it was also one of the
things which had solidified opposition against Jeremiah.

Did Jesus' prediction of the destruction of the Temple
include the idea that he would be the one to destroy it, and
did it include a self-reference about its being rebuilt in three
days, as the false witnesses at the trial of Jesus maintain (Mk
14:58//Mt 26:61; Mk 15:29//Mt 27:40)? The fact that these
accusations are placed in the mouths of false witnesses
creates a problem for interpretation. There is no reason to
think that the evangelists considered the entire prediction as
something falsely attributed to Jesus. They record it sepa-
rately elsewhere (Mk 13:1-2). Thus it seems to be more the
case that Mark is saying that the Sadducees relied upon
untrustworthy testimony. What in fact may have been false
in the charge is the fact that Jesus had prophesied that he
would destroy the Temple. This does not seem to be a part of
the prediction itself (Mk 13:1-2). On the other hand, it is
easily conceivable that reports of the prediction did carry
with them the impression that Jesus himself would be
involved. Reports may have implicated him, especially after
the Temple incident. The self-reference to rebuilding the
Temple in three days may stem from something Jesus said
which was falsely interpreted and which implicated him
further, or it may be influenced in an "after the fact" way.
There is no reason to exclude the likelihood that Jesus
predicted his resurrection. The historiographical kernel,
however, is Jesus' prediction of the destruction of the
Temple, and separate teachings concerning his impending
death and resurrection.

Even more offensive, however, more alarming, was the
Temple incident recorded by all the evangelists, whatever it
consisted in (Mk 11:15-17//Mt 21:12-13, Lk 19:45-46, Jn

2:13-17). It is not easy to determine the precise character and timing of this attack or outburst on Jesus' part. Underneath it, however, there is an incident from the life of Jesus. It is very possible that this event did not occur during Jesus' last visit to Jerusalem but rather during an earlier visit.[5] The Synoptics compress all of Jesus' Jerusalem activity into one visit. Therefore the Johannine setting may be more accurate (2:13-17). If it was during an earlier visit, it could account for Jesus' assurance that there would be opposition on his next visit and for the sensitivity toward Jesus which may have already existed in Jerusalem prior to his final visit as well as for the rumors which associated Jesus with being anti-Temple. Whatever the incident consisted in, its actual character escapes historiographical precision. The nature of such an incident lends itself to unreliable reports. It is quite possible, however, that the Temple police did get involved and intervene. An action as major as what Jesus seems to have undertaken would have met resistance.

But what was the nature of Jesus' concern? Although we cannot be sure, we can conclude at least that Jesus' motivation was *religious*. Temple officials could hardly avoid taking Jesus' attack personally, however. They were the ones responsible for the Temple and current practice. Thus Jesus' attack seems to have been felt as, and probably was, an attack on the Temple priesthood, especially the high priests. The accounts record chief priests and scribes conspiring against Jesus immediately after this episode (Mk 11:18-19//Lk 19:47-8).

Yet the attack seems to have been motivated not only by a religious sense, but also by (what is inseparable from true religion) *socio-economic* reasons as well. C.H. Dodd writes, "The charge is that the priesthood was exploiting the sanctity of the Temple to make it a stronghold of a powerful

---

[5]See Etienne Trocmé, *Jesus and His Contemporaries*, trans. R.A. Wilson (London: S.C.M. Press, 1973), 110-20; Albert Nolan, *Jesus Before Christianity* (Maryknoll, New York: Orbis Books, 1978), 101-6. Raymond Brown, *The Gospel According to John, XIII-XXI*, 114-25. Also Marcus J. Borg, *Conflict, Holiness and Politics in the Teachings of Jesus* (New York and Toronto: Edwin Mellen Press, 1984), 163-200.

and exclusive faction."[6] The chief priests benefited socially and economically from their control over the Temple. It was not simply their (Sadducean) theology which was being threatened but their socio-economic power and status. In other words, it was a question of authority. Jesus, known to speak and teach with authority, and even preaching authoritatively within the precincts of the Temple itself, was challenging the very authority of the chief priests in Jerusalem, the highest "legitimate" authority within Judaism. It was not a challenge that would go unnoticed. Nor was their authority, and the power and profit it carried with it, to go unprotected. Jesus was a false teacher (to some of the Pharisees); but even more, a political and economic threat (to the Sadducees). Any earlier opposition (Pharisaic, on religious grounds) was small by comparison to this opposition, that of the Jerusalem aristocracy, for whom Jesus' outrage cut away at the very structure of established Jewish society. This is the meaning of the Temple incident. Jesus did not preach against the Temple. He respected and loved it, although he could envision Judaism without it. Jesus' attack was not on the Temple, as it had not been on the Law. His accusation was against an establishment that benefited economically from poverty perpetuated through religion. Jesus' "attack" on the Temple was prophetic and symbolic.[7]

Roman Responsibility in the Trial of Jesus

One of the major questions for Christians about the death of Jesus is why it happened. Another important question, in the light of history, and especially the history of conflict

---

[6]C.H. Dodd, *The Founder of Christianity* (New York: The Macmillan Co., 1970), 146. See also W.R. Wilson, *The Execution of Jesus* (New York: Charles Scribner's Sons, 1970), 95-101.

[7]With different emphases, both E.P. Sanders and Edward Schillebeeckx interpret the Temple incident in terms of prophetic, symbolic actions. E.P. Sanders, *Jesus, An Experiment in Christology,* trans. Hubert Hoskins (New York: Seabury Press, 1979), 243-49.

between Christians and Jews, is the question of responsibility for the death of Jesus. Christians have used Jewish involvement to fuel the fire of anti-Judaism. Thus it has become difficult to free any discussion of the trial of Jesus from biases. Jewish interpretations of the trial tend to place the responsibility on Pilate and Rome, and understandably so, given their experience of a history of anti-Semitism accompanied by the Christian charge of deicide. At the same time, Christian interpretations, including the New Testament itself, have tended to place the responsibility more within Judaism.[8] In this discussion it is more difficult than usual to get to the facts behind the interpretation. Whatever tentative conclusions we come to can in no way be a basis for anti-Semitism. Whatever the facts and course of history, no such inquiry can or should support anti-Jewish polemic. Both Roman and Jewish authorities were involved. We will approach the question of Roman responsibility first. The Romans, in fact, were the ones who executed Jesus. In what way were they responsible for his death?

Pilate was the Roman procurator at the time of Jesus' execution. He was present in Jerusalem although he ordinarily resided at Caesarea Maritima. The death sentence which was passed was crucifixion, a Roman penalty. Thus the sentence, in the end at least, was given by Pilate and implemented with the assistance of Roman soldiers.

Now the tendency among Christians, and within the New Testament itself, is to exonerate Pilate. Critical inquiry, however, challenges that perspective. What we do know of Pilate from history is that he was his own man. The Gospel

---

[8]An excellent, respected, and scholarly treatment from the perspective of Jewish historiography is Paul Winter's *On the Trial of Jesus* (Berlin: Walter de Gruyter and Co., 1961). Also see the more recent *What Crucified Jesus?* by Ellis Rivkin (Nashville: Abingdon Press, 1984). An important study of Jewish approaches to the death of Jesus is David R. Catchpole's *The Trial of Jesus, A Study in Gospels and Jewish Historiography from 1770 to the Present Day* (Leiden: E.J. Brill, 1971). See Catchpole, 296, for a listing of significant reviews of Paul Winter's work. For a balanced summary of the varied approaches to this question, see Raymond Brown, *The Gospel According to John, XIII-XXI,* 791-802. Also see Fitzmyer, *A Christological Catechism, New Testament Answers* (New York: Paulist Press, 1981), 58-62; Hans Conzelmann, *Jesus,* trans. J. Raymond Lord, ed. John Reumann (Philadelphia: Fortress Press, 1973), 82-86.

portrait is not consistent with the facts of history. Pilate
could be ruthless. Philo describes him as "naturally inflexible,
a blend of self-will and relentlessness," and refers to his
conduct as procurator in terms of "briberies, insults, rob-
beries, outrages and wanton injuries, executions without
trial constantly repeated, ceaseless and supremely grievous
cruelty."[9] There was sufficient cause for Jewish authorities to
be cautious toward him. On the occasion of one clash
between Pilate and the Jews of Jerusalem, Pilate was ready
to slaughter them but decided not to. On a second occasion,
when he appropriated Temple funds to build an aqueduct,
he had many of them beaten with clubs. Later Pilate
slaughtered a group of Samaritans.[10] And who were the
Galileans Pilate had massacred (Luke 13:1)? Pilate was not
wishy-washy, and was sensitive about his own authority,
about any potential rebellion against Rome or threat to his
political career. The historiographical data indicate a
tendency in the Gospels to minimize Pilate's responsibility.
But why?

The Gospels were written in the first century. Tension
existed between Judaism and what was at first a Jewish sect
which later became Christianity. The painful split between
synagogue and church was probably inevitable, certainly
after the decision in Jerusalem concerning circumcision and
Gentile Christians, and also after the destruction of the
Temple in 70 C.E. and the Christian lack of support for the
Jewish cause. As Christians became more and more a
missionary and Gentile church, they also had to make their
rapprochement with Rome. The Christian faith spread
rapidly throughout the Empire but it was not a religion
welcomed by Rome. Already in the first centuries there were
persecutions and the charge of treason. Thus Christians had
no need to complicate their lives, to implicate themselves as

[9]Philo, "The Embassy to Gaius" (De Legatione ad Gaium), trans. F.H. Colson,
vol. 10 of Philo, Loeb Classical Library (Cambridge: Harvard University Press,
1962), chap. 38, par. 301-5.

[10]Josephus, *Jewish Antiquities,* trans. Louis H. Feldman, vol. 9 of Josephus,
Loeb Classical Library (Cambridge: Harvard University Press, 1965), book 18, par.
55-62, 85-89.

being anti-Roman or subversive, or to do anything to lend credence to the suspicions against them. Their leader had been sentenced to death by a Roman procurator as a subversive against Rome! It was to their advantage to play down this fact, and to place blame elsewhere. Thus the sociology of the Gospels' formation helps us to perceive the unhistorical portrait of Pilate they provide.

Was there any possibility that Pilate would have wanted the death sentence? The question of Roman and Jewish involvement in the trial is related to another question. Was the offense of Jesus more political or more religious? Apart from the difficulty of separating these aspects of life within first-century Palestine, there remains the fact that Pilate could have perceived Jesus' threat in political terms even if Jesus himself did not understand his mission in this way. Any allusion to messianism would more than likely have left the impression of political messianism. The more commonly held view of the awaited Messiah contained Davidic, national, political overtones. Resisting this particular messianic claim may have been a struggle for Jesus himself. Clearly his communication in this regard was not highly effective. Even those closest to him did not understand. One of his closest companions and outspoken followers, Peter, claimed that he was the Messiah (Mk 8:29). The sons of Zebedee, James and John, both close to Jesus, did not understand the kind of reign of which Jesus spoke. Are we to assume that a large number of those who heard or followed him did not think of him eventually in messianic terms? And would not the messianic misinterpretation of his mission be a particular possibility in Jerusalem? Could the people of Jerusalem easily have seen that he was not a leader in a Galilean resistance movement?

Why did Pilate come to Jerusalem at the time of the great Passover celebration of liberation from bondage in Egypt? The celebration itself calls to mind a God who liberates people from oppression. And Pilate was no fool. He had put down Jewish rebellion before and would hold in check what even appeared to be rebellion. How was Jesus received by the Jews as he entered Jerusalem on this particular visit?

There were Jews there who knew of Jesus from previous visits. Other Galileans had come with him while still others arrived before him who now also came out from Jerusalem to greet him. They ushered him into Jerusalem triumphantly, almost defiantly, as king of the Jews. They proclaimed him as the son of David. How would all of this have been perceived by the Jewish authorities? By Pilate himself? It would be foolish to think that Pilate knew nothing of what was going on. It would have been prudent to nip things in the bud, to set up an example quickly before things went too far. Pilate would have quickly asked to have this man delivered over to him.

Whatever else may be said, Jesus was tried before Pilate and executed as a messianic pretender. This was in Pilate's question to Jesus: are you the king of the Jews (Mk 15:2)? Jesus failed or declined at this point to defend himself adequately. Pilate had little choice but to execute him as an insurrectionist. At the very least Jesus was a threat to the peace at this festival time.

Thus one can plausibly argue that the primary initiative and responsibility was that of Pontius Pilate, and the argument is not merely hypothetical. A misinterpretation of Jesus could have led the Roman occupying authorities to see him as a menance for Rome—which to some degree he was whether he wanted to be or not.[11]

---

[11]One of the better presentations opening the door to the full role of the Roman authorities is that of Paul Winter, n. 8 of this chapter. It is well worth reading in order to balance traditional approaches which downplay Roman culpability. See esp. pp. 136-48. My major criticism of the book pertains to the chapter on the enemies of Jesus, 111-35, where he goes too far in eliminating the tension between Jesus and Jews of his own day although much of what he says in that chapter is also accurate. For both critical and appreciative comments on Winter, see Catchpole, index, also pp. 105-10, 113-26, 148-86, 203-20, 261-71, 296. The effort to interpret Jesus himself in political terms is exemplified in S.G. Brandon's *The Trial of Jesus of Nazareth* (New York: Stein and Day, 1968), to a great degree a misinterpretation of the trial. For comments critical of Brandon see Catchpole, 116-26.

The Role of the Jewish Sanhedrin

Given the plausibility of Pilate's own desire to execute Jesus, is there sufficient basis for maintaining any significant Jewish responsibility at all, or do the Gospel accounts simply represent a tendency within early Christianity to place the blame on the Jews? To suggest that the Gospel narratives' inclusion of leading Jewish authorities in the proceedings against Jesus was entirely the result of the tendency in the early church to attribute responsibility more and more to the Jews may overstate a case.[12]

The Synoptic Gospels do not consider the Jewish people themselves as involved in the arrest of Jesus and the proceedings against him. The enemies of Jesus were rather the power in Jerusalem. Opposition to Jesus during his ministry is focused by the Synoptics on the tension between Jesus and some of the Pharisees. When we come to his opposition in Jerusalem, however, during his final visit, the Pharisees go unmentioned. Given the Gospels' critique of Pharisaism, it is noteworthy that blame for the death of Jesus is never associated with them. The opposition of the Jerusalem establishment is primarily Sadducean. The Gospels themselves associated the Jewish responsibility with the chief priests, the elders of the people, and leading scribes.[13] At least the first two groups would have been Sadducees, the Jerusalem aristocracy. Although the Sanhedrin at this time contained some scribes of the Pharisaic party, it was still primarily Sadducean. However formally assembled the Sanhedrin was, the opposition to Jesus would have been primarily Sadducean. Historiographically it seems reasonable to limit Jewish involvement to the upper class, the powerful Jerusalem lay and priestly families.

A further question is the degree to which the Sadducean "trial" involved a sentencing of Jesus and what the charge

---

[12]Although the tendency to associate the responsibility more and more with the Jews is present in the Gospels, one must be careful not to urge this too much. It does not account for all references to Jewish involvement. See Catchpole, 263-71; Brown, *John XIII-XXI*, 793-94; Sloyan, 36-73.

[13]Note the contrast in references in Paul Winter, 121-26.

was. Was there consensus for a death sentence? Or did they only recommend such a sentence? What power did they themselves have? This last question remains disputed and unresolved. In the Gospel of John (18:32) the Sadducean leadership passed Jesus on to Pilate because they did not have the authority to execute him. Is this historical fact or Johannine explanation? The issue is important in any attempt to assess the role of the Jewish high priest and the role of Pilate. If the Sanhedrin had the power to pass the death sentence and execute Jesus but did not do so (for they passed him on to Pilate), then it would appear as if Pilate were the enemy and the Jews were not to blame.[14]

As we attempt to understand the role of the Sanhedrin, we must raise the unanswerable question of their motive. The usual assumption is that the Jewish motivation for getting rid of Jesus rested on *religious* grounds. If so, there could have been several charges and it does seem as if a mixture of accusations appeared during the proceedings. As we have seen above, Jesus' attitude with respect to the Temple seems to have been an issue (Mk 14:57-58//Mt 26:10-61). Was it Jesus' theology of the Temple? Was it his prediction about its

[14]With respect to the Sanhedrin's power in areas of capital punishment, distinguished scholars line up on both sides. For the argument that Jews did have the right to exercise capital punishment under the Roman occupation prior to 70 C.E., see T.A. Burkill, "The Competence of the Sanhedrin," *Vigiliae Christianae*, 10 (1956), 80-96, and also "The Trial of Jesus," *Vigiliae Christianae*, 12 (1958), 1-18; Paul Winter, *On the Trial of Jesus*, 9-15, 67-90. For the opinion that the Sanhedrin did not have power over the capital sentence, see P. Benoit, "Le procès de Jésus,"*Exégèse et Théologie* (Paris: Cerf, 1961), I, 265-89, also "Jésus devant le Sanhédrin," *Exégèse et Théologie*, I, 290-311, and *The Passion and Resurrection of Jesus Christ* (New York: Herder and Herder, 1970), 113-14; J. Blinzler, *The Trial of Jesus* (Westminster, Md.: Newman, 1959); W. R. Wilson, *The Execution of Jesus*, 1-16. A significant support for this latter view is A.N. Sherwin-White, *Roman Society and Roman Law in the New Testament,* (Oxford: Clarendon Press, 1963), esp. 1-47, and "The Trial of Christ," in *Historicity and Chronology in the New Testament,* Theological Collections 6 (London: SPCK, 1965), 97-116. Catchpole, 154, writes, "The distinction asserted by Blinzler, between the right to pass a sentence and the right to execute it turns out to be entirely justified. The conclusion which seems most in accord with the evidence is that the Sanhedrin could pass sentence but that the execution could not be in their hands but was restricted by and to the Romans."

destruction? Was it the Temple incident itself? The reaction
to Jeremiah's prediction concerning Jerusalem had been,
"This man deserves the sentence of death, because he has
prophesied against this city, as you have heard with your
own ears" (Jer 26:11).

Was it Jesus' messiahship, or his sonship, that was the
issue (Mk 14:61-64//Mt 26:63-66//Lk 22:67-71)? Had Jesus
claimed to be the Messiah? Apart from Jesus' own claim, is
this how he was seen, how his ministry was interpreted, how
his disciples spoke, what the people had come to believe?
Did the high priest see Jesus as a false messiah? Or was even
the possibility of Jesus' being perceived as a messianic zealot
too great a danger? Or was the charge of blasphemy based
on the way in which Jesus spoke about his relation with
God, his own authority to act in God's name, his power over
sin, or his talk about being God's very own son? At any rate
some held that he was guilty of blasphemy.

Or was Jesus convicted for being a false prophet (Mk
14:65//Mt 26:68//Lk 26:64)? According to the Scriptures, a
false prophet was deserving of the death penalty (Dt 13:1-5).
"But the prophet who presumes to speak a word in my name
which I have not commanded him to speak, or who speaks
in the name of other gods, that same prophet shall die" (Dt
18:20). There is no question that Jesus was seen by many as a
prophet. But was he a false prophet? Was the power by
which he acted that of Beelzebub? Was his teaching false?
Did he not deserve to die?

Or was it not so much false prophecy as his attitude toward
the priesthood, or toward the high priest, even contempt of
court? "One of the officers standing by struck Jesus with his
hand, saying, 'Is that how you answer the high priest?'" (Jn
18:22). Was it the established priestly elite he threatened?
How did Jesus perceive their authority? Did Jesus not fall
under the condemnation of Deuteronomy 17:12, "The man
who acts presumptuously, by not obeying the priest who
stands to minister there before the Lord your God, or the
judge, that man shall die; so you shall purge the evil from
Israel." Both John Bowker and Edward Schillebeeckx have

given this particular text a significant role in their understanding of the trial of Jesus.[15]

Or was Jesus' offensiveness to the Sanhedrin and threat to
the aristocracy something other than religious? Is it a valid
assumption that Jewish opposition was more religious than
political? While we generally grant that Pilate's motive was
political, perhaps the Sanhedrin's motive was also and
equally political. Was Jesus worth the risk of the Jewish
revolt, of a Roman slaughter, or Roman reprisals in the
sacred city, of potential loss of rights? Pilate was justifiably
to be feared. It may well be such fear rather than any
particular religious offense that was the final straw.

Or could the aristocracy's motivation have been even
more so *socio-economic?* The Sadducees were as much a
socio-economic elite as they were a religious party and these
interests seemed at stake. Jesus was unafraid of Herod in
Galilee, and unafraid of the high priesthood in Jerusalem.
His religious teaching and practice appeared to threaten
their social status and position in Judaism. Did not his
attack on Temple practice affect both their authority and
their source of revenue? Did not his political menace
threaten their preferential position with Pilate? How could
Caiaphas remain high priest for an unusual length of time,
during the entire procuratorship of Pilate, without being
careful not to anger or fail him? Was it for Caiaphas, or
Annas, a question of "better for one to die for the nation" or
"better for one to die than for us to go under?"

In the end, of course, one cannot on historiographical
grounds decide what motive may have most influenced the
chief priests, elders, and scribes. It is probable that all or a
variety of motivations and accusations came into play. One
was offended by Jesus' seeming blasphemy, another by his
seeming indifference to their authority, another by the
political risk they faced, another by sensitivity to position

[15]John Bowker, *Jesus and the Pharisees* (Cambridge: University Press, 1973),
42-52. Bowker writes, "The major category of offense into which Jesus appeared to
fall was that of the so-called 'rebellious elder'" (46). See Schillebeeckx, *Jesus,*
312-18, for his interpretation of Jesus' trial.

and power, another by false teaching. Probably many factors played a role and there may have been no one formal charge. Likewise there may have been no formal passing of the death sentence. Some may have argued that Jesus deserved to die but there may or may not have been consensus about either the charge or the sentence. The session(s) may or may not have been formal proceedings. But something about which there was agreement was the decision to pass Jesus over to Pilate. Whether they were passing the buck, or plotting for a death sentence, or seeking an execution of a sentence already passed, we will never know. What seems clear, however, is that some of the leaders of the Sanhedrin were involved.

Who Was Responsible?

We have seen solid reasons for not dismissing or diminishing Pilate's role in the proceedings against Jesus. Pilate was not simply a servant of the Jewish court, or at the mercy of the high priest. If anything, the reverse was the case. Pilate was quite able to assert his own authority; he was the Roman procurator in Judea; he was in Jerusalem on this occasion precisely out of concern for Roman interests.

At the same time there are solid reasons for not dismissing the role of the chief priest, and other high priests, along with some of the elders in the Jerusalem aristocracy, and some of the scribes, whether or not their own proceedings had the character of a formal trial or not. Here it is not a question of the Jewish people, nor the Pharisees, but of some of the leading authorities who where more or less Sadducean in sympathy. The Pharisees at this period had membership in but did not control the Sanhedrin. Nor can we say for sure that there was a formal trial of the Sanhedrin.

Thus any discussion of the responsibility for the sentence against Jesus is not a question of either/or, but a question of *both* Pilate's *and* Caiaphas' roles. The historical truth lies somewhere between. Further than this we cannot really go on historiographical grounds. We must reconcile ourselves to the inconclusiveness of all hypotheses. Among such hypotheses, we find: (1) the "misunderstanding" theory, based on Mark 12:17 and John 18:37. Jesus preached a non-political reign of God, but many, including his disciples, misunderstood him. Hence Jesus was perceived as a political menance and action was taken against him only because his message and activity were misunderstood. Initiative against Jesus here could have come from either Jewish or Roman authorities. (2) It may be that Pilate had ordered the high priest to arrest Jesus and hand him over, having heard rumors and reports concerning Jesus. Jewish deliberation was then a question of whether Jesus deserved to die, and whether they in fact should hand him over. This seems to have been one thing on which they agreed: hand Jesus over to Pilate lest the nation be destroyed. The politically wise decision was to collaborate with Rome. (3) It may be that Caiaphas had become concerned about the Jesus case and took the initiative. He may have misunderstood Jesus' political aims, or may have had other reasons to see Jesus as a danger to the nation. Jesus was dangerous to Judaism itself, and to priestly authority within Judaism. Thus Caiaphas' manifold fears led him in consultation with others to apprehend Jesus and to hand him over either as a preventative measure before Pilate became alarmed and to prove his own loyalty, or to get rid of Jesus who deserved to die according to the Law. In all these situations there were varied degrees of misunderstanding or misinterpretation on the part of Jewish and Roman authority. (4) The "popular unrest" theory in which Jesus is not so much misunderstood but recognized as posing a real threat. Jesus was not a zealot, nor did he have nationalistic political goals in mind, but because of his effect on the people he was nevertheless a political risk. Again here, as in the case of misunderstanding, the initiative for the arrest could have been with Pilate (as in 2 above) or with the chief priests (as in 3 above).

So, did Pilate exert pressure on Caiaphas, for whatever reasons, or did the Jewish authorities exert pressure on Pilate? We cannot know. Nor is there any way to know whether the action taken against Jesus was due to his being more a religious threat, a political threat, or an economic threat. Moreover, these are not easily distinguishable. Prophetic religion has socio-economic and political implications, and Jesus was a prophet, and more.[16] Perhaps our need to place blame at all is itself the fault. If our concern is with responsibility, we cannot finish such a discussion by surveying only Roman and Jewish involvement. We must raise the issue of the disciples' responsibility for Jesus' death. For were not Jesus' followers and disciples also equally at fault? And is not this image of his disciples part of the passion narratives as well?[17] The disciples were responsible, right up to the end, (a) for misrepresenting Jesus' cause and (b) for deserting Jesus and failing to come to his defense. How often did his closest disciples fail to understand Jesus' teaching about the (reign of) God to come (Lk 22:24-30//Mk 10:35-45//Mt 20:20-28)? How often did the people try to make him a king? Did not the disciples desert Jesus after his arrest? Could they not have brought testimony and witness in his favor? It was not only Judas who betrayed Jesus (Mk 14:10-11). Peter's betrayal is told in all four Gospels (Mk 14:66-72, Mt 26:69-75, Lk 22:56-62, Jn 18:25-27). And who is seen as betraying Jesus more, the high priest or Peter in the narrative of the Sanhedrin trial (Mk 14:53-15:1)? Who was more responsible, those who arrested him or those who deserted him? And is Peter not symbolic of all the disciples? The three disciples particularly close to Jesus are hardly models in Gethsemane (Mk 14:32-42). All the disciples protested "too much" that they would not deny Jesus (Mk 14:31), and twenty verses later "all forsook him and fled" (14:50). Whatever the disciples did, wherever they went, they were not with Jesus when he went through this ordeal (another wilderness) alone (Jn 16:32). If blame is to be assessed, Jesus' disciples as well as Jesus' opposition are to blame—and not one more than the other. We cannot defend the disciples who followed after Jesus in his life, but

---

[16]See A.E. Harvey, *Jesus and the Constraints of History* (Philadelphia: Westminster Press, 1982), 11-35, esp. 30-35. The decision to hand Jesus over was moreso political and judicial. Yet there may have been other underlying motives as well.

[17]See Schillebeeckx, *Jesus*, 320-9.

when the time came for them to go "into the wilderness" were not present.

The catch in any discussion of responsibility or guilt for the death of Jesus lies in our somewhat perverse need to assign blame. There is something significant in the passion narratives' inability to enable us definitively to blame anyone. Luke records a final perspective on the whole ordeal: "Father, forgive them" (Lk 23:34).[18] Forgive the Judases, the Peters, the Caiaphases, the Pilates. The desire to fix guilt is a direct contradiction to the teaching of Jesus as interpreted in the Fourth Gospel: Let the one without guilt cast the first stone (Jn 8:7). Also, attend to the two by four in your own eye before you inspect the sliver in your neighbor's eye: judge not lest you be judged (Mt 7:1-5). The purpose of the passion narratives is not to affix blame but to convey the passion of the passionate one, Jesus' ongoing call to an ordeal in the wilderness. The passion narratives tell the end to which Jesus' life and ministry came: a tragic one. Jesus is *the victim* of a variety of factors, including his own free choices. It is almost as if the power and forces of evil have won out. This man, who was God's man, in solidarity with God, and in solidarity with the people, and who was so completely a man for others, was sentenced to a cruel death. But will his cause die with him? Is the power of evil more powerful than the power of good?

A Death By Crucifixion

The more typical mode of execution among the Jews was death by stoning, although burning and slaying are also mentioned in the Hebrew Scriptures. There is some evidence

---

[18]There is a difficulty regarding Luke 23:34a. It is reasonable to hold on the grounds of textual criticism that the words do not belong to the original text of the Gospel of Luke. See Fitzmyer, *The Gospel According to Luke, X-XXIV*, 1503-1504.

for the use of crucifixion among the Jews, although it was never a typical Jewish method of execution. After being stoned to death (Lk 24:14), someone condemned for blasphemy or idolatry was also hanged, publicly exposed (Dt 21:22-3, Jos 10:26).[19]

Crucifixion was a method of execution commonly used by the Romans, widespread in the ancient world and was also used among the Greeks.[20] Among the Romans it was particularly used on the lower classes, for slaves, violent criminals, and rebels in the outlying provinces. As a public execution, degrading and brutal, it was considered an effective deterrent. After the sentence was passed, the condemned person was frequently flogged and scourged as well. Although the method of crucifixion varied, commonly a heavy wooden beam was placed upon the condemned person's neck and his arms stretched out and fastened to it. He was led thus to the place of execution where he was lifted up and the beam secured on another vertical one sufficiently

[19]The degree to which crucifixion was ever practiced among the Jews remains a disputed question. There is evidence of its use, but it does not appear to have been a common method of executing the death penalty. See Paul Winter, 62-74, for the thesis "that a sentence of death carried out in Judaea in the first century of our era by the mode of crucifixion was a sentence which had been passed by a Roman authority" (62). Fitzmyer maintains that "it is far from clear that crucifixion was never employed by Jews in Palestine," *A Christological Catechism,* 62. See Fitzmyer, "Crucifixion in Ancient Palestine, Qumran Literature, and the NT, *Catholic Biblical Quarterly,* 40 (1978), 493-513, esp. 503-4; also in *To Advance the Gospel, New Testament Studies* (New York: Crossroad, 1981), 125-46. A.E. Harvey writes, "We can say with absolute confidence that at the time with which we are concerned this form of execution in a Roman province could have been carried out only by the Roman officials, and only on the orders of the Roman governor" (*Jesus and the Constraints of History,* 12). For Jewish death sentences, see Gustaf Dalman, *Jesus-Jeshua* (New York: Ktav Publishing Co., [1929] 1971), 185-95; Paul Winter, 67-74. Also Josef Blinzler, "The Jewish Punishment of Stoning in the NT Period," 147-61, and Ernst Bammel, "Crucifixion as a Punishment in Palestine," 162-66, both in *The Trial of Jesus,* ed. Bammel, Studies in Biblical Theology, Second Series, 13 (Naperville; Alec R. Allenson, 1970).

[20]The best treatment on crucifixion in the ancient and Roman worlds available in English is Martin Hengel's *Crucifixion* (Philadelphia: Fortress Press, 1977). Also see Paul Winter, 62-66.

high so that his feet hung suspended in air. The arms were usually tied to the cross beam, though nails were sometimes used. The feet were left dangling, or sometimes fastened by ropes. The man was usually stripped, which added to his disgrace. As he weakened and was unable to support himself, the weight of his body pulled him down and death eventually came by suffocation.

It is hard for us to imagine the disgrace that Jesus' death involved for his contemporaries, Jews, Greeks and Romans. He was given the death sentence and executed in what was considered a most barbaric and brutal way. One can imagine what a "stumbling block" (1 Cor 1:23) this fact would be for the proclamation of the gospel. The early Christians were offering a condemned criminal, a crucified messiah, as the source of hope and salvation. Needless to say, it made of them a laughing stock in both Jewish and Gentile worlds. It is easy to see why interpreting, understanding, theologizing on the death of Jesus was one of the earliest and most difficult tasks of early preaching.

Anyone in the Roman world could easily refute or mock the Christian movement simply by reference to the cross of Jesus. What has become to us a sign of salvation would have been seen as simply folly, madness. When Paul "points out to the commuity which he founded that his preaching of the crucified messiah is a religious 'stumbling block' for the Jews and 'madness' for his Greek hearers, we are hearing in his confession not least the twenty-year experience of the greatest Christian missionary who had often reaped no more than mockery and bitter rejection with his message .... "[21]

Crucifixion can be contrasted with the "popular entertainment" of throwing people to the wild beasts. The latter was not a regular form of execution; crucifixion was much more common. Both, however, provided entertainment.

[21]Hengel, *Crucifixion*, 19.

Crucifixion was also more agonizing; the process of death could take several days. Often the victim was left to rot and was not buried. The family and relatives shared in the public disgrace. Crucifixion means little today other than to turn our thoughts to Jesus. In the first century, however, it evoked a sense of shame, whether in the East or West. The Christians' "Christ" and "Lord" had been sentenced to a shameful death by legitimate authority, a death reserved for lower class criminals, rebellious slaves, and rebels against Rome. This fact was a scandal which made "Jesus crucified" a stumbling block, madness, a challenge to be interpreted. This was the end of his life to which his faith, his mission, his ministry, his God had brought him. How were his disciples to feel or understand what had happened?

History and Its Interpretation

There are few facts about Jesus of Nazareth as historiographically unassailable as is the historicity of Jesus' death by crucifixion during the procuratorship of Pontius Pilate, 26-36 C.E. Jesus was probably crucified in April of 30 C.E.[22] At the same time there are few facts about Jesus of Nazareth more subject to interpretation. Although all the evangelists provide us with detailed historical information, none of them are primarily interested in a historical account as such. Few events in the life of Jesus were more important in the

---

[22]The dates 30 and 33 C.E. are the two dates for which there is support. More common is 30 C.E. See Conzelmann, *Jesus,* 23-25; Samuel Parsons, "The Mission of Christ," in Thomas Aquinas, *Summa Theologiae* (New York: McGraw Hill, 1971), vol. 53, 181-86. Hoehner, *Herod Antipas* (Cambridge: University Press, 1972), favors the year 33 as the date of the crucifixion, see pp. 171, 130-31, 180-83. The term of Pontius Pilate as procurator was 26-36 C.E.

life of the church or more subject to its theologization. This is why any effort at a chronology of these events will always remain a hypothesis.[23] To understand the passion narratives is to realize that one is not being given a report of events so much as an invitation to penetrate the meaning of that event, to understand it. The event is simply the death, and death by crucifixion, of God's chosen one. How does one make sense of that? We must remember that all our accounts of Jesus' death have come to us as interpreted in the light of the resurrection, and this has made all the difference in the world. The resurrection turned defeat into victory, disillusionment into hope. How different the narratives and interpretations would be, had there been no resurrection. What the disciples of Jesus experienced and understood after Jesus was apprehended and crucified but prior to his appearance to them was bewilderment, confusion, fear, sadness.

Thus we need not attempt to reconstruct what was even in history primarily a task for hermeneutics. With the death of Jesus, his *history became inseparable from hermeneutics* - a fact which has been true ever since and which makes any purely historiographical approach to his life inadequate. His "history" cannot be presented factually; his "Historie" is "Geschichte."[24] This man cannot be understood, even as a

[23]This does not mean that efforts to establish such chronology are without value. It simply means that they remain tentative and hypothetical. One of the more discussed chronological problems pertains to whether Jesus' last meal with his disciples was in fact a paschal/passover celebration and whether he celebrated this meal on Tuesday or Thursday evening. An earlier celebration and arrest allows more time for many of the events "compressed and telescoped" by the evangelist into less than one day and has a basis in the dispute over the calendar and thus the date of the Passover. For further discussion of this alternative of a chronology of three days, see Annie Jaubert, *The Date of the Last Supper* (Staten Island, New York: Alba House, 1958/1965), whose hypothesis formed the basis for later discussions; Matthew Black, "The Arrest and Trial of Jesus and the Date of the Last Supper," *New Testament Essays, Studies in Memory of T.W. Manson*, ed. A.J.B. Higgins (Manchester: University Press, 1959); Eugene Ruckstuhl, *Chronology of the Last Days of Jesus* (New York: Desclée Co., 1965).

[24]A further discussion of the distinction between "Historie" and "Geschichte" is contained in chapter six. See pp. 196-97.

historical phenemenon, by historiography alone. Thus history itself cannot be understood by historiography alone, but requires hermeneutics.

Jesus of Nazareth, the prophet and sage from Galilee, was taken into custody either by Roman soldiers, Jewish guards, or both. He was probably apprehended by Jewish officials, although we do not know who in fact took the initiative to order the arrest. He was then taken and held prisoner in the house of the high priest, Caiaphas. Perhaps prior to that he had been taken to the house of Annas for an unofficial preliminary questioning. Or perhaps such unofficial proceedings took place at the house of Caiaphas. This interrogation was not an official session of the Sanhedrin.

Early the next morning a definitive action was taken by the chief priests, elders, and scribes who had gathered to discuss the case. He was to be sent to Pilate. We cannot determine whether or not the morning session was an official session of the Sanhedrin either. We do not know whether it formally arrived at a death sentence. All we know is that the consensus was to turn Jesus over to the jurisdiction of Pilate. The case thereafter remained under the control and in the hands of Pilate. He may have had Jesus transferred to Herod to see whether Herod had any comment to make. But Pilate issued the death sentence on the grounds that Jesus was a potential rebel who claimed to be king of the Jews. Pilate ordered the customary preliminary scourging after which Jesus was led to the place of execution outside the walls and crucified. He died, a false prophet and false messiah. On Golgotha, his life on earth ended.[25]

[25]Most of the authors on whom this sequence of events depends have been mentioned. See especially W.R. Wilson, *The Execution of Jesus* (New York: Charles Scribner's Sons, 1970), for a fine readable introduction to the trial; and J. Blinzler, *The Trial of Jesus* (Westminster, Md.: Newman, 1959); David Catchpole, *The Trial of Jesus,* esp. 261-71; and Paul Winter, *On the Trial of Jesus,* esp. 136-48, for more advanced treatments. For a collection of valuable essays, see *The Trial of Jesus,* edited by Ernst Bammel, Studies in Biblical Theology, Second Series, 13 (Naperville: Alec R. Allenson, 1970), esp. the essays by Catchpole, "The Problem

The task of interpretation now begins—not interpretation as propaganda, but interpretation as understanding. Was Jesus a false prophet or a true prophet? Did Jesus ever claim to be Messiah, was he a false messiah, or was he truly a messiah? If a true prophet, how does one understand God's seeming abandonment of him?[26]

of the Historicity of the Sanhedrin Trial," 47-65; J.C. O'Neill, "The Charge of Blasphemy at Jesus' Trial Before the Sanhedrin," 72-77; Harold Hoehner, "Why Did Pilate Hand Jesus over to Antiphas? 84-90. Also see Harold Hoehner on Pilate and Herod in his *Herod Antipas,* 224-50.

[26]Schillebeeckx identifies three early efforts to understand the death of Jesus: (1) Jesus died the death of a prophetic martyr, (2) Jesus' death is included within God's plan of salvation as part of salvation-history, and (3) Jesus' death has a saving efficacy. The first of these was probably the earliest interpretation. See Schillebeeckx, *Jesus,* 272-319; also *Christ, The Experience of Jesus as Lord,* trans. John Bowden (New York: Seabury Press, 1980), 823-32. Also Wolfhart Pannenberg, *Jesus-God and Man,* trans. Lewis L. Wilkins and Duane R. Priebe (Philadelphia: Westminster Press, 1968), 246-51; Norman Perrin, *Rediscovering the Teaching of Jesus* (New York: Harper and Row, 1967), 181-85.

2

Jesus, Servant Of The Lord

In approaching any historical figure, we go back and forth between fact and interpretation, between data and understanding. Although these can be distinguished, they are in the end inseparable. What we ultimately seek in our pursuit of history is not fact alone, but understanding. Even when we approach the historical Jesus or the Jesus of historiography we still interpret in order to understand. In the previous volume we interpreted Jesus of Nazareth as a prophet and sage. We did so in order to understand his role in history.

I now suggest an additional interpretative category: Jesus as servant of the Lord. In speaking of him as a servant we are not setting aside but rather including our previous understanding of Jesus as both prophet and teacher.

Just as words like prophet, preacher, healer, teacher have a history, so does the word "servant." Jesus as healer was not like a twentieth-century physician. Nor was Jesus as teacher like a university lecturer or twelfth-century commentator. So likewise the word "servant" must be understood before we can use it to understand Jesus.

First, we will consider the background to the Israelite concept of servant. Second, we will look at four Deutero-Isaian servant poems. Third, we shall look at the data in the history of Jesus himself which urge us to speak of him as a servant of the Lord.

The Concept of Servant

Throughout the Hebrew Bible, the servant is the servant *of the Lord,* one whose life is lived in unfailing obedience to the Lord, one who does the will of the Lord, who lives in accord with the covenant of the Lord and the word of the Lord. Servanthood is obedience (Jer 7:23, 11:5).[1]

As the theology of suffering developed in Israelite and Judean history, it became more clear that sometimes suffering was a part of obedience to the Lord. Not all suffering was the result of a divine vocation and servanthood, nor does all obedience involve the call to suffering. However, sometimes the servant had to suffer. Not that suffering was desired by God, but that suffering was inevitable if the mission of God was to be accomplished. This suffering servanthood is the theology of servanthood which we find in the first three of the deutero-Isaian servant songs. Jeremiah is a supreme exemplification of this type of servanthood.[2]

Jeremiah was called by the Lord to be a prophet to Judah and to the nations during the final years of Judah's history prior to the Babylonian captivity, during the reigns of Josiah, Jehoiakim, and Zedekiah. He was called to be the Lord's prophet, the Lord's servant. This was in spite of his own resistance, his own distaste for the vocation (Jer 1:4-8). In spite of his resistance, Jeremiah was seduced by the Lord and accepted his call.

---

[1] W. Zimmerli and J. Jeremias, *The Servant of God,* SBT (Naperville: Alec Allenson, Inc., 1957) provides coverage of the servant concept in general, the four Deutero-Isaian songs in particular, as well as the meaning and use in early Judaism and the New Testament period.

[2] For a discussion of Jeremiah, see particularly John Bright, *Jeremiah,* Anchor Bible 21 (Garden City, N.Y.: Doubleday and Co., 1965). Although I quote from "Jeremiah's Confessions" in the text (e.g., 20:7, 15:10-11, 20:14-18), I am aware that the biographical information they provide is a disputed issue and that some exegetes interpret them as a product of later reflection on the exile.

> O Lord, thou hast deceived me, and I was deceived; thou
> art stronger than I, and thou hast prevailed. I have
> become a laughingstock all the day; everyone mocks me.
>
> (Jer 20:7)

From that moment onward, Jeremiah's life was one of
fidelity and obedience to the Lord. He was not yet twenty
when he was called and he continued to speak the Lord's
word until he was almost sixty years of age (from 627 until
after 587 B.C.E.). Jeremiah's obedience to the Lord brought
only one suffering after another throughout his life. There
was no respite (Jer 4:19-22, 11:19, 15:10-18, 20:1-18). Jeremiah was like Job (contrast Jer 20:14-18 and Job 3). The
people would not listen to him. His ministry seemed in vain.
He was repeatedly maltreated. Yet he continued to speak out
against the worship of false gods and the apostasy of the
people (Jer 2 and 3; 5:30-31; 14:14; 23:13-14, 16-17, 30). He
continued to speak out against the social injustices which
were a violation of the covenant with the Lord (Jer 5:1, 28,
30-31; 7:5-7; 22:3). He continued to call for interior repentance, the circumcision of the heart (Jer 4:4, 9:25-26, Dt
10:16). He even had the ill fortune of having to advise
surrender on the part of the chosen people to Nebuchad-
nezzar of Babylon (Jer 25:9, 27:6). He proclaimed the
destruction of Jerusalem, God's own city (Jer 9:11; 26:6;
38:4-5, 52). Jeremiah was judged to be both a traitor and a
heretic (Jer 26). This was the fate to which the Lord had
called him.

We can allow the pain of Jeremiah to speak for itself:
"My anguish, my anguish! I writhe in pain!" (Jer 4:19). But
there was no peace for this faithful servant. Ill begotten was
he who would have to preach the word of the Lord at this
time and place in history. Jeremiah himself knew that only
too well.

> Woe is me, my mother, that you bore me, a man of strife
> and contention to the whole land! I have not lent, nor
> have I borrowed, yet all of them curse me. So let it be, O
> Lord, if I have not entreated thee for their good, if I have

> not pleaded with thee on behalf of the enemy in the time
> of trouble and in the time of distress!   (Jer 15:10-11)

Jeremiah's vocation was one of prophecy and preaching, a ministry of the word. But it was a vocation to suffering, loneliness, inconsolable grief, anguish, imprisonment, pain and rejection as well. This was what the Lord had called him to by calling him to speak God's word. And the human soul of Jeremiah could only cry out.

> Cursed be the day on which I was born! The day when my
> mother bore me, let it not be blessed! Cursed be the man
> who brought the news to my father, "A son is born to
> you," making him very glad. Let that man be like the cities
> which the Lord overthrew without pity; let him hear a cry
> in the morning and an alarm at noon, because he did not
> kill me in the womb; so my mother would have been my
> grave, and her womb forever great. Why did I come forth
> from the womb to see toil and sorrow, and spend my days
> in shame?   (Jer 20:14-18)

Few texts of the Hebrew Scriptures move us as deeply or portray as completely the theology of suffering servanthood.

The servant in the Israelite tradition was anyone who did the will of the Lord, whose life is the prayer "Thy will be done." That ought at least be the king, the prophet, the priest, the sage, but also every Israelite or Jew, as well as the nation as a whole. Obedience characterized the Lord's servant. Sometimes that obedience was inseparable from suffering and rejection. The theology of the servant continues to be developed in the theology of the second Isaiah.

The Deutero-Isaian Servant(s)

The word "servant" has varied meanings, not only within the Bible, but even within Deutero-Isaiah. Walther Zimmerli points to five specifically religious uses of the word in Scripture: the self-description of the humble in the presence of the Lord; the pious; Israel; specific figures in Israel such as the patriarchs, Moses, the king, the prophet, Job; and the suffering servant of Deutero-Isaiah.[3] In Deutero-Isaiah, outside the four texts known as the servant songs to which we will shortly refer, the servant refers to Israel. The image of the servant in the four specific texts of our concern, however, goes beyond the image in the rest of Deutero-Isaiah in that the servant does not always appear to be simply Israel. Sometimes the servant has a mission to Israel.

The problems connected with critical exegesis of these four texts are many and there is little unanimity on most of the issues. For our purposes the critical issues are less pertinent than the theology (or theologies) of the "songs." Nevertheless, a summary of some of these issues may be helpful. Although there is discussion about which verses actually comprise the servant songs and how these are to be divided, scholars generally agree that the four servant songs comprise 42:1-4; 49:1-6; 50:4-11; 52:13 to 53:12.

First we should consider the question of authorship. Although all four texts are found within the corpus attributed to Deutero-Isaiah (Is 40-55), they form a sufficiently distinct unit from the rest of the prophecy and raise special problems. Sigmund Mowinckel argues for an authorship later than Deutero-Isaiah, very possibly the circle of which Trito-Isaiah was a member.[4] On the other hand, Christopher North argues for Deutero-Isaian authorship on the grounds that the relation of the songs to their contexts, their vocabulary, their metrical forms and their theological content do not necessitate an author other than Deutero-Isaiah.[5] North concludes that the songs are by Deutero-Isaiah, that there was a common author for all of them, that they represent development in the prophet's thought, and that

---

[3]Zimmerli and Jeremias, *The Servant of God*, 13-34.

[4]Sigmund Mowinckel, *He That Cometh, The Messiah Concept in the Old Testament and Later Judaism*, trans. G.W. Anderson (Nashville: Abingdon Press, 1954), 241-46, 253-55.

[5]Christopher North, *The Suffering Servant in Deutero-Isaiah* (London: Oxford University Press, 1956), 156-89.

they were not all composed at the same time.

The issue of authorship is closely related to the issue of how distinctive (and perhaps separable) the songs are in relationship to the rest of Deutero-Isaiah. There are two distinct opinions here. Peter Ackroyd argues, "Great damage appears to have been done to the understanding of the message of the prophet in the separating out of four so-called 'Servant Songs' from the remainder of the material."[6] But John L. McKenzie contends, "We have adopted the position that the Songs are not related to the context except for the response which follows the first three Songs (42:5-9; 49:7-13; 50:10-11)."[7] Although there is little agreement about how distinctive and separable the four songs are, there is more agreement that they cannot be seen as too self-contained a unit. As Ackroyd writes, "Considerable unreality is introduced into the discussion when attempts are made at finding a thought-sequence within the four single passages."[8] McKenzie concurs, "Yet it should be noticed that the four songs do not form a single literary unit. They cannot be read together. They are detached not only from the context but even more obviously from each other."[9]

If we separate the songs out someone other than Deutero-Isaiah appears to be the author, as Mowinckel and McKenzie maintain. If we integrate the songs into the context, we will more likely attribute authorship to Deutero-Isaiah, as do

---

[6]Peter Ackroyd, *Exile and Restoration,* The Old Testament Library (Philadelphia: Westminster Press, 1968), 127. Since Bernhard Duhm, it has been almost axiomatic to separate these four texts out from the rest of Deutero-Isaiah, but this consensus no longer stands. A recent effort to refute separating the songs from the larger context of the whole of Second Isaiah is Tryggve N.D. Mettinger, *A Farewell to the Servant Songs, A Critical Examination of an Exegetical Axiom,* trans. Frederick H. Cryer (Lund: C.W.K. Gleerup, 1983). Richard J. Clifford, *Fair Spoken and Persuading, An Interpretation of Second Isaiah* (New York: Paulist Press, 1984), also resists taking them out of their larger context. See pp. 30-33, 56-58.

[7]John L. McKenzie, *Second Isaiah,* Anchor Bible 20 (Garden City, N.Y.: Doubleday & Co., 1968), xxxix.

[8]Ackroyd, *Exile and Restoration,* 127.

[9]McKenzie, *Second Isaiah,* xxxix.

Ackroyd, North, Rignell.[10] For our purposes, we can leave the question of authorship open, and recognize both the differences and similarities between these four poems and the rest of Deutero-Isaiah. Authorities conclude that the texts were composed somewhere near the end of the Exile.

It is important to consider whether or not the texts are messianic. The messianic interpretation was the prevalent opinion in Christian theology prior to the development of critical exegesis and some continue to hold this interpretation. The majority of those who maintain a traditional messianic interpretation also hold for the unity of the book of Isaiah. Objections to the messianic interpretation include the fact that the servant is to lead Israel out of exile. And since the prophet expected this to happen soon, the servant must already have been born. Mowinckel's opinion in this regard is instructive: the servant prophecies are not messianic in the sense which that word had in Hebrew Scripture or in Judaism.[11] North would agree: "I do not think that anything is to be gained by attempts to prove that the Servant is the Divine Messiah of Isaiah 9 and 11."[12]

If we set aside the traditional messianic interpretation, there have been two major directions within critical exegesis about the identity of the servant: whether the servant is an individual or a collective reality. The collective theory has taken many forms: the entire nation Israel, the ideal Israel, a pious minority within Israel, the order of prophets, the order of priests. Today the collective theory is associated with H. Wheeler Robinson of England and Otto Eissfeldt of Germany. They base their modifications of the collective theory on the Hebrew concept of corporate personality and argue

[10]L.G. Rignell, *A Study of Isaiah, Ch. 49-55* (Lund: C.W.K. Gleerup, 1956). Gerhard von Rad separates the servant songs as a new servant concept but holds to Deutero-Isaian authorship. See *Old Testament Theology,* trans. D.M.G. Stalker, vol. 2 (New York: Harper and Row, 1965), 250-62.

[11]Mowinckel, *He That Cometh,* 213-33, 241-46, 155-57.

[12]North, *The Suffering Servant in Deutero-Isaiah,* 218.

for a composite in which the servant was both an individual historical person and Israel.[13]
Suggestions about the identity of the servant as an historical individual vary widely. Names proposed include the prophet himself (Deutero-Isaiah), Zerubbabel, Meshullam the son of Zerubbabel, Scheshbazzar, Jehoiachin, Moses, or someone now unknown. Advocates of an individual interpretation for the servant figure include Sellin, Mowinckel, Kittel. Sellin advocated Zerubbabel, Jehoiachin, and Moses, and then in turn abandoned each candidate, finally opting for Deutero-Isaiah himself. Mowinckel was the originator of the autobiographical theory, that the servant was the prophet Deutero-Isaiah himself, but Mowinckel himself later abandoned this view. He is still a strong advocate of the historical individual theory and now maintains that the servant was a definite person known to the prophet, a prophet from the same circle as the author, the Deutero-Isaianic circle from which the Trito-Isaian prophecies came.[14] Kittel's theory combines individual and messianic elements—that the servant was an anonymous contemporary of Deutero-Isaiah to whom the prophet looked as the promised Messiah. Since the claims for particular historical individuals have so far failed, North's argument is persuasive: if the servant is an individual, it must be someone anonymous.

North is ready, however, to abandon the historical individual theory altogether. Neither does he advocate the collective theory, however. He points, rather, to the fact that the contrast need not be between individual and collective theories but can be between historical individuals and an ideal figure, whether that be an ideal individual or the ideal Israel. For North, it is a question of a unique individual who has not yet appeared and a concrete ideal figure still to come.

---

[13]See H. W. Robinson, *The Cross of the Servant: A Study in Deutero-Isaiah* (London, 1926); also his *Corporate Personality in Ancient Israel* (Philadelphia: Fortress Press, 1964). Morna Hooker in her study also suggests a corporate interpretation. See note 30 of this chapter.

[14]Mowinckel, 246-55.

For North the question of whether the prophet expected the servant in the near or distant future is unimportant. He was expected, and he was still to come.[15]

Another issue in the whole discussion is what weight, if any, to give to the political role of the servant. On this issue Mowinckel, North, and von Rad all opt for the non-political, non-royal servant, distinguished from the political character of the Davidic Messiah. In this sense the expected servant was not the expected Davidic Messiah. For both Mowinckel and North the servant was a concrete individual, but for Mowinckel an historical individual, and for North an ideal future individual who was seen as a type for Israel. North would not insist on an either/or interpretation with respect to the individual and collective theories. For him, the servant really transcends both as an ideal of one to come. Although this figure was not messianic in the strict sense of the expected Davidic Messiah of later Judaism, North's interpretation of the servant as an ideal of one to come can be seen as a new quasi-messianic interpretation.

John Lindblom takes a different position from most other scholars. For him, the question is not: who was the servant of the songs? Rather it is: what did the servant figure signify? "In my opinion the principal question concerning the Ebed-Yahweh problem must be: *What is the literary character of the Ebed Songs?*"[16] For Lindblom, the songs form a special group not because there is a connecting servant figure but because there is a unifying literary character. Hence Lindblom discards the assumption that the subject of the songs must be the same throughout. The servant is different in different songs. Lindblom's conclusion then is to see the songs as allegorical or symbolic pictures depicting Israel's captivity and mission. The four songs do not describe a common figure but are all allegorical elucidations of varying historical realities. Lindblom divides all the oracles of Deutero-Isaiah into two groups, the missionary revelations

---

[15]North, 207-19.

[16]John Lindblom, *The Servant Songs in Deutero-Isaiah* (Lund: C.W.K. Gleerup, 1951), 10.

and the triumphal revelations, based on two homogeneous sets of ideas. The missionary revelations include, in addition to the four songs, 45:20-25; 51:7-8; 55:1-5; 48:1-11; 48:17-19. These oracles all express a mission of Israel to the Gentiles and culminate in the Servant Songs. The themes here are the salvation of the Gentiles, and Israel as the instrument of that salvation. In the triumphal revelations, the theme is triumphal deliverance of Israel from Babylonia and consequent vengeance on the enemy. Although the two groups of texts have much in common, the differences are significant. Israel's positive task in the world in the first set contrasts with Israel's deliverance from the triumph of her enemies in the second set. In the first group the Gentiles are seen as recipients of the true faith and in the latter as the object of judgment.

Thus, for Lindblom, the same prophet, Deutero-Isaiah, could not be the author of both groups of oracles, and yet it would be arbitrary simply to point to two authors. Rather the differences reflect the historical experience of Israel and depend on the fluctuating course of historical events. The prophet saw in history the incomprehensibility of the ways of God. Therefore there is no need to separate the four songs from the other oracles. Yet these four songs are alike in that they are allegorical pictures interpreting historical situations, Israel's present situation and her noble mission. The servant was neither individual nor group exclusively, but was a symbol, an individual who allegorically symbolized Israel in different roles.

H.H. Rowley presents a clear and succinct essay.[17] His own view is similar to North's. Rowley sees the corporate personality approach of Wheeler Robinson as helpful since there are both collective and individual traits in the servant concept. A single identity of the servant with Israel is not possible. In the second song the servant has a mission to Israel. Also, the sufferings of Israel were not innocent or

---

[17]H.H. Rowley, "The Servant of the Lord in the Light of Three Decades of Criticism," in *The Servant of the Lord and other Essays* (Oxford: Basil Blackwell, 1965), 1-60.

guiltless. Thus Rowley, like North, opts for development within the songs from a more collective to a more individual interpretation. The first song seems to be predominantly about Israel. In the second song we see purified Israel. Thus there was a mission both *to* and *through* Israel. The third song is less clear. It may be about the collective servant as a personification. The fourth song, however, is unmistakably individual. This individual servant was a future figure, not an historical one. Like North, therefore, Rowley concludes that the servant was a future individual.

Rowley differs from Wheeler Robinson in that Rowley sees development but not fluidity in the songs. Rowley perceives a development from the servant as Israel to the servant as a future individual, but not alternation. Rowley also distinquishes his view from that of North. He sees North's interpretation as a linear development (not a fluid back and forth movement), but Rowley argues neither for fluidity nor for a simple linear interpretation but for cumulative significance.

> I find the development from the thoughts of Israel as the Servant to the thought of the individual Servant *par excellence,* without abandoning the thought of Israel as still the Servant. If the fourth song is dominantly individual, the mission which the Servant fulfills is still not merely his own, but Israel's and Israel is still called to enter in some measure into it, so that the Servant may really be Israel's representative.[18]

Rowley is also more reluctant than North to use the term "messianic" to describe this future individual because that word suggests the Davidic Messiah and most would agree that the Servant and the Messiah were distinct concepts. The notion of suffering was not associated with the Messiah in pre-Christian Judaism, at least not in the more widespread, popular messianic hope. There is enough in common between

[18]Ibid., 56.

North and Rowley, however, to make their views merit special consideration.

As we conclude this brief survey of some of the critical issues, we can suggest that we need not or ought not impose one interpretation on all four of the poems, for the servant figure need not necessarily be the same in all four; and that the servant figure may refer both to an idealized Israel or remnant therein as well as to a figure to come whose mission was also idealized. The collective and individual connotations of the idealization are not mutually exclusive. Let us then look more closely at these four depictions of servanthood, not suggesting however that they can be truly separated from the rest of Second Isaiah.

Isaiah 42:1-4; The First Servant Song

¹Behold my servant, whom I uphold,
    my chosen, in whom my soul delights;
I have put my Spirit upon him,
    he will bring forth justice to the nations.

²He will not cry or lift up his voice,
    or make it heard in the street;

³a bruised reed he will not break
    and a dimly burning wick he will not quench;
    he will faithfully bring forth justice.

⁴He will not fail or be discouraged
    till he has established justice in the earth
    and the coastlands wait for his law.

Who the designated servant might have been is not our concern so much as the meaning of the image: the servant is *chosen* by the Lord, is one in whom the Lord takes delight, is pleasing to the Lord.[19] The Lord not only chooses who is to be the Lord's servant but he is one *on whom the Spirit of the*

[19]See especially Edward Kissane, *The Book of Isaiah,* vol. 2 (Dublin: Browne and Nolan, 1943), 35-36; George Knight, *Deutero-Isaiah* (New York: Abingdon Press, 1965), 70-74; John McKenzie, *Second Isaiah,* 37-38; and Claus Westermann *Isaiah 40-66,* The Old Testament Library (Philadelphia: Westminster Press, 1969), 92-97.

Lord descends and he takes his place among the charismatic figures of Israelite history. The gift of the Spirit does not necessarily mean that of prophecy, for judges and kings as well as prophets take their place among those who had been endowed with the spirit in the past.

He was to be called or chosen and endowed with the Spirit *in order to serve*. He was to be given a task to perform, a mission to fulfill, for others. It was for the sake of others that he was to be chosen. His mission was that of *mishpat,* translated in the RSV as justice (lines 1d, 3c, 4b), translated by others as judgment, or by George Knight as way of life, interpreted by Edward Kissane and John McKenzie as revelation. It must be left somewhat open as to what the mission consisted in, but communicating knowledge of the true God seems to have been part of it. Claus Westermann suggests that the judgment the servant was to bring was that the Lord of Israel alone is God, a judgment brought to the Gentiles.

The servant here contrasts with other servants of the Lord, whether the prophets or kings or others. He was not typical. *He would not impose his message on others by force.* He would not shout his prophecies in the street. The servant was to be non-coercive, non-oppressive. He would not burden or crush the poor and the helpless, the bruised reeds. Yet he would not fail.

Verse four returns to a theme in verse one—that *his mission was to be to all,* to the nations beyond Israel. The suggestion is that he will indeed be a revelation to the Gentiles. Several authors see in the figure "one like Moses,"[20] and verse four concludes that the nations wait for his torah (his instruction, revelation, perhaps a delineation of the *mishpat*).

Whether the figure is to be interpreted individually, collectively, ideally, or allegorically, we have the description of a chosen one, upon whom the Spirit rests, who is called to serve others, whose mission is to the Gentiles, whose message

---

[20]This is von Rad's interpretation. See *Old Testament Theology,* vol. 2, 250-62.

will not be imposed by force, whose *mishpat* is a true judgment, knowledge, and revelation of the Lord.

Isaiah 49:1-6: The Second Servant Song

[1]Listen to me, O coastlands,
  and hearken, you peoples from afar.
The Lord called me from the womb,
  from the body of my mother he named my name.

[2]He made my mouth like a sharp sword,
  in the shadow of his hand he hid me;
he made me a polished arrow,
  in his quiver he hid me away.

[3]And he said to me, "You are my servant,
  Israel, in whom I will be glorified."

[4]But I have said, "I have labored in vain,
  I have spent my strength for nothing and vanity;
yet surely my right is with the Lord,
  and my recompense with my God."

[5]And now the Lord says,
  who formed me from the womb to be his servant,
to bring Jacob back to him,
  and that Israel might be gathered to him.
For I am honored in the eyes of the Lord,
  and my God has become my strength.

[6]He says:
  "It is too light a thing that you should be my servant
  to raise up the tribes of Jacob
  and to restore the preserved of Israel;
I will give you as a light to the nations,
  that my salvation may reach to the end of the earth."

In the first of the songs, it is the Lord who speaks, "Behold my servant whom I uphold." Here it is the servant himself who speaks, "Listen to me, O coastlands." We see his sense of mission, specifically the mission to the nations, to the whole earth, to the Gentiles.[21]

The poem speaks of *a call.* The Lord has chosen his servant while he was still in his mother's womb. The call is reminiscent of that of Jeremiah: "Before I formed you, in the womb I knew you, and before you were born I consecrated you; I appointed you a prophet to the nations" (1:5).

As the call of the servant resembles that of the prophets, so does his approach. The mission is to be accomplished by word of mouth, through speech, in power, through *the power of the word,* the ministry of the word. The Lord equipped him with speech for his task.

The main exegetical problem of verse three is the reference to Israel. Westermann argues that it is a later addition.[22] It is the only time the word "Israel" appears in the four songs. It could be a gloss which represents the beginning of a collective interpretation for the servant. It could also portray the identity of the servant with Israel. The tone of the poem, however, is that of an individual speaking.

Verse four introduces the motif of *discouragement.* His work has been in vain. His strength is gone, he has accomplished nothing. Yet he does not despair. Surely *the Lord is still with him* and will vindicate him. This hope is even more strongly expressed in verse five (c and d). God is his continuing strength. He is honored in spite of failure or setback. One mission (to bring Israel back to the Lord) is being replaced by another—to be a light to the nations. The mission to Israel is too small a task; *his mission is to be to the nations.*

The servant has told his story, how he had been chosen from his mother's womb, how he had been given the power of the word, how he had been sent on a mission to Israel, how this mission was in vain, how he became discouraged, how the Lord remained with him and replaced his earlier

[21]Cf. Kissane, *The Book of Isaiah,* vol. 2, 121-28; McKenzie, *Second Isaiah,* 103-6; Westermann, *Isaiah 40-66,* 206-12.

[22]Westermann, 209.

mission with a greater one, how he was to bring the salvation and the word of the Lord to the whole earth.

Isaiah 50:4-11; The Third Servant Song

4The Lord God has given me the tongue of those
    who are taught
that I may know how to sustain with a word
    him that is weary.
Morning by morning he wakens,
    he wakens by ear
    to hear as those who are taught.

5The Lord God has opened my ear,
    and I was not rebellious
    I turned not backward.

6I gave my back to the smiters,
    and my cheeks to those who pulled out the beard;
I hid not my face
    from shame and spitting.

7For the Lord God helps me,
    therefore I have not been confounded;
therefore I have set my face like a flint
    and I know that I shall not be put to shame;

8   he who vindicates me is near.
Who will contend with me?
    Let us stand up together.
Who is my adversary?
    Let him come near to me.

9Behold, the Lord God helps me
    who will declare me guilty?
Behold all of them will wear out like a garment;
    the moth will eat them up.

10Who among you fears the Lord
    and obeys the voice of his servant,
who walks in darkness
    and has no light,

yet trusts in the name of the Lord
and relies upon his God?

[11]Behold, all you who kindle a fire,
who set brands alight!
Walk by the light of your fire,
and by the brands which you have kindled!
This shall you have from my hand:
you shall lie down in torment.

The speaker seems to be the servant as in the previous song, although some argue that it is Deutero-Isaiah who speaks, at least in verses ten and eleven. Verses four and five reflect the theme of *the call*, as in the two previous songs.[23]

The poem makes the point: my words are God's words. He taught me. I listened and obeyed. The prophetic character of his mission is again stated: *his is a ministry of the word*. Those who are weary may be the Israelites. The Lord is the instructor whose message sustains those whose burden is heavy ("My yoke is easy and my burden is light," Mt 11:30). The disciple is attentive, listens, hears, and is docile. Verse five points to the receptivity of this disciple. The sequence is call, discipleship, mission, servanthood, prophetic ministry, vindication.

As verses four and five describe the vocation and docility of the servant, verse six specifies adversities even more clearly than the previous two poems. He is *rejected* by those to whom he is sent. His mission encounters hostility and abuse. Verse six has something of the character of a lament such as we find in Jeremiah (11:10; 18:18).

As verse six describes the abuse, verses seven to nine express the servant's confidence. He is convinced: *God is with me*. He remains firm in the face of the adversities. He obeys. He neither runs nor rebels against the Lord: the Lord will vindicate him. Bold enough to challenge his adversaries, he, like Jeremiah, is confident (11:20; 15:15-16; 20:11, 12).

[23]Kissane, 151-52; McKenzie, 115-17; Westermann, 225-35.

Verses ten and eleven are more difficult. Are they the words of the servant or the author? Kissane sees verse ten as an address to the exiles, the Israelites, the oppressed. It can be seen again as reflecting the notion that he who hears the servant hears the Lord. Those addressed are called upon to trust in the Lord and to have confidence in him.

Kissane interprets verse eleven as an address to the oppressors, the pagans, specifically the Babylonians. If so, this is the only reference to other nations, a theme prominent in the other two poems. Yet the reference here is different. The nations are not the ones who hear the word of the servant but those who shall be defeated and laid low, perhaps the Babylonians. McKenzie sees verse eleven as still an address to Israelites, those who reject the prophetic word. This interpretation would be more consistent with the two previous poems.

Despite inconsistencies, common themes run through all three poems: call, mission, message, ministry of the word, presence of the Lord, discouragement and rejection, vindication.

Isaiah 52:13-53:12; The Fourth Servant Song

13Behold, my servant shall prosper,
    he shall be exalted and lifted up,
    and shall be very high.
14As many were astonished at him—
    his appearance was so marred,
    beyond human semblance,
    and his form beyond that of the sons of men—

15so shall he startle many nations;
    kings shall shut their mouths because of him;
    for that which has not been told them they shall see,
    and that which they have not heard they shall understand.

1Who has believed what we have heard?
And to whom has the arm of the Lord been revealed?

2For he grew up before him like a young plant,

and like a root out of dry ground,
he had no form or comeliness that we should look at him,
and no beauty that we should desire him.

3He was despised and rejected by men;
a man of sorrows and acquainted with grief;
and as one from whom men hid their faces
he was despised, and we esteemed him not.

4Surely he has borne our griefs
and carried our sorrows;
yet we esteemed him stricken,
smitten by God, and afflicted.

5But he was wounded for our transgressions,
he was bruised for our iniquities;
upon him was the chastisement that made us whole,
and with his stripes we are healed.

6All we like sheep have gone astray;
we have turned every one to his own way;
and the Lord has laid on him
the iniquity of us all.

7He was oppressed, and he was afflicted,
yet he opened not his mouth;
like a lamb that is led to the slaughter,
and like a sheep that before its shearers is dumb,
so he opened not his mouth.

8By oppression and judgment he was taken away;
and as for his generation, who considered
that he was cut off out of the land of the living,
stricken for the transgression of my people?

9And they made his grave with the wicked
and with a rich man in his death,
although he had done no violence,
and there was no deceit in his mouth.

10Yet it was the will of the Lord to bruise him;
he has put him to grief;

when he makes himself an offering for sin,
   he shall see his offspring,
   he shall prolong his days;
the will of the Lord shall prosper in his hand;

[11]he shall see the fruit of the travail of his soul
   and be satisfied;
by his knowledge shall the righteous one, my servant,
   make many to be accounted righteous,
   and he shall bear their iniquities.
[12]Therefore I will divide him a portion with the great,
   and he shall divide the spoil with the strong;
because he poured out his soul to death,
   and was numbered with the transgressors;
yet he bore the sin of many,
   and made intercession for the transgressors.

There are two speakers in the fourth song. The Lord is the speaker in the beginning (52:13-15) and again in the end (53:11-12). The bulk of the poem (53:1-10) is a comment by some Israelites or a group of Israelites other than the servant. The Lord was the speaker in the first of the servant songs; the servant was the speaker in the next two; here we are aware of another voice. McKenzie suggests that it may be that of the author. Westerman points out the common element of humiliation *and exaltation* in both parts of this fourth poem. This theme is not new but the vicarious nature of the humiliation is new.[24]

The fourth poem begins somewhat like the first. The Lord then declares that his servant will be highly exalted. This "vindication" is again indicated in 53:10.

Many (probably Israelites) are astounded at the servant's appearance: appalling, disfigured, distorted. He does not even appear to be human. Such was the toll that his suffering took on his very physical features. Those shaken by his physical disfigurement will be shaken by the story of his success. Verse thirteen pointed to the exaltation or the

[24]McKenzie, 129-36; Westermann, 253-69.

success of the mission, the vindication of the servant. The report of what has been accomplished in him will reach many nations and recalls his role as "light to the nations" mentioned in the first two poems. Westermann writes, "That a man who was smitten, who was marred beyond human semblance, and who was despised in the eyes of God and men should be given such approval and significance, and be thus exalted, is in very truth something new and unheard of, going against tradition and all men's settled ideas."[25]

The speaker shifts in verse one of chapter 53, but the verse begins with the exact theme with which the previous speaker ended: It is unbelievable and unheard of that the Lord was at work in this. The servant had grown up like a young plant, not particularly comely or stately, not one to take note of, more like a plant in a desert. He is lacking in beauty, insignificant. He was not simply an unattractive and un-noticed figure. He became despised, rejected, one of the wretched of the earth, isolated from others, shunned. The nature of the affliction or suffering is unspecified. The description here has even led some to postulate that the servant was a leper. We are also reminded of Job (19:1-22).

In verse four, we come to a central issue. Because of his tremendous affliction he was judged to be guilty, according to the prevailing theology of suffering as a punishment for sin. But this one was innocent. His suffering was *for our sake*. It is our sorrow he bore. He himself was innocent and God was indeed with him. The traditional theology of suffering is shattered. The source of the wonder revealed in verse four is continued. We are the ones who have erred, strayed away, sinned. He is the one who was afflicted and has borne the brunt of the chastisement for our sake. By his suffering we have been healed. This theology of vicarious suffering is new to Hebrew thought.

Although the nature of his suffering is unspecified, we see, as in the third poem, the docility and obedience of the servant. In verses three and four, he was rejected because he was so uncomely, as if diseased. Here he is oppressed and

[25]Westermann, 260.

maltreated and does not fight back. But he was the victim of misjudgment, a legal miscarriage of justice, as if he had been tried and found guilty of something. But how could his generation have understood innocence and that the righteous can suffer? Who realized, says the poet, that he was put to death for our transgressions?

He died, and was buried with the wicked. Again the poet acknowledges the servant's innocence in spite of the tale of his suffering, death and burial.

In verse ten, the narrator describes the vindication which the Lord had already mentioned in 52:13 and 15. His suffering was in fact in accord with the will of the Lord. His sufferings were a sin offering. Because he persevered in his mission even unto death, he will receive a reward; his days will be prolonged and he will see the fruit of his labors. These three themes are all significant: (1) The Lord had been with his servant throughout his life. (2) The suffering and death of the servant are comparable to a guilt offering. The servant is like the victim of an atonement sacrifice because through his death, others have been cleansed. (3) Although the work of the servant does not end in defeat, the nature of his vindication is unclear.

Either at the beginning or in the middle of verse eleven, the speaker becomes the Lord once again who simply repeats and confirms the report which has been given. The servant will see the fruit of his suffering. His servant is righteous in spite of the suffering heaped on him. He suffered for the unrighteous and bore the burden of their wickedness. He died, was buried as one of the transgressors, yet in fact was an intercessor for the transgressors, and therefore shall be numbered among the great. The Lord says that because of the vicarious suffering of his servant, many have been made righteous.

To conclude: Our primary concern is not with the critical problems of the texts (their distinguishability from the rest of Deutero-Isaiah, their authorship, their internal consistency, the identity of the servant) but with the theological content of the images. It is legitimate to see development within the four Songs; yet consistency need not be imposed in order to arrive at one servant figure. The following are ideas which flow from the texts, whether all these ideas refer to one figure or many, to an individual or to a group, to an historical reality or an ideal or future reality. The servant is chosen (Songs 1,2,3). He is given the gift of the Spirit (Song 1). He is given the power of the word (Songs 2,3). He is sent to serve, and has a consciousness of mission (Songs 1,3). The message is not imposed by force (Song 1). There is a mission to Israel, which does not bear much fruit (Song 2). There is also a mission to the Gentiles (Songs 1,2). The mission includes bringing true judgment, righteousness or salvation (Song 1). Discouragement and suffering and rejection are necessary for the mission itself (Songs 2,3,4). The humiliation and obedience extend even to death and burial (Song 4). The Lord remains with his servant and preserves him in the midst of all (Songs 2,3,4). The Lord vindicates and exalts the servant (Songs 3,4). The sufferings of the servant were undeserved, and are vicarious, an atonement for the many (Song 4).

It must also be emphasized that the fourth servant song gave rise to an Isaianic exaltation theme that continued to be present in later Jewish literature, such as the Book of Daniel, Second Maccabees, and the Book of Wisdom, as Judaism struggled with the question of the fate of its righteous and persecuted ones, the milieu in which the doctrine of resurrection was born as well. The stories and theology of the persecuted but vindicated righteous are found in Daniel 12:1-3, 2 Maccabees 7, and Wisdom 2:12-20, 4:18-5:14, and elsewhere. The Isaianic theme of the exaltation of the servant lay behind the later hope of post-mortem vindication. As G.W.E. Nickelsburg writes, "At some time between the writing of Second Isaiah and the time of Antiochus, civil persecution of [the religious leader of] the Jews fostered an interpretation of Isaiah 52-53 as a scene of the post-mortem exaltation of the persecuted ones and the [impending] judgment of their persecutors."[26]

---

[26]George W.E. Nickelsburg, *Resurrection, Immortality, and Eternal Life in Inter-testamental Judaism,* Harvard Theological Studies 26 (Cambridge: Harvard

Jesus of Nazareth, Servant of the Lord

One can see why Christians came to interpret Jesus and especially Jesus' death and exaltation through the images of servanthood. The many facets of that image helped them to understand the ministry, mission and death of Jesus: obedience, suffering, rejection, suffering on behalf of others, the ideal Israelite, a messianic figure, a prophetic figure, one sent to the Gentiles. The servant image connoted someone chosen by God, on whom the Spirit descended. One called in order to serve, who was given a mission, with a message that will not be imposed on others by force. One with a mission both to and beyond Israel, whose ministry was especially a ministry of the word. One who gathered disciples, with whom God was and whom God vindicated and even exalted. One who died and whose suffering was undeserved. We can see the reasons for interpreting Jesus as servant.

Jesus was a prophet, not unlike the prophets of old. Traditionally, the true prophet was a supreme example of the servant of the Lord. Jesus was also a teacher and his teaching was often concerned with service and servanthood.[27]

That the last will become first and the humble will be exalted was one of the central themes in the authentic teaching of Jesus. Similarly, Jesus' teaching about himself included the understanding of one who comes to serve and not to be served.[28]

Not only in his ministry to the word of the Lord does Jesus emphasize servanthood, but also in his life. In the wilderness, at prayer, with faith and trust in God, Jesus' will is to do the will of the one who sent him. And in being open

University Press, 1972), 81. Nickelsburg's is the most thorough treatment of the development of this Isaianic exaltation theme.

[27]See Mk 3:35/Mt 12:50, Lk 8:21; Mk 8:34-35/ Mt 10:38-39, Lk 9:23-24; Mk 9:33-37/Mt 18:1-5, Lk 9:46-48; Mk 10:31/ Mt 19:30, Lk 13:30; Mk 12:28-34/Mt 22:34-40, Lk 10:25-28; Mt 6:24/ Lk 16:13; Mt 10:24-25/ Lk 6:40; Mt 24:45-51/ Lk 12:42-46; Mt 20:16; Mt. 23:1-12; Lk 10:29-37; Lk 12:37; Lk 14:7-11; Lk 17:7-10; Lk 18:14.

[28]See Mk 10:41-45/Mt 20:24-28, Lk 22:24-27; Mk 2:17/Mt 9:12-13, Lk 5:31-32; Mk 14:36/Mt 26:42, Lk 22:42.

to his Father's will he allows himself to be someone who lives for others, through healing and exorcisms, through his presence to the blind and lame, through his readiness to respond to those who come or are brought to him, through his love for women and children, through his willingness to identify and be identified with the outcast and sinner. Jesus *was* what he proclaimed; he *became* what he preached. Jesus made incarnate in his praxis what it meant to be the Lord's servant.

Probably the most moving of Jesus' symbolic actions and the most clear exemplification of Jesus as servant and his own self-consciousness of being a servant is the acted out parable of the washing of the disciples' feet recorded in the Fourth Gospel and placed in the setting of their last meal together (Jn 13:1-20).[29]

There is sufficient reason to conclude that the footwashing has a basis in history, although the interpretative discourse surrounding the symbolic action within the Johannine narrative was not part of the original action. Whatever other associations or meanings there may be in the symbol, the primary symbolisation is of the humility of Jesus, the freely chosen humiliation in the life of a servant of the Lord, and the humiliation Jesus is soon to experience in his condemnation and crucifixion.

We must distinguish before going further between Jesus as *a* servant of the Lord and Jesus as *the* servant of the Lord. I am primarily asserting that Jesus is *a* servant, that he can be understood and must be understood within the servant tradition. When we speak about *the* servant, we mean the servant of the fourth Deutero-Isaian song and its depiction of the ideal individual still to come. One can also interpret Jesus in the light of this particular depiction of a servant. Jesus also exemplifies the ideal of servanthood as depicted in Isaiah 52-53. That particular conception of a servant helps us to understand and interpret the life and death of Jesus as

---

[29]On the footwashing, see M.E. Boismard, "Le lavement des pieds (John 13:1-17)," *Revue biblique* 71 (1964), 5-24; Raymond Brown, *The Gospel According to John, XIII-XXI,* Anchor Bible 29 A (Garden City, N.Y.: Doubleday and Co., 1970), 548-72.

well as his exaltation. We can justifiably see Jesus in that text. This does not mean, however, that Jesus is *the* Deutero-Isaian servant in the sense that the prophecy foretold his coming in particular, or that Jesus is the only (actual or possible) historical figure to fulfill that image of the Lord's servant. It is simply that the Jesus of history was in fact *a* servant of God, and a servant to a great degree in accord with the Deutero-Isaian pictures of the ideal servant.

Although it is valid to speak of Jesus as servant, would Jesus himself have thought of himself in that way? Although caution is necessary in any analysis of Jesus' self-understanding, it is probable that Jesus thought of himself as *a* servant in the Israelite tradition. Indeed, he thought of himself as a prophet. The life, prayer, ministry, and final humiliation of Jesus exemplify true servanthood. The teaching of Jesus often explicitly focuses on service and serving. It is hardly likely that Jesus did not see himself as exemplifying or embodying what it meant to be a servant. And he also explicitly spoke about his mission in such terms (Mk 10:41-45, 2:17).

Was Jesus' consciousness, prayer, and mission influenced in part by the image of servant found in Deutero-Isaiah? Again, there should be no hesitancy to say yes. A prophet who had such a strong self-awareness of being God's servant and whose teaching was so clearly about true servanthood would hardly have ignored the provocative depiction in the Book of Isaiah. Jesus was well acquainted with the Scriptures. He prayed them. He preached from them. He was recognized as learned with regard to them. And the Book of Isaiah in particular was a great source of nourishment for him. Although Jesus knew well the Law and the Prophets, some texts in particular formed a part of his consciousness. In the wilderness narratives in Matthew and Luke, Jesus is portrayed as having relied on Deuteronomy. It was to be expected that Jesus would know and have prayed over Deuteronomy often and carefully. On the cross he is portrayed as having relied upon the psalms. These too would have been part of his daily prayer, memory, and consciousness. And there is reason to believe that the Book of Isaiah was likewise particularly significant for Jesus.[30] It played an important role in Qumran. With the exception of Psalms, it is the book in the Hebrew Bible most often quoted in the New Testament. Jesus may have opened his Galilean preaching with a text from Isaiah (Lk 4:18). How often would Jesus not have prayed over and recited the verses from Isaiah about the Lord's servant whom the Lord upholds? Could he have avoided its helping him to see more clearly his own ministry and fate as his mission unfolded?

Jesus' servant consciousness manifested itself at his last meal with his disciples (Mk 14:24). It also clearly manifested itself when disputes about greatness and position and status surfaced among his disciples (Lk 22:24-27). "Here am I among you as one who serves! " has a claim to authenticity (Lk 22:27). And so does: "For the son of humanity also came not to be served but to serve, and to give his life as a ransom for many (Mk 10:45/ Mt 20:28).[31]

---

[30]Morna Hooker, *Jesus and the Servant, The Influence of the Servant Concept of Deutero-Isaiah in the New Testament* (London: SPCK, 1959), argues that Jesus did not see himself as the servant of Isaiah, see pp. 73, 77, 85.

[31]There are several difficulties with respect to Mk 10:45. Is it an authentic saying of Jesus? Does it reflect the servant theology of Is 53? One could answer yes to the first question and no to the second, or vice versa. Some divide the verse. Thus: Is Mk 10:45a an authentic saying of Jesus, or is Lk 22:27 the original, authentic Jesus material? Even so, can Mk 10:45b be dismissed as not authentic? Mk 10:45b may be an authentic Jesus saying which Mark has united to another saying on Jesus coming to serve (so F.W. Beare, *The Gospel according to Matthew* [San Franscisco: Harper and Row, Pub., 1981], 408-9). In a concise summary of arguments pro and con, D.E. Nineham remarks that the majority opinion is against the authenticity of 10:45b (*Saint Mark,* Pelican NT Commentaries [New York: Penguin Books, 1981], 280-281).

Morna Hooker's research has been influential *(Jesus and the Servant, The Influence of the Servant Concept of Deutero-Isaiah in the New Testament).* The fact that Mk 10:45b is not included in the Lucan version of the saying suggests that it may not be authentic (p. 75). Even apart from this, however, Mk 10:45 is unrelated to Is 53. For Hooker, there is no evidence that Jesus saw himself as *the* servant of Deutero-Isaiah, namely, one whose suffering expiates the sins of others (pp. 74-79, 134-63; also Morna D. Hooker, *The Son of Man in Mark* [London: SPCK, 1967], 140-47).

H.E. Tödt, *The Son of Man in the Synoptic Tradition,* trans. Dorothea Barton (Philadelphia: Westminster Press, 1965), 202-11, also argues against the authenticity of Mk 10:45b; Mk 10:45b, however, probably does have reference to Is 53 for Tödt. But the probable dependence of Mk 10:45b on Is 53 does not go back to an original saying of Jesus.

Again, this is not saying that Jesus saw himself as specifically fulfilling an Isaian prophecy, nor that he saw himself alone as exclusively exemplifying the Isaian proph-

Reginald Fuller, *The Mission and Achievement of Jesus* (London: SCM Press, 1954), 55-64, argued for the authenticity of Mk 10:45 and that the original material in the passion predictions formed a clear description of the servant of Is 53, and thus for Jesus' interpretation of his death in light of Is 53. However, later, influenced by Hooker and Tödt, in *The Foundations of New Testament Christology* (New York: Charles Scribner's Sons, 1965), 115-119, he changed his mind. Mk 10:45b is an allusion to Is 53, but Mk 10:45b is not an original saying of Jesus.

Maurice Casey, *Son of Man, The Interpretation and Influence of Daniel 7* (London: SPCK, 1979), 164-65, 205-6, 236-37, whose interpretation of the son of humanity problem I endorse as more accurate than Tödt's, lists Mk 10:45 among those sayings which are authentic examples of sayings spoken in accord with correct Aramaic idiom.

Barnabas Lindars, *Jesus Son of Man* (Grand Rapids, Mich.: William B. Eerdmans Pub. Co., 1983), 76-84, maintains that Mk 10:45 comprises two sayings, that 10:45b is an addition to an original saying on service, that the word "ransom" in 10:45b is not original but interpretative, that the expression "son of humanity" belongs to 10:45b, and that what Jesus said was, "A man may give his life for many." The "many" may recall Is 53:12. Thus Jesus *may* have been inspired by Is 53 to express his vocation to death. A connection with Is 53 remains incapable of being proved though it remains probable. Either way, the early church rapidly made use of Is 53 to explain the significance of Jesus' death.

In my opinion Mk 10:45a (certainly Lk 22:27) is most probably an authentic saying of Jesus. Mk 10:45b is more questionable but ought not be quickly dismissed; see Lindars' interpretation above. The relationship between Mk 10:45b and Is 53 remains an open question. That question, however, is not the only determinant of whether Jesus saw his death as a vicarious martyrdom. Apart from a strict connection between Mk 10:45 and Is 53, Jesus seems to have been influenced by the book of Isaiah. Also, even apart from Is 53, Morna Hooker, *The Son of Man in Mark*, 140-47; *Jesus and the Servant*, 78; and C.K. Barrett, "The Background of Mark 10:45," in *New Testament Essays, Studies in Memory of T.W. Manson*, ed. A.J.B. Higgins (Manchester: The University Press, 1959), 1-18; and J. Duncan M. Derrett, *Jesus' Audience, the Social and Psychological Environment in Which He Worked* (London: Darton, Longman and Todd, 1973), 44-45, point out that the concepts of suffering as atonement and vicarious merit were present and reflect Maccabean martyrdom theology. Also see Ps 118:22, and n. 26 of this chapter.

Morna Hooker, *Jesus and the Servant*, defines narrowly *the* servant of Deutero-Isaiah. I suggest that Jesus did not see himself as *the* servant of Deutero-Isaiah, but that he did see himself as *a* servant of the Lord, which concept was probably influenced by Isaian theology. At any rate, was there such a thing as *the* Deutero-Isaian concept for Jesus to identify with? Only moderns speak of Deutero-Isaiah and the four servant songs.

Jesus saw himself as *a* servant. Servanthood influenced how he saw his life, and thus most probably how he saw his death. The sources for Jesus' understanding would have probably included at least Psalms, Isaiah, and Deuteronomy, as well as later Maccabean theology and his own reflection on the death of John the baptizer.

ecy, or that he saw the Isaian servant or himself in messianic terms. It is simply saying that Jesus may have relied upon the Isaian prophecy in order to understand and interpret his own mission and destiny. The earliest post-resurrection interpretation of Jesus' death was in terms of a prophet's or martyr's death (cf. Ps 118:22), but the interpretation in terms of redemptive suffering (Is 53) was also early, Palestinian (4 Macc 6:29, 17:22, and 2 Macc 7:37 f), and fitted well the later theology of the vindication and exaltation of God's persecuted and righteous ones.

In Conclusion

Jesus' tragic death by crucifixion was a consequence of religious, political, and socio-economic factors closely interwoven. Jesus was a victim of his own integrity and fidelity to God.

Even before the resurrection or any experience thereof, Jesus' death would have sought for an understanding. He had been too sought out as prophet and too compassionate a sage to be simply dismissed. The tragedy and scandal of his crucifixion could easily be seen as the death of a righteous martyr and the fate of a prophet, not unlike that of John. After the experience of the resurrection, Jesus' faithful followers would penetrate even further into the mystery of his death. Its redemptive significance would become more apparent.

But in one sense Jesus' death was simply a capsule of his whole life: a man in solidarity with God and the people. This is what the cross came to signify. It was the symbol par excellence for the integrity and fidelity of this man, and eventually for his victory as well.

But the cross demands that we and the first disciples go beyond our previous understanding of Jesus as prophet to Israel and sage for his disciples, and beyond Jesus as simply a victim of a system, which he was, and to recognize in Jesus' mission and ministry and above all in his tragic end a true servant of the Lord. Jesus was a servant in his life and above all in his death. Whether he himself saw his death as redemptive or not,[32] he saw himself as faithful to the darling God whom he served and the people to whom he had been sent—a servant par excellence.

[32]See J.C. O'Neill, "Did Jesus Teach That His Death Would Be Vicarious as Well as Typical?" in *Suffering and Martyrdom in the New Testament, Studies Presented to G.M. Styler*, ed. W. Horbury and B. McNeil (Cambridge: Cambridge University Press, 1981), 9-27.

Part Two

The Resurrection of Jesus

3

Resurrection From the Dead

There was no event in the life of Jesus more significant than his resurrection, nor any event more significant for the later church. The resurrection of Jesus was not just one more event in his life alongside others, nor is it an event historiographically accessible in the same way as other events in his life. The "Risen Lord" is no longer "of history" in the same way as the earthly Jesus was. But the resurrection was not a completely new beginning either. It was the culmination of Jesus' life on earth. It was an historical event which transcends the methods of historiography.

The resurrection of Jesus was an event that could be closely drawn into the eschatology of the Jewish people. Was it in fact an eschatological event more than it was an historical event? With the resurrection of Jesus, we can begin to distinguish "the eschatology of the nation" from "the eschatology of the individual." In this second sense, the resurrection of Jesus was certainly an eschatological event *for Jesus*. Was it more than that?

It is helpful to introduce another distinction. The "end" of history can be its culmination or consummation, whether on earth or in heaven; or it can be its goal, purpose, inner meaning, having more to do with *telos* than *chronos*. Eschatology, as I use the term, refers to the end of history in the chronological sense, not the teleological sense, although these two words are not mutually exclusive. In other words, eschatology refers to the end times, our ultimate, human, collective future. An event which discloses the inner meaning or final goal of history is not an eschatological event but a revelatory event. I prefer not to use the word eschatology too widely to cover anything that has to do with hope, with the future, or with the inner meaning of history.[1] Eschatology is concerned with collective hopes and expectations concerning the *finis* of history. In this sense, it is more appropriate to describe Jesus' resurrection as a revelatory event, an eschatological event for him but a revelatory event for others. It was not and has not been the end of history.

As we approach our discussion of the resurrection of Jesus I will begin with an inquiry into the doctrine of resurrection in general rather than with the specifics of the resurrection of Jesus, from resurrection as a category in the history of religion rather than as a specific christological fact. This approach to the resurrection of Jesus corresponds to the Pauline perspective on a relationship between Jesus' resurrection and our own. It is not as if Jesus' resurrection is completely in a category by itself. Jesus' resurrection is rather an exemplification of what is elsewhere true—that we too will be raised from the dead. This is not to imply that there was nothing special or even unique about Jesus' being raised. Rather it implies a link between what Jesus experienced and what other human beings have experienced or will experience.

"Now if Christ is preached as raised from the dead, how can some of you say that there is no resurrection of the dead? But if there is no resurrection of the dead, then Christ has not been raised" (I Cor 15:12-13). Jesus' resurrection is distinguishable but not separable from the doctrine of a more general resurrection. Thus, methodologically, we will first ask what resurrection means, and then inquire into the resurrection of Jesus in particular. If Jesus' resurrection is an exemplification of resurrection in general, as Paul suggests,

---

[1]In this regard, see Volume One of this series, *The Mission and Ministry of Jesus* (Wilmington, Del.: Michael Glazier, 1986), 68-83.

then our understanding of resurrection can help us to understand Jesus.

If we begin with the question of how humankind has historically and religiously conceived its future beyond death, we find that humankind has spoken of such future life primarily in three ways: as reincarnation or rebirth, as immortality of the soul, and as resurrection from the dead.[2] These three need not be seen as exclusive of each other or as ultimately irreconcilable. Yet, historically they manifest distinctive traditions, reincarnation being especially Eastern or Indian (Hindu), immortality being especially Hellenistic, and resurrection Semitic. They are varied cultural as well as religious ways of approaching the question of human destiny.

Although all three are deserving of serious attention in any religious anthropology, our concern here will be the concept of resurrection—not because it is necessarily more true, but because it will help us better to understand the language used to interpret the destiny of Jesus. Our concern is what happened to Jesus at his death. And we are told: he was raised from the dead.

Some forms of the doctrine of rebirth (reincarnation) are philosophically conceivable and not to be too quickly dismissed as we in the West tend to do.[3] It is simply that the doctrine of rebirth is not of immediate help to us here. The Greek concept of immortality will not be our starting point either. Given the Hellenistic influence on Judaism, however,

---

[2] A further possibility spoken of today is that of being immortalized in the divine memory, a theological opinion prominent in process theology. For a critique of this option, see John Hick, *Death and Eternal Life* (New York: Harper and Row, 1976), 215-21. The best effort to develop a globally responsible theology of death and an eschatology which seriously considers varied cultural approaches to life after death is Hick's *Death and Eternal Life*. Also see Hans Küng, *Eternal Life?*, trans. Edward Quinn (Garden City, N.Y.: Doubleday and Co., 1984).

[3] Reincarnation itself need not be seen as incompatible with Christianity even though it has never been a part of Christian orthodoxy. A good introduction to the concept of reincarnation and its compatibility with Christianity is Geddes MacGregor's *Reincarnation* (Wheaton, IL.: The Theosophical Publishing House, 1978). Also see John Hick, *Death and Eternal Life*, 297-396, for a discriminating discussion of the concept of reincarnation, 365-73, in particular for his reflection on Christianity's compatibility with the doctrine of reincarnation, and 399-466 for his own effort to construct a global theology of the future after death.

we ought not be surprised that we will meet the concept of immortality within Jewish history, but we do not begin with it.[4]

The Jewish Background
for Life After Death

Sheol was the final abode for the dead of Israel, but Sheol eventually came to be conceived as an abode for the dead of all the nations. Already early, in pre-Mosaic and pre-prophetic Israelite religion, probably under the influence of ancestor worship, death meant an end of earthly life, but not the end of all existence as such. Yet Sheol was considered to be outside Yahweh's rule. The Lord reigned over the living, and over the nation, but not over the dead.

There were throughout Israel's history varying and conflicting views about the type of life in Sheol. R.H. Charles distinguishes between (1) an older, more primitive, pre-prophetic, non-monotheistic conception in which a certain degree of knowledge and power were attributed to the dead, and (2) a later conception, influenced by monotheism, prophetic and post-prophetic, in which there was neither knowledge nor life in the grave, but simply a shadowy and negative kind of existence, this view being an ancestor of later Sadduceeism.[5] It is important to note that neither of

---

[4]The polarization between the concept of immortality as Hellenistic and resurrection as Jewish was emphasized by Oscar Cullmann. Cullmann's perspective is widely recognized as inadequate today. On the contrast between these two ideas, see John Hick, *Death and Eternal Life*, 177-81. Also see Hans Clemens Caesarius Cavallin, *Life After Death, Pt. I, An Enquiry into the Jewish Background* (Lund, Sweden: C.W.K. Gleerup, 1974), a doctoral thesis at Uppsala University, 15-18, 103-70, 199-200; George W.E. Nickelsburg, *Resurrection, Immortality and Eternal Life in Intertestamental Judaism* (Cambridge: Harvard University Press, 1972). For the essay by Cullmann, see *Immortality and Resurrection*, four essays by Cullmann, Wolfson, Jaeger, Cadbury, edited with an introduction by Krister Stendahl (New York: Macmillan Co., 1965).

[5]R.H. Charles, *Eschatology, The Doctrine of a Future Life in Israel, Judaism and Christianity* (New York: Schoken Books, [1899/1913] 1963), 33-50, 160-64, 217-20, 244, 290-94, 357.

these views, nor indeed the doctrine of Sheol itself, was the ancestor of later Jewish teaching about the resurrection of the dead, the source of which came later.

The sense of the individual in Israelite religion emerged most notably with Jeremiah and Ezekiel. Prior to this it was not the individual but the family or tribe which was the basic religious unit. This was true even for the great eighth century prophets: their messages were for the nation. Granted, the translations of Enoch (Gn 5:22-24) and Elijah (1 Kgs 2:11) manifest an awareness of individuals and their future. But these translations were exceptional and based on their lives of union with God on earth. They depict an immortality *with* the body, not without it, *before* death, not after it, and were narrated in a time when the reign of the Lord was seen as limited to the living and did not extend to Sheol. The first manifestations of the belief that the power of the Lord extended to Sheol are in 1 Kings 17:22 and 2 Kings 4:35, 13:21, where the Lord restores the dead to life through the prophets. But any real sense that the individual is the object of the Lord's concern awaits Jeremiah and Ezekiel and their effort to wrestle with the theology of individual retribution.

Jeremiah rejected the previous, prevalent theology of retribution in which the individual was seen simply as a member of the family. Jeremiah 31:29-30 suggests a relationship between the Lord and the individual Israelite. Jeremiah came to this conviction on the basis of his own personal experience of God and in the face of the impending destruction of the nation.

Likewise Ezekiel taught a direct relationship between the Lord and the individual (18:4). Given the individual's relation to God (18:4) the individual who is faithful to the Lord is unaffected by the sins of one's ancestors (18:20-28). There is strictly an individual basis for reward and punishment. For Ezekiel, reward and punishment were limited to this life. There was no doctrine of life after death. Hence, outward and material fortunes and misfortunes give witness to the individual's condition before God. Ezekiel seems not to have expected the righteous to perish in the destruction of Jerusalem (9:3-6). Ezekiel's theology is manifest in the

Psalms as well as in the Book of Proverbs.

Ezekiel's perspective is questioned in Job and Ecclesiastes. The present condition is not necessarily a true manifestation of an individual's righteousness before the Lord. Yet, even with Job, the issue is not resolved by a development of the doctrine of a future life for the individual. R.H. Charles writes:

> Job declares that God will appear for his vindication, and that after his death (i.e., without the body) he shall witness this vindication, and enjoy the vision of God. But we cannot infer that this divine experience will endure *beyond the moment of Job's justification by God.* It is not the blessed immortality of the departed soul that is referred to here, but its actual entrance into and enjoyment of the higher life, however momentary its duration.[6]

In Job, although the individual is not cut off from union with God by death, there is still no doctrine of a future life.

With Jeremiah and Ezekiel, Israel became aware of the individual. With Job and Ecclesiastes, traditional theology was called into question. The stage was set for the development of an awareness of a future life—that there was more to life after death than Sheol. This is seen in Psalms 69 and 73 where Sheol became the abode only for the wicked and heaven becomes an abode for the righteous. After death the future lot of the righteous and the wicked is not the same. God preserves the righteous from Sheol.

Exactly when the doctrine of the resurrection from the dead appeared in Judaism is a disputed question. The clearest reference is the book of Daniel, second century B.C.E., which reference is considered the only "universally accepted statement of an eschatological resurrection from the dead within the Hebrew Bible."[7]

---

[6]*Ibid.,* 71.

[7]Cavallin, *Life After Death,* 26. Also see Maurice Casey, *Son of Man, The Interpretation and Influence of Daniel 7* (London: S.P.C.K., 1979), 46.

> And many of those who sleep in the dust of the earth shall awake, some to everlasting life, some to shame and everlasting contempt. And those who are wise shall shine like the brightness of the firmament; and those who turn many to righteousness, like the stars forever and ever.
>
> (Dn 12:2-3)

Here we have a doctrine of the resurrection of both the righteous and the wicked. It is not necessarily a doctrine of universal resurrection; it may refer only to Israelites, or only to exceptionally good or evil Israelites, or even include outstanding good or evil non-Israelites. Isaiah 26:19 is in the background of the Danielic verse.[8] In the book of Daniel, the righteous seem to be raised to a heavenly type of future life and not simply resuscitated to life on earth. The use of the heavens and stars in the text symbolize the life to come. In addition to these verses, Daniel 12:13 seems to contain a promise of the future resurrection for Daniel himself.

The development of the doctrine of resurrection affected the doctrine of Sheol, depending upon whether it was envisioned as an eternal abode for all the dead, or an intermediate abode for the righteous Israelites but an eternal abode for others. These two meanings predominated, but later, in apocryphal and apocalyptic literature, Sheol was sometimes seen as a final abode of eternal punishment or fire and then had the meaning of a hell.

After Sheol was no longer seen as the eternal abode for all, but rather as an intermediate place, or as an eternal one for some only, other expressions such as Paradise and Heaven described the destiny of the righteous, and Gehenna and Hell described the fate of the wicked. These terms too were variously conceived.

The word Gehenna derived from the "Valley of Hinnom" south of Jerusalem, which had once been the scene of idolatrous sacrifices. Jeremiah prophesied that it would be called the Valley of Slaughter. It was later designated as the

---

[8]Cavallin, 27

place of punishment for apostate Jews. In I Enoch 27 it became a place of punishment and judgment for the wicked after Sheol.

We thus already have some idea of the many questions which the concepts of future life will present:

Who will be raised from the dead? Only the righteous? Both the righteous and the wicked? Only Jews, or both Jews and Gentiles? All of the people or some of them?

When will they be raised? At the final consummation? At the beginning of the messianic kingdom? Immediately after death? And, is one's situation determined at death, or is there hope for moral development after death?

Are the dead to be raised with their bodies or without them? Will it be a resurrection of the body or only of the spirit? If bodily, what will the risen body be like? Which body will it be? If it is to be a transformed body, when will this transformation take place?

Will the dead be raised to life on earth? In heaven? On a new earth? If there is to be a kingdom of the Messiah on earth, how long will it last? How will this world end?

What is the relationship between the fate of the individual and that of the community, between the individual and all of Israel?

If there is to be an intermediate state after death and before the resurrection, in what will it consist? Where will it be?

Will the fate of the Gentiles differ from the fate of the Jews?

All of these were questions within the eschatology of Early Judaism, and the variety of opinions within Judaism points to the fact that various options were entertained. H.C.C. Cavallin researched the biblical and post-biblical Palestinian, Diaspora, and Rabbinic literature of Judaism with respect to the doctrine about life after death.[9] Here we can

---

[9]For Cavallin, see n. 4 in this chapter. Also see D.S. Russell, *The Method and Message of Jewish Apocalyptic* (Philadelphia: Westminster Press, 1964), chapter 14.

only indicate some of his conclusions. Most important, and contrary to a common enough assumption, there was no such thing as *the* Jewish doctrine about life after death in pre-Christian Judaism, nor *the* Jewish conception of resurrection of the body.[10] It is also incorrect to contrast a *Jewish* doctrine of the resurrection of the body with the *Greek* doctrine of the immortality of the soul.[11]

It seems probable that the Essenes believed in some form of life after death although the question is disputed. Resurrection as something already realized by one's initiation into the community of the righteous was the view prominent among them.

Rabbinic Judaism, the final stage in a developing doctrine on the future life, affirmed belief in the resurrection of the body. Both the schools of Shammai and Hillel believed in the resurrection of the earthly body, although Shammai may have been more literal in its understanding than Hillel. An important text of Rabbinic orthodoxy states that among those Israelites who have no such share in the world to come are those who say that there is no resurrection of the dead.[12] The second benediction of the *Shemoneh Esreh* also proclaims belief in the resurrection. But this clear belief of later Rabbinic Judaism, which is still not precise about the nature of the resurrection, cannot be read back into the period from 100 B.C.E.-100 C.E. when a wide variety of views existed.

Not all Jews believed in some form of afterlife.[13] Many Jewish documents from this period say nothing about afterlife at all. The Sadducees themselves consciously denied any form of afterlife, whether that of immortality or resurrection. The Pharisees did accept the doctrine of resurrection

[10]See Cavallin, 15-21, 197-202; C.F. Evans, *Resurrection and the New Testament*, Studies in Biblical Theology, Second Series, 12 (London: SCM, 1970), 14-19.

[11]Cavallin, 60-72, 200; C.F. Evans, 27-30; and note 4 of this chapter.

[12]M. Sanhedrin 10:1. See *The Mishnah*, trans. and introduced by Herbert Danby (Oxford University Press, [1933] 1980), 397.

[13]Cavallin is cautious, but sees the doctrine of resurrection as fairly widespread in pre-Christian Judaism. See pp. 193-96. C.F. Evans, 19-20 (esp. n. 34), 30-34, gives some of the reasons for being cautious in one's judgement on this question.

from the dead. Belief in some form of afterlife was probably more widespread than its denial but it was by no means universal. What we often think of as Jewish belief was not established until some decades after Paul, toward the close of the first century C.E., and even then it appeared with variations.

In the two centuries before Jesus Christ as well as during the first century C.E., there was a major concern with the question of the vindication of the righteous. It is in this context that the notion of resurrection appears and develops. Yet resurrection remains only a minor part of the eschatology in the apocalypses. It manifests itself in a primary way in Daniel, the Enoch literature, The Testaments of the Twelve Partriarchs, 4 Ezra and 2 Baruch. In addition to the theme of resurrection, we also find a focus on immortality in first century Judaism, particularly in Philo of Alexandria and the Book of Wisdom.[14] The concept of immortality simply adds to the variety of conceptions of the afterlife in Early Judaism. Here we will look at that variety only as it is manifest in the Jewish apocalypses.

Chapters 1-36 of *I Enoch* comprise the first part of the book and are a unit in themselves, often dated to the late third or early second century B.C.E.[15] Chapter 22 describes the waiting places of the dead prior to final judgment. There is an elaborate understanding of this intermediate stage. There are two distinct abodes for the wicked, one for those who receive their just punishment in life on earth and thus

---

[14]Cf. David Winston, *The Wisdom of Solomon*, Anchor Bible 43 (Garden City, N.Y.: Doubleday and Co., 1979). See Philo, *On the Special Laws (De Specialibus Legibus)*, trans. F.H. Colson, vol. 7 of Philo (Cambridge: Harvard University Press, 1950), Book 1, par. 68.

[15]See R.H. Charles, *Eschatology, The Doctrine of a Future Life in Israel, Judaism and Christianity*; H.C.C. Cavallin, *Life After Death*. For an introduction to the apocalyptic and apocryphal literature, see Martin McNamara, *Intertestamental Literature,* Old Testament Message 23 (Wilmington, Del.: Michael Glazier, 1983); and George W.E. Nickelsburg, *Jewish Literature Between the Bible and the Mishnah* (Philadelphia: Fortress Press, 1981). For a translation as well as introduction, see *The Old Testament Pseudepigrapha*, vol. 1, *Apocalyptic Literature and Testaments*, ed. James H. Charlesworth (Garden City, N.Y.: Doubleday and Co., 1983).

are punished more mercifully after death, and another for those sinners who did not receive justice during their lifetimes. There is a third abode for the righteous, and Cavallin interprets the text as implying two abodes for the righteous, the second abode of the righteous being for the martyrs. This first section of I Enoch manifests belief in life after death and in God's justice. The immortality of souls seems to be the basis for an intermediate state before the final judgment. Some conception of resurrection may be present but is not central.

Chapters 91-104 of I Enoch comprise the fifth part of the work, a section of the work extremely difficult to date. This section contains several references to afterlife. A resurrection for the righteous with no indication of how this resurrection is to be conceived is indicated in 91:10 (also in 92:3-4; 102:4). In 102:3-9 belief in justice and a future for both the righteous and the wicked is expressed. The text does not speak, however, of a resurrection of the body.

Chapters 37-71 comprise the second part of I Enoch and are known as "The Parables of Enoch." They are more and more being assigned a date in the first century C.E. Chapter 51:1-5 seems to imply the resurrection of the body, something which is not clear elsewhere in I Enoch. Chapter 51 also suggests a resurrection for both righteous and wicked. The description in 58:1-3 and 62:15-16 indicates an eternal life for the righteous and a transformation into glory.

In the *Testaments of the Twelve Patriarchs* there are varied allusions to resurrection, from references to the resurrection of the patriarchs (Simeon 6:7; Judah 25:1; Zebulun 10:2; Benjamin 10:6) to a general resurrection of the righteous and the wicked (Benjamin 10:8). The texts give no further details as to whether this is a resurrection of the body or in what it consists.

4 Ezra, an apocalypse dated toward the end of the first century C.E., considers a resurrection from the dead and seems to envision two resurrections. The text of 7:31, reflecting Daniel 12:2, implies a resurrection of the body. A final resurrection will occur at the end of history and is combined with a final judgment (7:26-44, 112-15). But there also seems to be a preliminary judgment after death with its consequent beatitude or torment. This may already reflect the classical harmonization in Judaism and Christianity where death was a separation of body and soul, followed by an intermediate state anticipating future joy or damnation, followed by a final resurrection and judgment.

In 4 Ezra we have a concept of the messianic kingdom (7:26-36). The Messiah will come, and there will apparently be a preliminary resurrection (of patriarchs, heroes, martyrs), and the reign of the Messiah for 400 years. At the end of the messianic reign, all, including the Messiah, will die. After that will come a universal resurrection and final judgment.

2 Baruch is closely related to 4 Ezra and is also dated toward the end of the first century C.E. or early second century. Chapter 30:1-5 implies the survival of the souls of the righteous and the wicked after death, a messianic reign on earth, a universal resurrection for a final judgment, and the annihilation of the wicked rather than eternal torment. The bodily aspect of the resurrection is not stressed.

Chapters 49-51 explicitly treat the question of what the resurrected bodies will look like. The text is important and contains some similarities to First Corinthians 15.

49¹But further, I ask you, O Mighty One; and I shall ask grace from you who created all things. ²In which shape will the living live in your day? Or how will remain their splendor which will be after that? ³Will they, perhaps, take again this present form, and will they put on the chained members which are in evil and by which evils are accomplished? Or will you perhaps change these things which have been in the world, as also the world itself?

50¹And he answered and said to me: Listen, Baruch, to this word and write down in memory of your heart all that you shall learn. ²For the earth will surely give back the dead at that time; it receives them now in order to keep them, not changing anything in their form. But as it has received them so it will give them back. And as I have delivered them to it so it will raise them. ³For then it will be necessary to show those who live that the dead are living again, and that those who went away have come back. ⁴And it will be that when they have recognized each other, those who know each other at this moment, then my judgment will be strong, and those things which have been spoken of before will come.

51 ¹And it will happen after this day which he appointed is over that both the shape of those who are found to be guilty as also the glory of those who have proved to be righteous will be changed. ²For the shape of those who now act wickedly will be made more evil than it is (now)so that they shall suffer torment. ³Also, as for the glory of those who proved to be righteous on account of my law, those who possessed intelligence in their life, and those who planted the root of wisdom in their heart—their splendor will then be glorified by transformations, and the shape of their face will be changed into the light of their beauty so that they may acquire and receive the undying world which is promised to them. ⁴Therefore, especially they who will then come will be sad, because they despised my Law and stopped their ears lest they hear wisdom and receive intelligence. ⁵When they, therefore, will see that those over whom they are exalted now will then be more exalted and glorified than they, then both these and those will be changed, these into the splendor of angels and those into startling visions and horrible shapes; and they will waste away even more. ⁶For they will first see and then they will go away to be tormented. ⁷Miracles, however, will appear at their own time to those who are saved because of their works and for whom the Law is now a hope, and intelligence, expectation, and wisdom a trust. ⁸For they shall see that world which is now invisible to them, and they will see a time which is now hidden to them. ⁹And time will no longer make them older. ¹⁰For they will live in the heights of that world and they will be like the angels and be equal to the stars. And they will be changed into any shape which they wished, from beauty to loveliness, and from light to the splendor of glory. ¹¹For the extents of Paradise will be spread out for them, and to

them will be shown the beauty of the majesty of the living beings under the throne, as well as all the hosts of the angels, those who are held by my word now lest they show themselves, and those who are withheld by my command so that they may stand at their places until their coming has arrived. [12]And the excellence of the righteous will then be greater than that of the angels. [13]For the first will receive the last, those whom they expected; and the last, those of whom they had heard that they had gone away. [14]For they have been saved from this world of affliction and have put down the burden of anguishes. [15]Because of which men lost their life and for what have those on the earth exchanged their soul? [16]For once they chose for themselves that time which cannot pass away without afflictions. And they chose for themselves that time of which the end is full of lamentations and evils. And they have denied the world that does not make those who come to it older. And they have rejected the time which causes glory so that they are not coming to the glory of which I spoke to you before. (2 Baruch 49-51)[16]

In this passage we have two different types of resurrection faith. How will the dead be raised; what will they look like? (49:1-3). The body is literally restored. As one was when one died, so will one be raised. We have here "one of the most extreme expressions of literal faith in the resurrection of the body."[17] This resurrection is for the purpose of recognition (50:1-4). Then some time after the resurrection, transformation takes place (51:1-12). The wicked shall be tormented, and the righteous shall be exalted and glorified and be like angels. It is "the most explicit expression concerning a spiritually resurrected body."[18] The resurrection in 2 Baruch is first very physical, then very spiritual.

---

[16]Translation from *Old Testament Pseudepigrapha*, vol. 1, ed. James H. Charlesworth. Translation by A.F.H. Klijn, pp. 637-38.

[17]Cavallin, 88.

[18]*Ibid.*, 88.

We can easily see even in our overly brief survey that the emerging belief in life after death did not rest upon an agreed upon, commonly accepted anthropology or view of the relationship between body and soul. Hence the character of the future life was variously conceived. The faith underlying the doctrine was that "righteousness is finally vindicated" and "God is proven to be just."[19]

> The point of the hope of life after death in Early Judaism is this transformation of the weak, imperfect, unjust, and often miserable existence of the righteous in the present world to the glory and joy in God's presence, in a situation of justice and undisturbed peace. The hope of a radically transformed life after death was born or at least planted in Israel in a period of suffering for those who trusted in God's promise and tried to keep his laws.[20]

Some Preliminary Observations

Few topics admit of such complexity, controversy, and variety as do topics which pertain to our personal and collective futures. Human interest in eschatology is understandable. Yet there is relatively little that we can say about it with certainty. Varied conceptions of the future have been sources of intense division among people. Even today apocalyptic expectations persist along with other ways of expressing hope for the future and faith in God's justice. Fundamental presuppositions of any Christian eschatological perspective include: (1) the belief that there is more to life than death; (2) the awareness that we cannot be clear or dogmatic about the character of that life; and yet (3) that the future beyond death is reason for a hope that will be fulfilled. These are three significant cornerstones for any eschatology: faith, a certain kind of skepticism, and hope.

[19]*Ibid.*, 213.
[20]*Ibid.*, 214.

1. Here is not the place to argue the reasonableness of faith in life after death. That has been critically and reflectively done by others.[21] Here it stands more as a presupposition. Yet it is a presupposition in the context of faith, and the same faith which provided the context for the emergence of belief in resurrection in Judaism: faith in God, in the justice of God, and that God is a Lord of the living. It is faith in God, theology, and not a particular conception of the human person, anthropology, which is the basis for belief in future life in the Judeo-Christian tradition.

2. At the same time that we affirm faith in our future, God's future for us, we must also strongly and clearly say that we know little if anything with respect to its details. Our faith is in God, who has a future in store for us, the particular character of which has not been revealed.

This eschatological skepticism which is but a corollary of faith (here also, in eschatology, we live by faith) is Pauline. Paul writes in his great discussion of the resurrection:

> But some one will ask, "How are the dead raised? With what kind of body do they come?" You foolish person! What you sow does not come to life unless it dies. (1 Cor 15:35-36)

What Paul is affirming is faith in the resurrection from the dead, but skepticism with respect to further details. How can we know what the resurrection body will be like? Paul himself does not know. These multitudinous expectations and questions are unnecessary (the 1966 Jerusalem Bible translated the text: "They are stupid questions").

These questions are foolish because they are ultimately unanswerable. Yet, we all ask them. We all speculate and wonder. Paul himself, after replying that the question about the nature of the resurrection body is foolish and unanswerable, goes on, nevertheless, in an effort to make the doctrine of resurrection more understandable. But Paul's

[21]One of the better contemporary studies in this regard is that by John Hick, *Death and Eternal Life*. See his bibliography and references to further studies. Also see Hans Küng, *Eternal Life?*

fundamental, intuitive response is that questions such as these are foolish. Why? Paul believes in God, in the power and justice of God, that God will restore the dead to life, and that God has already, in fact, done this for Jesus. The individual here must rely upon faith and trust in God. In death, as in life, one is in the hands of God. Nothing more is known than that God will be faithful.

Paul's response to the questions about resurrection is based upon his own careful reflection, his familiarity with the Jewish traditions, and his own personal experience of Jesus as raised from the dead. Yet even after all this, he does not place too great a confidence in his own effort to conceptualize the mystery. We also may not be able to arrive at precision and consistency here. Paul understands the concern and attempts to help, but is still aware that we do not know the future. The value of trying to flesh out the details of an eschatology is that *this effort helps us.* It helps to conceptualize possibilities. The danger is to place too great a weight on human constructs. Eschatological faith with respect to the fact of a future life must be balanced by eschatological skepticism with respect to its nature.

3. This skepticism is in no way, however, a lack of faith or an occasion for despair. Eschatological faith not only implies hope; it is hope. It is a hope beyond conceptualization. Paul hesitates to respond too confidently about the nature of the resurrection body but his hope is in a God who is faithful. Earlier in his first letter to the Corinthians, he writes:

> But, as it is written, "What no eye has seen nor ear heard, nor the human heart conceived what God has prepared for those who love him." (1 Cor 2:9)

No one can conceive how God will fulfill God's promises, but Paul's faith in God remains firm.

> For I am sure that neither death, nor life, nor angels, nor principalities, nor things present, nor things to come, nor powers, nor height, nor depth, nor anything else in all

creation, will be able to separate us from the love of God in Christ Jesus our Lord. (Romans 8:38-39)

And who is Paul's God?

O the depth of the riches and wisdom and knowledge of God! How unsearchable are his judgments and how inscrutable his ways! "For who has known the mind of the Lord, or who has been his counselor?" "Or who has given a gift to him that he might be repaid?" For from him and through him and to him are all things. To him be glory forever. Amen. (Romans 11:33-36)

Paul's faith and hope are unshakable. He cannot imagine precisely how God will restore the dead to life and reward the righteous. Paul's eschatology is based on faith and hope. And thus all the human speculations, whatever their value may be, are not to be taken too seriously. Our faith is not in these concepts, but in God. But let us see what else Paul has to teach us.

Paul's Theology of Resurrection

Belief in Jesus as raised from the dead permeates Pauline preaching and theology. Our concern here will be with four texts—I Thessalonians 4:13-18; 1 Corinthians 15; 2 Corinthians 5:1-5; and Philippians 1:23, 3:20-21. There is general agreement that Paul's thinking on the resurrection exhibits development. However, there is not agreement on the degree of development or on what caused it.[22] There are differences

---

[22]Among those who recognize development in Paul's thought are C.H. Dodd (1934), W.D. Davies (1948), C.F.D. Moule (1964), and Pierre Benoit (1977). Benoit represents a moderate approach to the question of how Paul's thinking changed, and he makes the valuable observation that the major development in Paul's thought would have taken place with his conversion and during the fifteen-year period prior to his literary activity. Cf. P. Benoit, "L' évolution du langage apocalyptique dans le corpus paulinien,"*Apocalypses et théologie de l'espérance*, 299-335, Association Catholique Française pour L'étude de la Bible, Paris, 1977; "Genèse et évolution de la pensée paulinienne," in L. de Lorenzi (ed.), *Paul de Tarse, Apôtre du notre temps*, 75-100, 1979; "Resurrection: At the End of Time or

as one moves from I Thessalonians to I Corinthians to 2 Corinthians to Philippians, Colossians, and Ephesians (leaving open the question of the authorship of Ephesians).[23]

In I Thessalonians Paul thinks that he and most Christians will still be alive at the Parousia. In I Corinthians, those who will be alive will be the exceptions, but Paul still thinks he will be one of them. By the time of 2 Corinthians, Paul has realized that he himself will die as well. By the time one comes to Colossians and Ephesians there is a greater emphasis both on union with Christ already now in the present and on the cosmic extent of Christ's influence.[24] There are many sources which may have contributed to a shift or development in Paul's thinking: the delay of the Parousia, the varied crises in his churches, his own close calls with death, and the personal experience of aging.[25] A much discussed question is whether Hellenistic or Jewish thought was more influential as Paul advanced in years, traveled more widely in the Hellenistic world, and saw more and more of a rift between Christianity and Judaism. Yet the

Immediately after Death?" in *Immortality and Resurrection*, 103-14, eds. Benoit and Murphy, Concilium (New York: Herder and Herder, 1970). Also see notes 24-26 below. A more recent discussion of this issue which argues for a lack of persuasive evidence that Paul's teaching on the resurrection of the dead underwent significant development is Ben F. Meyer, "Did Paul's View of the Resurrection of the Dead Undergo Development?" *Theological Studies*, 47 (1986), 363-87. Also see Victor Paul Furnish, "Development in Paul's Thought," *Journal of the American Academy of Religion*, 38 (1970), 289-303.

[23]One must still leave open the question of the date for Philippians. For an up-to-date study of the chronological problems in Pauline studies, see Robert Jewett, *A Chronology of Paul's Life* (Philadelphia: Fortress Press, 1979).

[24]C.H. Dodd made the point that there is a shift in Paul from a future eschatology with an awareness of the imminence of the Parousia to an emphasis on the present spiritual union possible with Christ here and now. See Dodd, "The Mind of Paul, Change and Development, " *Bulletin of the John Rylands Library*, vol. 18 (1934), reprinted in *New Testament Studies*, a collection of essays (New York: Charles Scribner's Sons, 1952), 67-128. This shift is a shift in emphasis. Both realities are present throughout Paul -- union with Christ now and the resurrection from the dead. Also see William Baird, "Pauline Eschatology in Hermeneutical Perspective," *New Testament Studies*, vol. 17 (1971), 314-27.

[25]See Benoit, n. 22 above. Also C.F.D. Moule, "The Influence of Circumstances..." *Journal of Theological Studies*, 65 (1964), 1-15; "St. Paul and Dualism," *New Testament Studies*, 12 (1965-66), 106-123.

dominant cultural influence in Paul's life remained Judaism.[26] This does not deny Hellenistic influence on him, nor the Hellenistic influence on Judaism itself.

> [13]But we would not have you ignorant, brethren, concerning those who are asleep, that you may not grieve as others do who have no hope. [14]For since we believe that Jesus died and rose again, even so, through Jesus, God will bring with him those who have fallen asleep. [15]For this we declare to you by the word of the Lord, that we who are alive, who are left until the coming of the Lord, shall not precede those who have fallen asleep. [16]For the Lord himself will descend from heaven with a cry of command, with the archangel's call, and with the sound of the trumpet of God. And the dead in Christ will rise first; [17]then we who are alive, who are left, shall be caught up together with them in clouds to meet the Lord in the air; and so we shall always be with the Lord. [18]Therefore comfort one another with these words. (1 Thes 4:13-18)

The Thessalonians, as well as Paul, lived in expectation of an imminent arrival or return of Jesus. They expected to be alive at the Parousia. Thus something of a crisis had developed for them: the fate of those who had died. The concern seems to have been not only with the fact of death and whether those who had died would share in the benefits of the Parousia, but also whether they would share fully or equally in the benefits. Would those who had died be at some disadvantage? In 4 Ezra 13:16-24, those who were to be alive were considered to have been more fortunate than those who had died. Thus Paul had to address a very concrete and pastoral concern. He did so in terms of the doctrine of the resurrection of the dead and the assumption or rapture of the living, and suggests no disparity between the two situations.

---

[26]Paramount among those who have emphasized Paul's relationship to Judaism is W.D. Davies, *Paul and Rabbinic Judaism* (New York: Harper and Row, 1948); *The Gospel and the Land* (Berkeley: University of California Press, 1974), 208-220.

In verse 13, Paul exhorts the community not to grieve as those do who live without hope of resurrection. He does not tell them not to grieve but not to grieve as unbelievers do. In verse 14, Paul recalls their faith in the resurrection of Jesus through whom their own dead will also be raised: the resurrection of Jesus is the basis for hope. We see in this verse the close link between Jesus' resurrection and our own which Paul later emphasizes in I Corinthians 15 as well.

Paul consoles those who grieve for the dead. In verse 15, however, he goes further. The problem is not that the Thessalonians disbelieve the doctrine of resurrection, but that they seem to think of those who have died as being at some disadvantage. Paul resolves this problem: those who are alive when the Lord comes will not precede those who have died. Paul seems to believe that most of them, including himself, will still be alive; but that condition would not be to their advantage.

In verses 16-17, Paul provides something of a scenario, centering around the three events of the Parousia, the resurrection, and the rapture or assumption of the living. The first are closely linked together. Jesus will descend from heaven and those who have died will be raised. The phrase, "dead in Christ," indicates that Paul is talking only about the resurrection of Christians.

After the descent of the Lord and the resurrection of the dead comes the assumption of the living into the clouds. Neither group has an advantage. The dead will be raised first and then those who are living will be taken together with them, and all together will meet the Lord in the heavens. Then they will all be consoled: we shall all, living and dead, be with the Lord always.

> [1]Now I would remind you, brethren, in what terms I preached to you the gospel, which you received, in which you stand; [2]by which you are saved, if you hold it fast—unless you believe in vain. [3]For I delivered to you as of first importance what I also received, that Christ died for our sins in accordance with the scriptures, [4]that he was buried, that he was raised on the third day in accordance

with the scriptures: [5]and that he appeared to Cephas, then to the twelve. [6]Then he appeared to more than five hundred brethern at one time, most of whom are still alive, though some have fallen asleep. [7]Then he appeared to James, then to all the apostles. [8]Last of all, as to one untimely born, he appeared also to me. [9]For I am the least of the apostles, unfit to be called an apostle, because I persecuted the Church of God. [10]But by the grace of God I am what I am, and his grace toward me was not in vain. On the contrary, I worked harder than any of them, though it was not I, but the grace of God which is with me. [11]Whether then it was I or they, so we preach and so you believed. (I Cor 15:1-11)

First Corinthians 15 is a self-contained unit on the resurrection and is the most important of the four Pauline texts we are considering. It can be divided into three major sections: verses 1-11 on the resurrection of Jesus, verses 12-34 on the fact of the resurrection of the dead, and verses 35-58 on the how of the resurrection, the nature of the resurrection body.

In this first section of I Corinthians 15, Paul reminds the Corinthians that he has preached the gospel to them as he received it, preaching first things first. He then gives a dense summary of the proclamation—an early creed—with reference to the death, burial, resurrection and apprearances of Jesus (at least 3b-5). In addition to the appearances to Peter and the twelve, Paul includes others not included in the Gospels, forming a series of six appearances; Cephas, the twelve, a group of more than 500, James, all the apostles, Paul himself. Paul includes Jesus' appearance to him as one of the sequence of varied appearances. He also reflects upon his own apostleship.

[12]Now if Christ is preached as raised from the dead, how can some of you say that there is no resurrection of the dead? [13]But if there is no resurrection of the dead, then Christ has not been raised. [14]If Christ has not been raised, then our preaching is in vain and your faith is in vain.

15We are even found to be misrepresenting God, because we testified of God that he raised Christ, whom he did not raise if it is true that the dead are not raised. 16For, if the dead are not raised, then Christ has not been raised. 17If Christ has not been raised, your faith is futile and you are still in your sins. 18Then those also who have fallen asleep in Christ have perished. 19If for this life only we have hope in Christ, we are of all men most to be pitied.

(I Cor 15:12-19)

Just as there had been concern among the Thessalonians which prompted a response from Paul, so here among the Corinthians there is also a problem in the community. There are Corinthians who deny the resurrection from the dead, and Paul reflects upon the consequences of their opinion. Paul sees the resurrection of Jesus as closely related to the resurrection of others and to the doctrine of a general resurrection. Jesus' resurrection is not an exception within humanity. Thus, if there is no general resurrection, then Jesus was not raised. But if Jesus has not been raised, faith in Jesus is foolish. The implication is that faith in Jesus is not foolish, that Jesus was in fact raised by God. Therefore, our hope is for resurrection and is not for this life only.

20But in fact Christ has been raised from the dead, the first fruits of those who have fallen asleep. 21For as by a man came death, by a man has come also the resurrection of the dead. 22For as in Adam all die, so also in Christ shall all be made alive. 23But each in his own order: Christ the first fruits, then at his coming those who belong to Christ. 24Then comes the end, when he delivers the kingdom to God the Father after destroying every rule and every authority and power. 25For he must reign until he puts his enemies under his feet. 26The last enemy to be destroyed is death. 27"For God has put all things in subjection under his feet." But when it says, "All things are put in subjection under him," it is plain that he is excepted who put all things under him. 28When all things are subjected to him, then the Son himself will also be subjected to him who put all things under him, that God may be everything to every one. (I Cor 15:20-28)

Jesus has in fact been raised. Paul reflects on Jesus as a contrast to Adam. Jesus Christ is another Adam. The Adam typology is a central feature of Paul's christology (Romans 5:12-21). Thanks to Adam, there is death. Thanks to Jesus, there is life. Paul then presents his own eschatological version of things to come which culminates in a mystical, panentheistic union of God with creation (I Cor 15:27-28).

> [29]Otherwise, what do people mean by being baptized on behalf of the dead? If the dead are not raised at all, why are people baptized on their behalf? [30]Why am I in peril every hour? [31] I protest, brethern, by my pride in you which I have in Christ Jesus our Lord, I die every day! [32]What do I gain if, humanly speaking, I fought with beasts at Ephesus? If the dead are not raised, "Let us eat and drink, for tomorrow we die." [33]Do not be deceived: "Bad company ruins good morals." [34]Come to your right mind, and sin no more. For some have no knowledge of God. I say this to your shame. (I Cor 15:29-34)

Paul returns to the question at hand, which he had been discussing in verses 12-19, and continues to argue on behalf of the doctrine of resurrection, exhorting the unbelieving to accept it. What baptism on behalf of the dead was is not known, although there have been many hypotheses.[27] The quotation in verse 32 is Isaiah 22:13 and verse 33 is from Menander's *Thais*. The major section of 15:12-34 is now complete. Paul has attempted both logically and rhetorically to convince the Corinthians that the resurrection of the dead will take place. He now proceeds to help them understand this fact by discussing *how* the dead will be raised.

---

[27]For a fairly recent interpretation, see Jerome Murphy-O'Connor, "Baptized for the Dead (1 Cor. 15:29), A Corinthian Slogan?" *Revue Biblique* 88 (1981), 532-43. For the history of the interpretation, see B.M. Foschini, "Those Who Are Baptized for the Dead," *Catholic Biblical Quarterly* 12 (1950), 260-76, 379-99, and 13 (1951), 46-78, 172-98, 276-83.

35But some one will ask, "How are the dead raised. With what kind of body do they come?" 36You foolish man! What you sow does not come to life unless it dies. 37And what you sow is not the body which is to be, but a bare kernel, perhaps of wheat or of some other grain. 38But God gives it a body as he has chosen, and to each kind of seed its own body. 39For not all flesh is alike, but there is one kind for men, another for animals, another for birds, and another for fish. 40There are celestial bodies; but the glory of the celestial is one and the glory of the terrestrial is another. 41There is one glory of the sun, and another glory of the moon, and another glory of the stars; for star differs from star in glory. 42So is it with the resurrection of the dead. What is sown is perishable, what is raised is imperishable. 43It is sown in dishonor, it is raised in glory. It is sown in weakness, it is raised in power. 44It is sown a physical body, it is raised a spiritual body. If there is a physical body, there is also a spiritual body. 45Thus it is written, "The first man Adam became a living being"; the last Adam became a life-giving spirit. 46But it is not the spiritual which is first but the physical, and then the spiritual. 47The first man was from the earth, a man of dust; the second man is from heaven. 48As was the man of dust, so are those who are of dust; and as is the man of heaven, so are those who are of heaven. 49Just as we have borne the image of the man of dust, we shall also bear the image of the man of heaven. (1 Cor 15:35-49)

I Corinthians 15:35-58 contains the most significant passage in Scripture on the nature of the resurrection. Paul begins with the familiar question which he was probably frequently asked. As we have seen, he first dismisses it as a foolish, unanswerable question; then he answers it. He elaborates his understanding of the resurrection with the analogy of the seed (vv. 36-39); and by reference to different or analogous kinds of flesh (v. 39), bodies (v. 40a), and glory (vv. 40b-41). He then returns to the image of sowing (vv. 42-44). Verse 44 contains the classical contrast between a physical body and a spiritual body. Paul concludes his effort to help the Corinthians understand by returning to Adam and an Adam/Christ contrast. This section (vv. 35-38) is not unrelated to the previous section (vv. 12-34). *If* Paul can help the Corinthians to see or understand more clearly what the resurrection means or consists in, if they can picture it better, then he has also helped those who deny the resurrection to come one step closer to accepting it. Thus Paul's effort to answer the question of how the dead are raised and what kind of body they will have is a part of his overall objective to convince the Corinthians of the doctrine of the resurrection, and of a bodily resurrection. "How the dead are raised" and "what they will look like" is really not important in itself (it is foolish to speculate). But it is important pastorally in that it may help some to accept the resurrection who otherwise would not because of their inability to comprehend it. It is in this context that Paul attempts to articulate what cannot really be known. Paul has, however, his own experience of the risen Jesus to go on. The implication is that "It is possible to make a reasonable estimate of what the resurrection body will be like, and that this estimate is verified in the resurrection body of Christ."[28]

Paul's interpretation is not overly literal or physical. He points out that there are different kinds of flesh, bodies, and glory, and so it should not appear so strange or incomprehensible to talk about two particular kinds of bodies, the earthly body and the resurrection body, or the physical and spiritual bodies.

The contrast between the earthly body and the resurrected body is quite a contrast for they are the reverse of each other. The one is perishable, inglorious, weak and physical. The other is imperishable, glorious, powerful, and spiritual (vv. 42-44). The seed image suggests this contrast; what you sow is not the same as what comes forth. There has been much debate about whether the seed analogy suggests a continuity

---

[28]Jerome Murphy-O'Connor, *1 Corinthians*, New Testament Message, 10 (Wilmington, Delaware: Michael Glazier, 1979), 147.

and identity or discontinuity and novelty, and there will probably be no end to the debate. It is not a question of either/or, but of *both* continuity *and* discontinuity. One cannot deny that Paul presents the two bodies as a contrast. In all of this Paul is trying to help the Corinthians understand the *how* of the resurrection (vv. 35-58) so that they can accept it (vv. 12-34) and thus the full gospel as he preached it to them (vv. 1-11).

50I tell you this, brethren: flesh and blood cannot inherit the kingdom of God, nor does the perishable inherit the imperishable. 51Lo! I tell you a mystery. We shall not all sleep, but we shall all be changed, 52in a moment, in the twinkling of an eye, at the last trumpet. For the trumpet will sound, and the dead will be raised imperishable, and we shall be changed. 53For this perishable nature must put on the imperishable, and this mortal nature must put on immortality. 54When the perishable put on the imperishable, and the mortal puts on immortality, then shall come to pass the saying that is written: "Death is swallowed up in victory." 55"O death, where is thy victory? O death, where is thy sting?" 56The sting of death is sin, and the power of sin is the law. 57But thanks be to God, who gives us the victory through our Lord Jesus Christ. 58Therefore, my beloved brethren be steadfast, immovable, always abounding in the work of the Lord, knowing that in the Lord your labor is not in vain. (I Cor 15:50-58)

Paul has already explained that the resurrection body is not the same as our earthly bodies. It is as different from the earthly body as the grain is from the seed. This should not be alarming since there are many different kinds of bodies anyway. As we now live with earthly bodies, later we will live with spiritual bodies. But now Paul goes further to explain the change that must take place if we are to live the life to come and inherit the reign of God.

Two interpretations can be seen in verse 50, depending upon whether one sees the verse as containing synonymous parallelism or synthetic parallelism.[29] "Flesh and blood," *(sarx kai haima)* is a Semitic expression denoting the whole person, but the person as weak, frail, corruptible, the naturally finite and fragile human being. Thus the human being as is cannot enter into the reign of God to come.

If the two expressions, "flesh and blood" and corruption or "reign of God" and incorruption are read as synonymous expressions, the latter could be seen as a translation for a more Hellenistic audience. Joachim Jeremias, however, does not see synonymous parallelism here. In addition to "flesh and blood" referring to the whole human being, as weak and distinct from God, it also refers only to those who are alive, not to the dead. "Flesh and blood cannot inherit the reign of God" does not refer at all to the resurrection of the dead, but to the condition of the living who must be changed before or at the Parousia. We thus have an awareness not unlike that of I Thessalonians where there are two groups that concern Paul: neither those still living (flesh and blood) nor those who have died (corruption, the perishable) can enter into God's reign without some kind of transformation. Jeremias writes:

> That means: the two lines of v. 50 are contrasting men of flesh and blood on the one hand, and corpses in decomposition on the other. In other words, the first line refers to those who are alive at the parousia, the second line to those who died before the parousia. The parallelism is thus not synonymous but synthetic and the meaning of v. 50 is: neither the living nor the dead can take part in the Kingdom of God—as they are.[30]

---

[29]Joachim Jeremias argues for synthetic parallelism. See Jeremias, "Flesh and Blood Cannot Inherit the Kingdom of God," *New Testament Studies* 2 (1965), 151-59. For further discussion of the text see the doctoral dissertation by John Gillman, *Transformation into the Future Life: A Study of 1 Cor. 15, 50-53, Its Context and Related Passages*, Catholic University of Louvain, 1980, pp. 433, 495, 763-5. The entire dissertation is a very helpful study of 1 Cor. 15 as well as other Pauline texts.

[30]Jeremias, "Flesh and Blood ...," 152. Jeremias also mentions, 154, that those who have died undergo a transformation like unto Jesus' resurrection, and those who are still living, a transformation like unto Jesus' transfiguration.

Paul may be asserting something similar to I Thessalonians. There will be no major difference in situation for the living and the dead. Both must undergo a change, and both will enter the reign of God together.

But why must the living as well as the dead be changed? The living already have bodies and are alive. "Flesh and blood" as well as corpses in the process of decomposition cannot enter what God has in store for us without transformation. Whether verse 50 is read as synonymous parallelism or synthetic parallelism, however, the fact remains that for Paul the future life requires a transformation of men and women as we now are in our earthly existence. This fact follows from what Paul has already said about different kinds of bodies: perishable bodies cannot enter the reign of God. They must put on imperishable bodies. Not all bodies are the same. There are earthly bodies and heavenly bodies. A new body is necessary for the new environment.

Verse 50, like the preceding verses, emphasizes a discontinuity between "this life" and its way of being embodied, and "the life to come" and its way of being embodied. The resurrection is not the revivification of the corpse, nor of the flesh, but a transformation or change. Paul's understanding seems to fall between two poles of thinking, between (1) a view which sees the risen person as restored to the same type of bodily life as that which we have lived on earth, and (2) a denial of the risen life as being embodied. Paul is not describing an immortal, disembodied soul or person. Nor is he describing bodies as we now have. That is his point: there has to be a change before we enter the reign of God.

In verses 51-52 Paul refers to what he has to say as a mystery. I referred earlier to an eschatological skepticism within Paul's own response to the questions put in 15:35. Now again we note that Paul sees these future events as a mystery which transcends human understanding, and he avoids any detailed description of the events to come. He simply makes the point that we will all in some way be changed. Perhaps Paul's awareness was influenced by his own earlier ecstatic experience which is narrated in 2 Corinthians 12:1-4, which is also inexpressible.

"We shall not all sleep," shows an awareness similar to 1 Thessalonians. The Parousia is imminent. Not all of us will die. Paul still sees himself among those who will be alive. The all, *pantes*, refers to all believers; Paul is not concerned here with the future state of non-believers. The future tense and the reference to the last trumpet shows that Paul has the Parousia in mind. Verses 51-52 also indicate the situation of equality between those who have died and those who are alive that Paul emphasized in 1 Thessalonians. There is no temporal distinction. It all will happen instantaneously and simultaneously. The dead will be raised into the imperishable life, and the living will simultaneously be transformed. Paul's use of the concept of transformation in order to articulate the mystery is not something uniquely Pauline. Some wrongly assert that the Jewish doctrine of the resurrection was very material, a resurrection of the flesh, and Paul's teaching here more spiritual. But we have seen that this characterization is not true. Diversity and pluralism characterized Judaism with respect to its understanding of the future life. The concept of transformation was present in Judaism as well. R.H. Charles wrote, "Paul was not altogether an innovator but an able and advanced expositor of some current Jewish views."[31] And W.D. Davies wrote as well, "There would be many Pharisees prepared to argue, as Paul does, for a transformed resurrection body."[32]

The text of 1 Corinthians 15 shows that there is both continuity and discontinuity between the present state and the life to come, that we must undergo a change or transformation to participate in the life to come, and that the life to come will still be an embodied or somatic existence. We can see the reality of the discontinuity as well as the basis for a continuity in the Pauline images and language: (1) Vv. 36-38, the seed analogy, show that what comes forth is not the same as that which is sown, yet is indeed in continuity with it. An apple tree does not look like an apple seed. There is

---

[31]R.H. Charles, *The Apocrypha and Pseudepigrapha of the Old Testament* (Oxford: Clarendon Press, 1913), vol. 2, p. 508, note on 2 Baruch 50-51.

[32]W.D. Davies, *Paul and Rabbinic Judaism*, 308.

discontinuity. Yet, an apple seed doesn't bring forth an orange tree or produce tomatoes. There is continuity. (2) Vv. 42-44, the four antitheses, point to the contrast, the discontinuity. yet the *it* that is sown and raised remains the same *it*. (3) V. 49, the Adam typology, shows that we are continuous, we bear the images, yet the images that we bear are quite different. (4) V. 50, that flesh and blood cannot inherit the reign of God, emphasizes the discontinuity. (5) V. 53 uses clothing language which implies the same person but a different garment.

Studies of Paul's use of the word *sōma* indicate that he did not mean body as we may think of body, namely, in contrast to soul, as simply materiality or physicality.[33] The Hebrew understanding of the human being is that of a psychophysical unit in contrast to a Platonic perspective which sees the body and soul as separable entities. Thus *sōma* does not refer to the physicality of the human person in itself, but to the person as a complete yet physical being. This emphasis on a wholistic understanding of *sōma* can be extended too far, however, to meaning person alone and not embodiment as well. *Sōma* does have the connotation of a physically embodied individual, but an individual who is still a psychosomatic unit, not an individual composed of "a body" and "a soul."[34] Rather I *am* a body; I do not *have* a body. As *sōma*, I am an individual person but an embodied person. *Sōma* is *me*, not my body, but me as being embodied. Thus *sōma* is a person, an individual, but an

---

[33]Murdoch E. Dahl, *The Resurrection of the Body, A Study of 1 Corinthians 15* , SBT 36 (Naperville, Ill.: Alec Allenson, 1962). Robert H. Gundry, *Soma in Biblical Theology, with Emphasis on Pauline Anthropology* (Cambridge: Cambridge University Press, 1976). Robert Jewett, *Paul's Anthoropological Terms, A Study of Their Use in Conflict Settings* (Leiden: E.J. Brill, 1971), 201-50; J.A.T. Robinson, *The Body, A Study in Pauline Theology* (London: SCM Press, 1963); E. Schweizer, "Pneuma," *Theological Dictionary of the New Testament*, trans. G.W. Bromiley, 6 (Grand Rapids: William B. Eerdmans Pub. Co., 1968), 389-455; "Psyche," *TDNT*, 9 (1974), 637-66; "Sarx," *TDNT*, 7 (1971), 1024-94.

[34]See Gundry, *Soma in Biblical Theology*. Gundry's study is significant in providing an emphasis often dismissed. Yet he goes too far in identifying *sōma* with the physical at the expense of the total. The two, a physical understanding and a wholistic understanding, need not be opposed.

individual as physically embodied and relationally extended. Much of the discussion of *sōma* is inflicted with either/or conceptual categories, rather than the awareness that the concept *sōma* integrates what we tend to oppose. Thus *sōma* can refer both to an individual (I am sown a physical body and raised a spiritual body) and to the individual as a person organically related to others and to God. *Sōma* means an individual, but can be extended to mean a supra-individual, psychophysical unity such as Christ. (There is but one body and we are members of it.) Likewise *sōma* can refer both to the whole person and to the person as physical. *Sōma* is both personal and physical. One cannot be a person without being embodied; yet "personality" and "physicality" are distinguishable, even if not separable. Thus *sōma* refers to a relationally structured, physically embodied, individual person. *Sarx*, flesh, refers to the person as fragile, weak, distant from God and others, and *sōma* refers to the person as a physical whole in relationship to God and others. The individual as *sōma* can experience transformation, not so the individual as *sarx*. One can speak of the resurrection of the body (*sōma*), but not the resurrection of the flesh (*sarx*).

Not only does *sōma* connote both individual and relational aspects, both a totality as well as physicality, but it also allows for both continuity and discontinuity when used with respect to resurrection. Murdoch Dahl's study is particularly helpful.[35] There is both continuity and discontinuity between this life as a *sōma psychikon* and the life to come as a *sōma pneumatikon*. Dahl points to two contrasting views and then presents his own.

One view, heterosomatism, tends toward discontinuity between the body now and the future, glorified body. In this exegesis of Paul, the body with which we are raised (or with which Jesus was raised) is not the same body that was buried (the corpse). We do not have our earthly, physical bodies restored in a glorified way but we are rather given new

---

[35]Murdoch Dah. s study, *The Resurrection of the Body*, maintains a rightful balance. It has been criticized for not delineating more clearly what somatic identity means. See Hick, *Death and Eternal Life*, p. 192, n. 47, also pp. 185-90. Also see Hick's replica theory for his own effort to resolve this issue, 278-96.

bodies, new creations. A second view, autosomatism, is more traditional, namely, that the physical body which we now possess is to be restored. There are not two contrasted bodies, but only one, and the spiritual body is my present body miraculously transformed.

Both of these perspectives pose problems. The seed analogy suggests continuity between what is sown and what is raised, even if it is radically different. Likewise the word *sōma* is basic to both the physical body and the spiritual body; it is sown a *sōma psychikon* and raised a *sōma pneumatikon*. That does not sound like a completely new *sōma* but the *sōma* transformed. Yet autosomatism carries with it the difficulty of a crude material identity of physical particles.

Dahl attempts to establish a position between these two. It is Paul's concept of transformation that is his solution to the relationship between the two ways of being embodied. For Dahl, the resurrection of the dead is neither a revivification of the corpse nor a new creation of the individual person. "Although the resurrection body will not be *materially identical* with the one we now possess, it will be what I choose to call *somatically identical*."[36] Our risen bodies will not be materially identical, not the same matter, not the same physical particles. Dahl rejects such a "crude materialism" as the basis for the identity and continuity. Yet we will be the same persons. It will be none other than I who am raised. This is somatic identity. "If I say, this is the *same man* I met in London seven years ago, I mean he is the *same person* (in Pauline terms the same 'body'), knowing that the particular cells of his 'body' (in the modern sense) have completely changed since then."[37]

Dahl's effort attempts to do justice both to continuity (somatic identity, the same person) and to the transformation involved (materially speaking, discontinuity). One ought not misread Dahl and see the raised person (*sōma*) as not being physically embodied. The one raised to new life with God is

---

[36] M. Dahl, *The Resurrection of the Body*, 10.
[37] *Ibid.*, 94.

not only the same prson, but an embodied person, but not
with a materially identical physicality. In other words,
somatic identity includes embodiment. It is *me* as a psycho-
physical unit, but not the physical matter of the corpse
restored or transformed.

One weakness in Dahl, as in most efforts to re-construct
what Paul means by *sōma*, is the danger of overprecision in
what Paul means. We must return to our eschatological
skepticism. We cannot answer all the questions about how
the dead are raised or with what bodies they will live forever.
These are foolish questions in the first place. What we
believe is that God will raise the dead and our hope is in the
Lord. Yet Paul's effort to discuss these questions indicates
that he saw both a newness, a change, a necessary transformation in order to inherit the reign of God, and yet that
those to be raised will be the same people who died, and also
embodied. But while it is not clear that it is the same material
body, it is clear that it is the same person.

There is no major change in Paul's conception or eschatology between 1 Thessalonians and 1 Corinthinans. In 1
Thessalonians the people seem to have expected to be alive
at the Parousia. It was thus a critical and disconcerting
problem that some had died. Those who had died would
have been seen as the exception, minority. With 1 Corinthians we do not have the same issue. Many had died and
more would die. However, they were consoled with the
doctrine of the resurrection of the dead. But some were
denying this doctrine which Paul saw as cutting at the very
core of his preaching. At any rate, being alive at the Parousia
was no longer something so ardently expected, although
there still would be some who would survive until then, and
Paul still expected to be among them.

In 1 Corinthians Paul speaks at greater length about the
transformation that is necessary, but this transformation is
in no way inconsistent with what Paul had taught in 1
Thessalonians.[38] Perhaps his thinking is more developed, or

[38]See John Gillman, "Signals of Transformation in 1 Thessalonians 4:13-18," *The
Catholic Biblical Quarterly*, 47 (1985), 263-81.

perhaps Paul already understood the resurrection and rapture of 1 Thessalonians to involve the kind of transformation he articulated in 1 Corinthinans. If Paul's effort helped some of the Corinthians to understand more clearly and thus accept the resurrection of the dead, it served a valid purpose: if we are not raised, Jesus has not been raised, and our faith is in vain.

> [16]So we do not lose heart. Though our outer nature is wasting away, our inner nature is being renewed every day. [17]For this slight momentary affliction is preparing for us an eternal weight of glory beyond all comparison, [18]because we look not to the things that are seen but to the things that are unseen; for the things that are unseen are eternal. [1]For we know that when the earthly tent we live in is destroyed, we have a building from God, a house not made with hands, eternal in the heavens. [2]Here indeed we groan, and long to put on our heavenly dwelling, [3]so that by putting it on we may not be found naked. [4]For while we are still in this tent, we sigh with anxiety; not that we should be unclothed, but that we would be further clothed, so that what is mortal may be swallowed up by life. [5]He who has prepared us for this very thing is God, who has given us the Spirit as a guarantee. [6]So we are always of good courage; we know that while we are at home in the body we are away from the Lord, [7]for we walk by faith, not by sight. [8]We are of good courage, and we would rather be away from the body and at home with the Lord. [9]So whether we are at home or away we make it our aim to please him. [10]For we must all appear before the judgement seat of Christ, so that each one may receive good or evil, according to what he has done in the body.
>
> (2 Cor 4:16-5:10)[39]

---

[39]I have followed the RSV in these translations of the Pauline texts. However, here, in 2 Cor. 5:1, I have changed the RSV in accord with my interpretation. I have translated *ean* as *when* rather than *if*. Note the translation of the New Jerusalem Bible is *when* as well.

We now move from the first letter to the Corinthians to Paul's second letter. At times our focus on a passage can lead us to urge a text to answer questions which are significant to us but not to the text. These dangers are especially true in the present passage. Paul's emphasis here is his conviction of life with Christ both now and in the life to come. The details of when and how are not his major concern, just as they were not the major concern of 1 Corinthians 15. Paul's concern is expressed in 4:16, that we do not lose heart.

Some argue that the passage refers to our present, earthly life with its possibility of inner transformation, and others argue that it refers to our future life and the hope of resurrection. Verse 16 refers to a transformation already begun. We do have both kinds of transformation in Paul: the transformation already begun with our incorporation into Christ and the community of believers through baptism, and the transformation still to come with the Parousia. Verses 16-18 make us aware that something is already happening to us, that our inner natures are being renewed and that our present afflictions are preparing glory for us. But the major emphasis in the passage is on the life to come after death. Verse 1 of chapter five turns our attention in that direction.

Another point of dispute is whether the passage envisions an individual or corporate future. Some have argued that the heavenly dwelling which we put on is the body of Christ itself, a corporate body rather than an individual one. While this passage clearly seems to be thinking of our future as individuals, one cannot dismiss the strong corporate emphasis in Paul. In 1 Corinthians 12, Paul had spoken about one body in Christ. Being with Christ and in Christ also includes being embodied. Thus the body concept in Paul is both individual and corporate. The focus of this passage, however, is more addressed to our individual, personal futures.

A much more disputed question is whether we receive our heavenly dwelling at the time of death or at the time of the Parousia. If the text is pushed it seems to reflect a shift or development in Paul's thinking by saying that the heavenly dwelling is received at death. In 1 Corinthians 15, the dead and those still alive are transformed at the Parousia; in 2 Corinthians 5, the dead seem to receive a new dwelling at death.

The passage seems much more conscious of death.[40] If the earthly tents we live in (our present bodies or ways of being in the world) are destroyed (presumably at death or by death, although Paul may still be thinking of those who will still be alive at the Parousia as well), we have a new, eternal, heavenly building. The sense of the present tense in verse 1 (*ekhomen*, we have) does suggest that *when* our earthly tents are set aside, we *then* receive our heavenly ones. There is no suggestion of waiting or of something intermediate. If and when this present body passes away, we have (present tense) our new bodies. This sense is suggested by verses 2-4 as well. Already there is a longing for this heavenly dwelling. Paul senses that he does not want ever to be without this heavenly home for to be without it is to be naked. There is again a present emphasis in the passage. Surely death cannot leave us naked. What we have already begun to put on will be put on even further at death so that we may not be found naked. When the earthly body is destroyed, there will be the gift of heavenly bodies. While still in this body (tent), there is a longing to be further clothed. With the desire to be further clothed, to put on our heavenly dwelling, Paul could hardly have in mind that being naked is in fact what will happen to those who die.

We can only speculate about what led Paul toward this new emphasis or consciousness. W.D. Davies writes, "Far more likely is it that two factors had constrained Paul to give more thought than he had previously done to what happened

---

[40]Some of those who see the heavenly body as received at death in 2 Corinthians include R.H. Charles and W.D. Davies. See Davies, *Paul and Rabbinic Judaism*, 309-20. Ben Meyer, "Did Paul's View of Resurrection of the Dead Undergo Development?" 379-81, argues against 2 Cor. 5 as implying the acquisition of a resurrected body immediately upon death, but this is less convincing to me than other parts of his essay.

to the Christian at death; he himself had been at the gates of death and the problem of Christians who died was becoming a pressing one; and Paul was thus led to state the fact that the Christian at death was not left naked but received a heavenly body."[41]

There is no true inconsistency in the two emphases of Paul. We have a both/and situation in which Paul attaches significance to both the moment of death and the moment of Parousia. Both may even be present in this passage from 2 Corinthians. Paul sees a future which begins at death for the Christian but which still is incomplete without the Parousia.

It is no longer an instantaneous moment but a new phase or age that dawns, indeed has already dawned with the resurrection of Jesus, and will last or not be complete until the Parousia. Thus there are several key moments in history or in the life of the individual for Paul. There is the Resurrection of Jesus, the Parousia, and the age between the two in which the Christians now live.[42] For the individual, there are the moments of baptism or incorporation into Christ, of death or transformation into glory, and the Parousia when Jesus will come and God will be all in all. These events flow from the resurrection of Jesus. An emphasis on one key moment of the Christian mystery does not deny another; baptism, death, and Parousia are all key moments. Death does not leave us naked, although we all still await the Parousia. We have been given our heavenly dwellings, but Christ's work is not yet complete. In what the Parousia consists, or the time between death and the Parousia for those already raised, Paul does not say. It is just that we can be expected to be raised when we die, when this earthly tent is put away.

It is not that Paul attaches less significance to the Parousia, but that he is more conscious of death, of the

---

[41]W.D. Davies, *Paul and Rabbinic Judaism*, 311.

[42]An interesting suggestion can be found in Davies, *Paul and Rabbinic Judaism*, 314-19. I am not sure it is accurate, however, to say as Davies does (318), that "there is no room in Paul's theology for an intermediate state of the dead."

many more who have died whom he did not expect to, of the probability now that even he himself will die before the Parousia, and that Jesus will not withhold his eternal life from those who love him, a life which cannot be totally disembodied.

There are several significant texts in Paul's letter to the Philippians but they will not add further to our understanding. The letter to the Philippians is also more difficult to date with precision, and thus cannot be used to argue any particular development in Paul's thought. In 1:19-26, Paul expresses his own heartfelt desire to die in order to be more fully with Christ (1:21-23). Here we see Paul's theology of death clearly developed and the moment of death as quite significant. At death Paul will be with Christ and he looks forward to this union. The implication is that life after death is also bodily existence (1:20).

> [19]Yes, and I shall rejoice. For I know that through your prayers and the help of the Spirit of Jesus Christ this will turn out for my deliverance, [20]as it is my eager expectation and hope that I shall not be at all ashamed, but that with full courage now and always Christ will be honored in my body, whether by life or by death. [21]For to me to live is Christ, and to die is gain. [22]If it is to be life in the flesh, that means fruitful labor for me. Yet which I shall choose I cannot tell. [23]I am hard pressed between the two. My desire is to depart and be with Christ, for that is far better. [24]But to remain in the flesh is more necessary on your account. [25]Convinced of this, I know that I shall remain and continue with you all, for your progress and joy in the faith, [26]so that in me you may have ample cause to glory in Christ Jesus, because of my coming to you again.
>
> (Phil 1:19-26)

Although Paul does not mention resurrection in the above passage, there is no inconsistency. His teaching on resurrection can be presumed, and later in the letter he does refer to resurrection from the dead (3:10-11). Another passage in Philippians is significant in that it not only refers once again to Paul's teaching about the future transformation but also brings us back to the close union between Jesus' resurrection and our own (3:20-21).

> ²⁰But our commonwealth is in heaven, and from it we await a Savior, the Lord Jesus Christ ²¹who will change our lowly body to be like his glorious body, by the power which enables him even to subject all things to himself.
>
> (Phil 3:20-21)

This is a succinct and impressive summary of Paul's teaching. Our true home which we Christians all await is in heaven. As in 1 Thessalonians, we still await the coming of Jesus from the heavens. The link between the coming of Jesus (1Thes) and the future transformation (1 Cor) is acknowledged. The transformation is here associated with the Parousia. Our earthly body will be transformed into a glorified body. In 3:21 the word Paul uses is *metaschēmatizō* which literally means "transform."

In this passage, more clearly than elsewhere, we see the close connection between Jesus' resurrection and that of his disciples. This connection was already suggested in 1 Corinthians 15. If we are not raised, Jesus has not been raised. But here we have quite clearly the principle, "as Christ, so the Christians."[43] Our transformed body will be like Jesus' resurrected body. Jesus' resurrected body is raised to glory. In 1 Corinthians Paul taught that our future embodiment will be as glorified bodies; in Philippians Paul indicates that Jesus' resurrected body is a glorified body. Our bodies will be like his. Paul's conceptualization of our resurrection flows from his understanding and experience of Jesus as raised. We will be like Christ.

In Philippians we see the importance Paul attaches to the moment of death (1:23) and the importance of the Parousia (3:20-21). We can presume that at death Paul did not expect

---

[43]John Gillman, *Transformation into the Future Life*, 1043-93, esp. 1097 and 1132.

to be naked but to put on Christ even more fully (2 Cor 5; Phil 1). Yet Paul still awaits the future coming of Jesus at the Parousia (1 Thes 4; Phil 3) at which time the final transformation will be fully accomplished and God will be all in all (1 Cor 15; Phil 3). Thus our transformation which began at baptism, which continued during our lives in our sufferings with Christ, which gave us a new heavenly dwelling to put on at death, is finally completed with the Parousia.

The Teaching of Jesus About Resurrection

As noted in our discussion on the teaching of Jesus in Volume One of this series, there is very little in Jesus' teaching about the resurrection from the dead. One must be careful not to construct more than the tradition offers. As is evident in his encounter with the Sadducees (Mark 12:18-27), Jesus believed in the resurrection. In general, Jesus' thinking was closer to Pharisaism than to Sadduceeism, and the Pharisees believed in the resurrection. Thus even apart from the recorded encounter with the Sadducees, one could presume Jesus' acceptance of some form of faith in future life.

As I mentioned earlier, Jesus seems to have spoken about his own resurrection. Even if the passion predictions in their present form manifest development after the event, there is sufficient reason to maintain that Jesus would have looked forward to or even spoken of his resurrection in association with the suffering and death he envisioned. The fact that the disciples seem not to have understood and were later surprised with Jesus' resurrection is not an argument against Jesus' teaching about his own resurrection. The disciples may have thought of Jesus as expressing belief in the general resurrection on the last day without their being conscious of its imminent application to Jesus himself. Resurrection itself was not a precise doctrine in Judaism and as far as we can tell was not all that precise for Jesus either. There is no reason to assume that the disciples should have understood clearly.

Jesus believed in the resurrection, in his own future resurrection, and in his vindication by God, but resurrection was not a prominent theme in his preaching or teaching. In fact, Jesus had little to say about it. As Henry Cadbury has written, "(Jesus') allusions (to afterlife) do not allow us to reconstruct any very definite or circumstantial impression of this future. They were innocently unprecise, intimations rather than descriptions, and were employed in connection with other matters on which Jesus had something emphatic and significant to say."[44]

As far as we can tell, did Jesus not envision the resurrected life as transformed and spiritualized? He did not envision being embodied as we are embodied now. Our first text, and really the only one in which Jesus directly addressed the question of future life, is that of his discussions with the Sadducees (Mk 12:18-27, // Mt 22:23-33, // Lk 20:27-40).[45]

> [18]And Sadducees came to him who say that there is no resurrection; and they asked him a question, saying, [19]"Teacher, Moses wrote for us that if a man's brother dies and leaves a wife, but leaves no child, the man must take the wife, and raise up children for his brother. [20]There were seven brothers; the first took a wife, and when he died left no children; [21]and the second took her, and died leaving no children; and the third likewise; [22]and the seven left no children. Last of all the woman also died. [23]In the resurrection whose wife will she be? For the seven had her as wife." [24]Jesus said to them, "Is not this why you are wrong, that you know neither the scriptures nor the power of God? [25]For when they rise from the dead, they neither marry nor are given in marriage, but are like

---

[44]Henry Cadbury, "Intimations of Immortality in the Thought of Jesus," in *Immortality and Resurrection*, 139-40, ed. Krister Stendahl. Also see Martin Rist, "Jesus and Eschatology," in *Transitions in Biblical Scholarship*, 193-215, ed. J.C. Rylaarsdam (Chicago: University of Chicago Press, 1968).

[45]I accept this text as a valid expression of the teaching of Jesus. Cf. Joachim Jeremias, *New Testament Theology, The Proclamation of Jesus*, trans. John Bowden (New York: Charles Scribner's Sons, 1971), 184, n. 3. Also John Gillmann, *Transformatin into the Future Life*, 1099.

angels in heaven. [26]And as for the dead being raised, have you not read in the book of Moses, in the passage about the bush, how God said to him, 'I am the God of Abraham, and the God of Isaac, and the God of Jacob'? [27]He is not the God of the dead, but of the living; you are quite wrong." (Mark 12:18-27)

The question put by the Sadducees may appear somewhat ridiculous, but it is valid. The questioners may see it as a jibe at Jesus or as a challenge pointing out illogicality in the doctrine of resurrection. The first part of Jesus' response (v. 25) is almost said in passing in order to get to the more important point Jesus makes (vv. 26-27). The response readily reflects Jesus as a teacher, how his teaching often flows spontaneously from situations. His response is at two levels: disposing of the question (v. 25), and then taking advantage of the situation to teach what he wants (vv. 26-27). Jesus answers and disposes of the question by pointing out how the Sadducees don't understand the resurrection in their making it too physical a life, too much a carbon copy of this world. In the resurrection from the dead there will not be marriage, husbands and wives as there are now. We will be like angels. However, we ought not place too much emphasis on this verse as such: it is not the heart of what Jesus is going to say. But it does appear as if Jesus, without giving any precise understanding of the *how* of the resurrection and what kind of bodies we will have, does provide a remark that is compatible with Paul's perspective on the resurrection as transformation, an understanding of resurrection that was also present in pre-Christian Judaism.

Did Jesus envision the resurrection to have already taken place, or to take place at the moment of death, or at least to take place for some at the time of death? Had some already been raised prior to the resurrection of Jesus himself? Here we must be careful not to push Jesus' intimation into saying something too precise in order to answer *our* questions. But does Jesus' teaching and considered responses intimate something along these lines?

In the above text Jesus continues (vv.26-27). What is at stake is one's own image of God. The Lord is not the Lord of the dead, but of living beings, of life. The power and justice of God require that at least the righteous be raised to further life. And, Jesus intimates, is this not the implication in the text from Exodus 3:6, "I am the God of your father, the God of Abraham, the God of Isaac, and the God of Jacob?" The Sadducees fail to understand the Scriptures. If the Lord reveals himself as the God of Abraham, Abraham must be alive. The Lord is not a God of the dead. Thus Jesus' response and understanding of Scripture is that at least the patriarchs are still alive. One could question whether their life is the life of the resurrected, however. Yet Jesus' response about Abraham, Isaac, and Jacob's being alive is completely in the context of a question about the resurrection and Jesus' response about how the Sadducees misunderstood resurrected life. It appears as if Jesus assumes or believes that at least the patriarchs have been already raised to their new life and are not awaiting a resurrection on the last day. We saw similar opinions in our discussion of the Jewish background, that some texts gave special place to the patriarchs, prophets, and martyrs of Israel (e.g. 4 Mc 13:17; 16:25).[46] Although Jesus affirms his faith that the patriarchs are already living with God, he says nothing about the kind of life they live. We can presume, however, that they are like angels. Is Jesus' belief that only the patriarchs have already been raised, or is this the fate of all the righteous at death?

Something suggestive of this line of thinking can be found in the Lucan parable about the rich man Lazarus (Lk 16:19-31), although some question its authenticity. Jesus, in the

---

[46]The Epistle to Rheginos (48:3 f) maintains that the resurrection of the righteous has already taken place but needs to be revealed. Elijah and Moses with Jesus at the Transfiguration are an expression of this. See C.F. Evans, *Resurrection and the New Testament*, 32. See "The Treatise on Resurrection" (Epistle to Rheginos), in *The Nag Hammadi Library*, ed. James M. Robinson (New York: Harper and Row, 1977), 50-53. Also M.L. Peel, *The Epistle to Rheginos, A Valentinian Letter on the Resurrection* (Philadelphia: Westminster, 1969). On the special emphasis given to the patriarchs in Judaism's doctrine of the future life, see H.C.C. Cavallin, *Life After Death*, 117, 206-10.

telling of the story, gives away something of his way of thinking: that immediately after death people attain their state of future life. There is nothing to suggest that Jesus would have thought of a future life for a soul as separate from the body. Thus upon death the righteous enter into life in the bosom of Abraham. They are raised to life from the dead. The unrighteous go to Hades.

According to the parable, Lazarus dies and "was carried by the angels to Abraham's bosom" (16:22). One does not get the impression that Lazarus has gone to Sheol. Rather it would seem that he is in Paradise. The implication in verse 31 is that Lazarus has been raised from the dead and that his return to earth would be fruitless to those who are there:

> He said to him, "If they do not hear Moses and the prophets, neither will they be convinced if some one should rise from the dead." (Luke 16:31)

Jesus believes in the resurrection because of his faith in God as a God of the living and implies in the telling of this parable that the righteous come to their final state at death. This is the impression also given in Luke 23:43, where the repentant criminal is promised Paradise immediately upon his death.

The rich man in the parable went to Hades after he died (v. 23). We do not know if this place of punishment was eternal in Jesus' mind or not. Any speculation is on very tenuous grounds. R.H. Charles maintained that the teaching of Jesus held that there would be a resurrection of the righteous only, that punishment was not conceived of as everlasting, and that forgiveness was still available to someone after death.[47] Matthew 12:31-32 implies that forgiveness is still possible to the sinner in life after death. The sin against the Holy Spirit cannot be forgiven in this life nor in the life to come. The implication is that other sins can be.

---

[47]R.H. Charles, *Eschatology, The Doctrine of a Future Life in Israel, Judaism, and Christianity*, 395-400.

Although the evangelists tend to picture punishment as eternal, this may reflect the language and concepts of the evangelist and of apocalypticism and not of Jesus. Jesus' concept was that of a just punishment, not an eternal one (Lk 12:47-48).

Thus one could hypothesize that Jesus believed in the doctrine of resurrection, believed that the righteous would be raised at the time of death, that they would have an angelic existence in Paradise, that he himself would be so raised at the time of his death, that he would go straight to the bosom of Abraham, that the unrighteous would go to Hades or hell where they would receive a just but temporal punishment (after which they would either be forgiven and raised to heavenly life or cease to exist at all).

These "intimations" in the teaching of Jesus are suggestive and tentative. Jesus never taught anything directly about the resurrection of the dead. He believed in it, but it was not prominent in his proclamation. Given the nature of the texts we have looked at, a response to the Sadducees and a parabolic story, we cannot conclude anything beyond Jesus' belief in the resurrection. Some of our suggestions may be based on redactional material. Yet there are therein suggestive hints about how Jesus thought of the life to come to the degree that he thought about it at all. His preoccupation was God's reign on earth.

4

Jesus Is Raised From The Dead

Although there is factual material contained within the Christian proclamation and in the Gospel naratives, we have learned not to assume too quickly that a chronological sequence in the Gospels necessarily manifests factual history. We saw in the passion narratives that one cannot easily determine the sequence of events since many factors other than the facts of history have influenced the accounts. So it is with the resurrection narratives. Literary and theological concerns have influenced the accounts as much as the facts of history.

As one studies the resurrection narratives in the four Gospels, one becomes aware of two types of narratives or two different kinds of material: narratives associated with the tomb of Jesus and narratives of Jesus' appearances to his followers. In our discussion we will begin with the appearance narratives first and then move to those associated with the tomb.[1]

---

[1]Excellent introductory studies pertinent to the resurrection narratives include Raymond Brown, *The Virginal Conception and Bodily Resurrection of Jesus* (New York: Paulist Press, 1973), 69-129; Reginald Fuller, *The Formation of the Resurrection Narratives* (New York: The Macmillan Co., 1971); Gerald O'Collins, *The Resurrection of Jesus Christ* (Valley Forge, Penn.: Judson Press, 1973); and Pheme Perkins, *Resurrection, New Testament Witness and Contemporary Reflection* (Garden City, New York: Doubleday and Co., Inc., 1984).

The Appearance Narratives

As we discuss the varied accounts of the appearances of the risen Jesus, we must keep in mind that we have already looked at the earliest written account that we have, 1 Corinthians 15. As we have seen, Paul lists there a sequence of six appearances, including his own experience on the road to Damascus (see Acts 9:22-26). On the basis of this he gives us a description of the risen body, with the implication that Jesus' risen condition is to some degree like unto what ours will be: a transformed and spiritual but embodied way of being. We will return to Paul's account later and first consider the Gospels.

One system of classifying the appearance narratives in the Gospels is based on a geographical detail—where the evangelists locate them. Some of the narratives place the experiences in Galilee, others in or near Jerusalem. Another system of classification is a division into apostolic christophanies or mission appearances (appearances that give a commission) and private christophanies or recognition appearances. Each approach has its merits.[2] Although the geographical details are not always to be taken literally, and may well be subordinate to other literary and theological concerns, neither are they to be completely disregarded. Simply in order to proceed, I shall discuss first those

---

[2]See Gerald O'Collins, *The Resurrection of Jesus Christ*, 18-28. The division into mission appearances and recognition appearances goes back to M. Albertz, "Zur Formgeschichte der Auferstehungsberichte," *Zeitschrift für die neutestamentliche Wissenschaft* 21 (1922), 159-69. Pierre Benoit prefers this classification in *The Passion and Resurrection of Jesus Christ* (New York: Herder and Herder, 1969), 183-87, 323-42. So does Jerome Murphy-O'Connor, "Recognizing the Risen Lord, The Historical Genesis of Belief in the Resurrection," N.C.R. Cassettes (Kansas City: National Catholic Reporter, 1978). From a literary point of view, this is the classification to be preferred. Raymond Brown, *The Virginal Conception and Bodily Resurrection of Jesus*, 99-111, follows a geographical classification. One may make a point of this difference in the narratives if one is attempting to sift out some historical material from within them. C.H. Dodd, "The Appearances of the Risen Christ: An Essay in Form Criticism of the Gospels," *Studies in the Gospels*, ed. D.E. Nineham (Oxford University Press, 1957), 9-35, reprinted in C.H. Dodd, *More New Testament Studies* (1968) offers still another system of classification into concise narratives (short stories) and circumstantial narratives (long stories).

narratives which place the appearances in Galilee, then those which locate them in Jerusalem, and as we proceed also indicate whether the narrative presents a mission or recognition appearance.

Appearances in Galilee. Here we are concerned with Mark 16:7; Matthew 28:9-10, 16-20; and John 21:1-23.

1. Mark 16:7. In Mark we have no appearance narrative at all. We have only the hint or suggestion of appearances to come. If so, they are seen as about to take place in Galilee. The Gospel of Mark ends at 16:8. Verses 9-20 are a later addition and not part of the original Gospel. We do not know whether Mark intended to end his Gospel at 16:8 or not.[3] If not, either something happened to Mark or something from his Gospel has been lost. It is possible, however, that Mark did end his Gospel at verse 8.

The conclusion of the orginal Gospel as we now have it (Mark 16: 1-8) is a narrative associated with the tomb of Jesus, not an appearance narrative. Yet verse 7 may be the suggestion of appearances to come:

> But go tell his disciples and Peter that he is going before you to Galilee; there you will see him, as he told you.
>
> (Mk. 16:7)

This particular verse has come to be interpreted in three ways and it is difficult to choose from among them. Does it refer at all to future appearances of Jesus as is commonly thought? If we do not read Mark 16: 1-8 in light of the later appendix (vv. 9-20) and in the light of Matthew, what leads one to believe that Mark is referring here to *appearances* in Galilee? Some have suggested rather that it refers to the imminent Parousia which Mark's community expected and

[3]Norman Perrin argues that Mark intended to end his Gospel at 16:8. See *The Resurrection according to Matthew, Mark and Luke* (Philadelphia: Fortress Press, 1977), 16-19. The question is a quite complicated one, however. See C.F. Evans, *Resurrection and the New Testament*, SBT, Second Series, vol. 12 (London: SCM Press, 1970), 67-75. Also see Fuller, *The Formation of the Resurrection Narratives*, 64-68, 155-59; Brown, *The Virginal Conception and Bodily Resurrection of Jesus*, 97-98.

which they expected to take place in Galilee. Mark 16:7 then may be referring to the return of the Son of Humanity in glory and not to Galilean appearances.[4]

Galilee does play a significant role in Mark's Gospel, both geographically and symbolically. Galilee, not Jerusalem, is the focus of salvation. Thus others see Mark 16:7 as referring neither to appearances, nor to the Parousia, but to the leadership which Jesus promised to his disciples in their mission to the Gentiles.[5] Galilee symbolizes the Gentile mission. We will see what Matthew does with the Marcan narrative precisely along this line (28:16-20). Mark 16:7 must be interpreted along with Mark 14:28, as the verse indicates: 16:7 refers back to 14:28. Do both of these refer to the Parousia, to the Gentile mission, or to appearances?

Still others argue that the reference does refer to Jesus' intent to appear to the disciples in Galilee to which they had fled after the fiasco in Jerusalem. Matthew interprets Mark in this fashion by including the appearance narrative that our Gospel of Mark lacks, and the Marcan reference to "his disciples and Peter" seems to refer to the first two appearances listed by Paul, that Jesus appeared first to Peter and then to the Eleven.

It is difficult to know what Mark had in mind and the three interpretations are not necessarily exclusive of each other. Mark may have seen the Risen Jesus as appearing to the disciples in Galilee, guiding them in their mission which would then begin from there, and later returning there in glory. He would rejoin them as Risen Lord in Galilee. Given the difficulty of the verse, however, we can only say that the

[4]A strong proponent of the Parousia interpretation is Perrin, *The Resurrection according to Matthew, Mark, and Luke*, 18-34. This is also the interpretation of Willi Marxsen, *Mark the Evangelist*, trans. Boyce, Juel, Poehlmann, with Harrisville (Nashville: Abingdon Press, 1969), 83-92, 111-16, and *The Resurrection of Jesus of Nazareth* (Philadelphia: Fortress Press, 1970), 162-64. For a criticism of this position, see Gerald O'Collins, *The Resurrrection of Jesus Christ*, 36-38.

[5]See specially C.F. Evans, *Resurrection and the New Testament*, 75-81; and "I will go before you into Galilee," *Journal of Theological Studies*, New Series, 5 (1954), 3-18. Also E.C. Hoskyns, "Adversaria Exegetica," *Theology* 7 (1923), 147-55.

Marcan Gospel does not contain an appearance narrative as such. It may contain a reference to appearances and, if so, the appearances were envisioned as having taken place in Galilee.

2. Matthew 28:9-10, 16-20. We have here two appearances of Jesus, the first to the women outside of Jerusalem, which is a recognition appearance, and the second to the Eleven, in Galilee, a mission appearance. The first seems preparatory to the second, with the women instructed to tell the disciples to go to Galilee. The second, the appearance to the Eleven, is also recorded in Luke's and John's accounts but for them the appearance occurs in Jerusalem. The appearance to the Eleven seems to be a central appearance, recorded by Paul and three evangelists, and perhaps suggested in Mark as well. We can see quite clearly how Matthew builds upon Mark. Matthew 28:7 parallels Mark 16:7.

> Then go quickly and tell his disciples that he has risen from the dead, and behold, he is going before you to Galilee; there you will see him. Lo, I have told you.
>
> (Mt. 28-7)

The response of the women in Matthew 28:8 is different from the response in Mark 16:8. In Mark the women are frightened and say nothing, whereas in Matthew they are full of joy and wish to tell the disciples. Matthew then includes an appearance of Jesus himself to the women (28:9-10) over and above the instruction of the angel (28:5-7).

Matthew's account of the appearance to the Eleven completes what is lacking in Mark and shows how Matthew brings Mark to another conclusion.

> Now the Eleven disciples went into Galilee, to the mountain to which Jesus had directed them. And when they saw him they worshipped him; but some doubted. And when Jesus came and said to them, "All authority in heaven and on earth has been given to me. Go therefore and make disciples of all nations, baptizing them in the name of the Father and of the Son and of the Holy Spirit,

> teaching them to observe all that I have commanded you;
> and lo, I am with you always, to the close of the age.
>
> (Mt. 28:16-20)

Jesus appears to the disciples in Galilee and also commissions them to the Gentile mission. The appearance to the Eleven in Matthew is mission-oriented. There are no details about the nature of the appearance, although Jesus seems quite recognizable.

3. John 21:1-23. Chapter 21 of John, the so-called Johannine appendix, was probably not composed by the evangelist, but by a later writer, perhaps a disciple of the evangelist.[6] The Gospel, as written by John or the evangelist, ended with chapter 20. The setting of chapter 21 is an appearance to seven disciples on the shore of the lake in Galilee after they had gone fishing. It continues with a dialogue between Jesus and Peter. The author of chapter 21 links his narrative to the previous chapter. Chapter 20 contains, as we will see, an account of two appearances to the disciples, both in Jerusalem, the first in the absence of Thomas and the second in his presence. Verse 14 of chapter 21 thus indicates that this is Jesus' third appearance, this one in Galilee. Reginald Fuller suggests that the ultimate source of the appearance in John 21 is the tradition of two appearances, one to Peter and another to the Eleven.

The author of John 21 has also combined the story of the miraculous catch of fish (Luke 5) and the Eucharistic setting for an appearance (Luke 24). Thus there are some affinities between Luke and John 21, a fusion of Lucan and Johannine material. Verses 15-18 contain the charge to Peter to look after the community of Jesus' disciples. It is not a separate appearance but a continuation of the appearance to the Eleven. It has an affinity to Matthew 16:17-19 in which Peter is established as the overseer of the church; Jesus' words are

---

[6]See Fuller, *The Formation of the Resurrection Narratives,* 146-54. Also Raymond Brown, *The Gospel according to John XIII-XXI,* Anchor Bible 29A (Garden City, New York: Doubleday and Co., Inc. 1970), 1063-1132.

a command, not exactly to mission but to a pastoral role with respect to the community. The earlier catch of fish, however, may symbolize the call to mission.

Appearances in Jerusalem. Here we are concerned with the appearance narratives in Luke 24:13-49, John 20:19-29, and Mark 16:9-20.

1. Luke 24:13-49. This section of Luke contains two appearance narratives, an account of Jesus' appearance to two disciples on the road to Emmaus, which is but a short distance of approximately seven miles from Jerusalem, a recognition appearance (vv. 13-35); and Jesus' appearance to the Eleven assembled together with their companions in Jerusalem, a mission appearance (vv. 36-49).[7] The narratives which locate the appearance to the Eleven in Jerusalem are the Lucan narrative and John 20. These narratives have other elements in common as well, not unlike the Lucan and Johannine passion narratives.

That the appearance to the Eleven took place in Jerusalem is only indicated in the transition from the Emmaus story (v. 33) and in the instruction (v. 47). The fact that Jerusalem is not mentioned in the narrative description of the appearance itself (vv. 36-43), along with the reference to eating fish (v. 43), may indicate an appearance originally described as located in Galilee and at a later (but still pre-Lucan) date transferred to the Jerusalem setting.

In addition to the Jerusalem location, another common element in the Lucan account and that of John 20 is their emphasis on the physical aspects of Jesus' appearances. Most scholars see Luke 24:39-43 and John 20:19-23 as narratives rooted in a common tradition. We find in this tradition and in the Lucan Emmaus story elements of both physical continuity and discontinuity with the earthly Jesus. The physicality of the appearance and the continuity between the earthly Jesus and the risen Jesus are emphasized. Jesus

---

[7]Fuller, *The Formation of the Resurrection Narratives*, 103-23. Also Joseph A. Fitzmyer, *The Gospel according to Luke X-XXIV*, Anchor Bible 28A (Garden City, New York: Doubleday and Co., Inc. 1985), 1553-85.

walks and talks in the Emmaus story. In the appearance to the Eleven, Jesus eats, refers to his hands and feet, flesh and bones, and invites them to touch him. Yet there are also elements of a transformed, or more spiritual type of bodily presence as well. Jesus is transfigured and is not exactly the same. In the Emmaus story Jesus is not recognized in the beginning, and he disappears in the end. In the appearance to the Eleven, the disciples at first think they are seeing a ghost (a *pneuma*).[8]

A common and significant element in both the Emmaus story and the appearance to the Eleven is that the heavily physical presence does not lead to belief and understanding. The disciples on the road to Emmaus did not recognize Jesus (v. 31) until after the Scriptures were opened up and explained to them (v. 32) and they broke bread together (v. 30). In Jerusalem, the disciples were at first both frightened and doubtful. Jesus convinces them, but they still can hardly believe, until they see intellectually (v. 41), that is understand - which again happens as a consequence of Jesus' opening their minds to understand the Scriptures (vv. 44-46).

In the two appearances in Luke we have very physical appearances of the risen Jesus, yet elements in the appearances suggest that we are not looking at an exact replica of the earthly Jesus. Faith, recognition, and understanding follow not upon the physical presence of Jesus but upon the disciples' deeper understanding of the Scriptures and an experience of the familiar meal.

2. John 20:19-29. In the Johannine account of the appearances, we also have two narratives: the appearance to the disciples, a mission appearance (vv. 19-23), and the appearance with Thomas present, a recognition appearance (vv. 24-29). Chapter 21 of John, as indicated above, is an independent narrative written by someone other than the author of the Gospel as a whole. Thus the evangelist's account itself contains these two appearances from chapter 20.

---

[8]See the doctoral dissertation of John Gillman, *Transformation into the Future Life: A Study of 1 Corinthians 15, 50-53, Its Context and Related Passages* (Ph.D. dissertation, Catholic University of Louvain, 1980), 1118-19.

In John as in Luke, the physicality of Jesus is very real. Jesus shows his hands and his side (v. 20) and Jesus invites Thomas to touch him and seemingly appears with the wounds left from the crucifixion (vv. 25-27). At the same time, however, Jesus' bodily presence is not exactly the same as it was on earth. In both of the Johannine appearances, the doors are closed and Jesus seems able to pass through them at will. As C.K. Barrett writes, Jesus is able "to pass through solid matter, or perhaps, to cause his body to materialize where he will."[9]

A definite role is given to Thomas in the Johannnine tradition. Thomas is only a name among the Twelve in the Synoptics. In John, he stands for misunderstanding and doubt, whereas in the Synoptics this role is assumed by Peter. The Johannnine tradition's assigning the role to Thomas may be the beginning of the Thomas legend and the Thomas writings, for example the *Gospel of Thomas*.

The significance of the appearance to Thomas lies in v. 29, "Blessed are those who have not seen and yet believe." The faith of the second and third generation Christians is validated, those in the generation for whom the fourth evangelist wrote but who were not able to see Jesus. The narrative does not discredit Thomas but rather credits all who believe whether they have seen the earthly Jesus or not.

Similarities between Luke and John include the greeting of peace (Luke 24:36; John 20:19), Jesus showing his hands and feet (Luke 24:20) or hands and side (John 20:19), the joy of the disciples (Luke 24:51; John 20:20), and the gift of the Spirit. In Luke 24:49 the Spirit is promised but not given, for Luke separates the appearances and the actual sending of the Spirit which occurs at Pentecost. In John 20:22-23, the Spirit is given during the appearance of Jesus. This raises the question whether the christophanies and the gift of the Spirit were originally one event or two.

Both Luke and John affirm the physicality of Jesus' presence, but for neither is that the significant point of the

[9]C.K. Barrett, *The Gospel according to St. John* (London: SPCK 1978), 567.

narrative. In Luke faith or recognition follows upon understanding the Scriptures. In John the narratives lead to a
commissioning (vv. 21-23), the gift of the Spirit (vv. 22-23),
and the affirmation of the faith of all who believe (v. 29). In
Luke there is also the suggestion of the commissioning to
come (vv. 47-49). In both Luke and John 20, the appearance
events take place in Jerusalem.

3. Mark 16:9-20. These concluding verses to our present
canonical Gospel of Mark were not originally part of the
Gospel. They have come to be called the Marcan appendix
and were added at a later date. Mark 16:8 was the original
ending. In spite of the fact that these verses are a later
addition, it is worthwhile to take note of the appearance
accounts which they contain. There is an ordered sequence
of three: first to Mary of Magdala, next to two disciples
walking in the country, and finally to the Eleven while they
were at table. The appearance to Mary of Magdala is
reported as an appearance.

> Now when he rose early on the first day of the week, he
> appeared first to Mary Magdalene, from whom he had
> cast out seven demons. (Mk. 16:9)

It has a parallel in the Gospel of John, 20:11-18, but this
does not mean that it is derived from the Fourth Gospel. In
John the incident takes place at the tomb. When Mary
reports the appearance to others, they do not believe that
Jesus is alive and that she has seen him (16:11).

Jesus next appears *under another form* to two of his
disciples as they were on their way into the country (v. 12).
This appearance is reminiscent of the Emmaus episode in
Luke 24. Again, as in the previous case, these two tell the
others who still do not believe (v. 13).

The final appearance is to the Eleven (vv. 14-20). There
are parallels for this appearance in Luke 24:36-49, John
20:19-22, and Matthew 28:16-20. Herein Jesus commissions
the disciples to go and proclaim the gospel to the whole
world (vv. 15-18), paralleling the mission appearances. The
Marcan appendix concludes with an ascension (vv. 19-20),

which otherwise is only recorded by Luke (24:51 and Acts 1). Although the longer ending of Mark contains parallels to the other Gospels, this does not necessarily mean that it is a summary of them. It may be an independent composition.[10] The appearances in the Marcan appendix all seem to take place in Judea.

Observations on the Appearances. Before we discuss the narratives associated with the tomb of Jesus, it will be helpful to bring together some observations. In so doing, we bring into consideration not only the appearance narratives in the Gospels but also Paul's record of the appearances as well. Paul's letters are the earliest written accounts that we have. Written in the early fifties, approximately twenty years before the first Gospel, they are historiographically significant. My observations here concern the historicity of the appearances, their nature and their location.

1. Historicity. However one may interpret the historical or non-historical character of the resurrection of Jesus itself, I would suggest that there is an historical dimension underlying the appearances of Jesus. We can point to a change in the disciples and to the emergence of their faith in Jesus as raised from the dead. This is an historical fact. Jesus' disciples came to believe in Jesus as raised, began to proclaim his resurrection from the dead, all as a result of an experience or conversion which led to faith. The documents themselves attribute the source or cause of this conversion of faith to the appearances of Jesus, to personal encounters with the risen Lord.

Thus historiography can take us back to the emergence of faith, to a change in the disciples after the death of Jesus, and to the disciples' articulation of this change resulting from the self-presentation of the risen Jesus to them. Historiography can probably go no further, although it can inquire into the nature or character of these experiences which are described as appearances. Consistent elements in

---

[10]For C.H. Dodd's understanding of the independent character of the narrative in the Marcan appendix, see "The Appearances of the Risen Christ: an Essay in Form Criticism of the Gospels," fn. 2 in this chapter.

the recognition appearance narratives include a lack of expectation for such on the part of those to whom Jesus appears and an initiative taken by Jesus.

The earliest Christians had a tradition about a period of time after the resurrection during which Jesus was still with them but in a new way, not exactly as Jesus had been with them before the crucifixion nor as he would later be with them in the Spirit but in a mode intermediate between the two. There is no way of knowing how long this period of self-manifestations of Jesus lasted. Luke confines it to a period of forty days but he is the only one to do so and the time period is symbolic. If we follow Paul, our earliest testimony, who includes his experience as one of the appearances, the period lasted for three or six years. Paul's conversion was in the mid-thirties. The primary period during which the appearances recorded in the Gospels took place (to the women, to Peter, to the Eleven and to other disciples) may have been much shorter, much earlier than Paul's. There is no way of knowing how long the period was, but the documents attest to this period in the life of Christianity.

Just as it is difficult to date the appearances, it is difficult to establish a chronology for them. If we set the experience of the women aside (which we shall be discussing shortly as we consider the narratives associated with the tomb) and if we set the experience of Paul aside, was there one appearance or more than one? There is no way of judging with certitude. The most reliable guide is Paul. If we follow Paul, we may want to accept his account of six appearances as having a basis in the history of this very early period. If so, Peter was the first of the men to experience the risen Lord. This conviction is not only Paul's but is also indicated in Luke 24:34. The appearance to the Eleven is the most historically attested appearance. It is contained in all our accounts. After this we are less clear. Some have identified the appearance to the five hundred as Pentecost. It is very probable that Jesus may have appeared to James. Our question is not so much whether something historical actually happened (the faith did emerge and the disciples were changed into believers) but rather what did happen to the disciples to bring about their change from disillusionment to faith.

2. The Nature of the Appearances. It is difficult to say anything certain about the nature of these experiences other than that all the accounts understand them as something that happened to the disciples involving the self-presentation of Jesus to them. We may consider Paul's experience as paradigmatic. Paul considers his conversion to be one of these events and seems to see all of these events as at least analogous. On the other hand, there is nothing to exclude variety. They need not all have been of the same sort. In some Jesus is portrayed as almost immediately recognizable, in others as unrecognizable. Jesus may have appeared to his disciples not always in exactly the same fashion. What they all have in common is the understanding that Jesus takes the initiative in manifesting himself. They are personal encounters with the risen Jesus with Jesus manifesting himself in a bodily or somatic way. But this tells us little. If we go to the earliest testimony of Paul, we see the difficulty of trying to be too precise about the resurrection body. If the risen body of Jesus was akin to the description Paul gives us, we can only say that Jesus was raised a glorious, spiritual body. What it means to have experienced this, however, is not clear.

The appearances recorded later in the Gospels, especially in Luke and John, suggest a more physical appearance than does Paul's text. It may be that Paul is the more reliable basis upon which to understand the experiences, or it may again be a question of analogous but diverse realities. The characteristic Greek verb used to describe these experiences was *ōphthē*: he appeared.[11] It remains an open question whether these events involved a physical being. Events such as angelophanies and theophanies in the Hebrew Scriptures are often accompanied by verbal communications. These are revelations, but they need not be auditory in any ordinary

[11]Gerald O'Collins, *The Resurrection of Jesus Christ*, 7-9.

sense. How one "sees" or "hears" when another dimension of our world contacts our space-time is not clear. This is why our language at this point becomes analogical and metaphorical. Fuller describes these experiences of appearances as revelatory self-disclosures or revelatory encounters.[12] In these events something is communicated from outside our ordinary way of experiencing our world, and this communication may involve a visual element such as light. Light can describe both the message and the medium.

In the appearance experiences, the disciples *recognized* Jesus and it was *Jesus* whom they recognized, the person whom they had known from his ministry. Thus the disastrous defeat to which Jesus had come during the Passover in Jerusalem had been overcome. On the basis of their experiences, the disciples were able to say that Jesus was alive. But the exact nature of the appearance-experiences is still difficult to describe. In these events, whatever phenomena (such as light) may have been present within them, the disciples came to believe because they had met the living, risen Jesus. This language is metaphorical because the appearances move one to the boundaries of history and what is historiographical. But we can say with Wolfhart Pannenberg: "The Easter appearances are not to be explained from the Easter faith of the disciples; rather, conversely, the Easter faith of the disciples is to be explained from the appearances."[13] On this point I am inclined to agree more with Pannenberg than Schillebeeckx.

The major difference between Schillebeeckx[14] and myself in this matter is that he clearly speaks of "the Easter

---

[12]See Raymond Brown, *The Virginal Conception and Bodily Resurrection of Jesus*, 83-92; Reginald Fuller, *The Formation of the Resurrection Narratives*, 30-34; Wolfhart Pannenberg, *Jesus—God and Man*, trans. Wilkins and Priebe (Philadelphia: The Westminster Press, 1968), 92-100; Ulrich Wilckens, "The Tradition-history of the Resurrection of Jesus," in *The Significance of the Message of the Resurrection for Faith in Jesus Christ*, ed. C.F.D. Moule, SBT, Second Series 8 (London: SCM Press, 1968), 51-76, esp. 61-69.

[13]Pannenberg, *Jesus—God and Man*, 96.

[14]Edward Schillebeeckx, *Jesus, An Experiment in Christology*, trans. Hubert Hoskins (New York: Seabury Press, 1979), 320-97.

experience" as a conversion experience that precedes the appearance traditions and tomb traditions, whereas I prefer to speak of the appearances as the experiences which induced faith -- the appearance-experiences. The appearances were the experiences of the Risen Lord's self-presentation, granting of course Schillebeeckx's distinction between the experience and its being put into language.

Schillebeeckx asks the question of what took place between the historical events of Jesus' death and the preaching of the first disciples. The disciples' failure of faith provided the context for a potential repentance, and Jesus' forgiveness was constitutive of the grace or conversion they experienced. That which took place after Jesus' death was the conversion of the disciples.

This "conversion" was first of all an experience of grace. The core of Jesus' self-manifestation was grace. This means that Jesus took the initiative for calling the disciples back. The conversion was a personal experience interpreted as Jesus' initiative. Jesus thus stood at the source of this conversion or "Easter experience." This grace of conversion was also a concrete experience of forgiveness.

The conversion experience contains not only the element of grace, but also of recognition. Jesus is experienced as One Who Lives. This does not necessarily imply seeing Jesus in a visual sense (which is perhaps why Schillebeeckx is at pains to distinguish between the "conversion" as an experience and "an appearance" as a later linguistic expression of the experience). The conversion involves, however, illumination. The "seeing of Jesus" is a christological seeing, an understanding of Jesus as the Christ, as alive, as present. This is the content then of the Easter experience—being converted on Jesus' initiative to Jesus as the Christ. They all of a sudden "saw" it.

An effect of this recognition, of this "seeing," is that the spiritual contact with Jesus which had been ruptured by his death was restored. Jesus could again be addressed in intimate, personal terms. Following after Jesus was restored.

For Schillebeechkx, this Easter experience and Easter faith emerged prior to and independent of the two traditions, namely, those of appearances and that of the tomb. The *reality* denoted by the Easter experience was independent of the two traditions. (I grant that this is in a sense true, but I prefer to speak of the Easter experience as the reality underlying the appearance. The experience is what the appearances were. The appearances were not only the language and interpretation but also the experiences themselves. For me, Schillebeeckx separates them too much. What he says about the conversion process helps us get at the core of what the appearance-experiences were.)

Schillebeeckx, of course, is making a point of distinguishing the spontaneous experience of conversion from the language in which it is expressed, a distinction between the experience and the articulation factor or resort to language. The experience is brought to expression through a "language filter" and also within given models of comprehension.

A question then is whether to speak of the appearances as the experiences of the Risen Lord (which of course had to be expressed in language and thus involved an interpretative element), as I prefer to do, or to make the experience antecedent to and independent of the appearances, which are then the interpretative narratives and models and a later tradition, as Schillebeeckx does. Thus, for Schillebeeckx, the faith existed before there were any appearances. For me, the appearance-experiences gave birth to the faith. The appearance-experiences and the appearance narratives, however, cannot be simply identified or separated. The appearances are more than just the linguistic, interpretative factor. For Schillebeeckx, the conversion to Jesus is structured along the line of a Jewish conversion vision which gradually became an appearance accompanied by the motif of commissioning. The appearance and tomb traditions are later interpretative elements of earlier experiences.

I myself see the appearance-experiences as foundational for the emergence of the Easter faith, not of course to an exclusion of a foundation in the mission and ministry of Jesus as well.[15]

---

[15]On this point, see the dicussion by Francis Schüssler Fiorenza in *Foundational Theology, Jesus and the Church* (New York: Crossroad, 1984), 18-24.

3. The Location of the Appearances. The appearance-experiences were real events in the lives of the disciples. Given what we have already said, it is not of great significance whether they took place in Jerusalem and its environs or in Galilee or in both. Paul provides us no information about where the appearances took place. We must also admit that we do not know.

It may well be that some such events took place in Jerusalem and other appearances took place in Galilee. I am not here suggesting a harmonization of the Gospel narratives nor a duplication of the appearance to the Eleven. But there was a tradition of appearances in Jerusalem, and Jesus may have appeared there to the women. Paul's record of an appearance to James may be a record of a Jerusalem appearance. Other appearances, perhaps one to Peter and one to the Eleven, may have taken place in Galilee.

If we consider only the appearance to the Eleven, the experience probably took place only once. We do not know whether in Jerusalem or Galilee. Galilee is a more frequently suggested hypothesis, but it is only hypothesis.[16] After the arrest or crucifixion of Jesus, the disciples fled back to Galilee. There Jesus appeared to Peter and later to the Eleven and the post-resurrection faith was born. On this occasion Jesus may have given the gift of the Spirit as well, and the preaching began. Another hypothesis is that Peter became detached from the rest of the disciples. He remained longer in Jerusalem. Thus the appearance to Peter may have taken place while he was *en route* and the appearance to the others back in Galilee after Peter had arrived.[17] These hypotheses are not conclusive however.

[16]For the Galilee hypothesis, see Brown, *The Virginal Conception and Bodily Resurrection of Jesus*, 99-111, esp. 108-111; and O'Collins, *The Resurrection of Jesus Christ*, 22-28, 36-38. Also see, Kirsopp Lake, *The Historical Evidence for the Resurrection of Jesus Christ* (New York: G.P. Putnam's Sons, 1907), chap. 6. For a critique of the Galilean hypothesis, see C.F. Evans, *Resurrection and the New Testament*, 128-31.

[17]See Fuller, *The Formation of the Resurrection Narratives*, 34-35. Also see Fuller, "The 'Thou Art Peter' Pericope," *McCormick Quarterly* 20 (1967), 309-315. Also F.C. Burkitt, *Christian Beginnings* (London: University Press, 1924), 87f.

The Tomb Narratives

Many have argued that the narratives associated with the tomb of Jesus represent a tradition later than that of the appearance narratives. Reference to the tomb is absent from Paul and the pre-Pauline kerygma that Paul records (1 Cor 15:3-5). There are many characteristics of legend as well as inconsistencies in the tomb stories (the young man in Mark and an angelophany in Matthew and two men in Luke; the concern over the stone in Mark and its being miraculously rolled away in Matthew). Even if the traditions associated with the tomb are later than the tradition of Jesus' appearances, and even if legendary features are part of their development, the empty tomb references testify to a Jerusalem based tradition for which we already have evidence in the appearance narratives. This Jerusalem based tradition is associated with women and with the tomb.

1. Mark 16:1-8. As stated above, these verses are the conclusion of Mark's Gospel.

> [1]And when the sabbath was past, Mary Magdalene, and Mary the mother of James, and Salome, bought spices, so that they might go and anoint him. 2. And very early on the first day of the week they went to the tomb when the sun had risen. 3. And they were saying to one another, "Who will roll away the stone for us from the door of the tomb?" 4. And looking up, they saw that the stone was rolled back—it was very large. 5. And entering the tomb, they saw a young man sitting on the right side, dressed in a white robe; and they were amazed. 6. And he said to them, "Do not be amazed; you seek Jesus of Nazareth, who was crucified. He has risen, he is not here; see the place where they laid him. 7. But go, tell his disciples and Peter that he is going before you to Galilee; there you will see him, as he told you." 8. And they went out and fled from the tomb; for trembling and astonishment had come upon them; and they said nothing to anyone for they were afraid. (Mk 16:1-8)

We spoke previously about verse seven. It may be a Marcan addition to the tradition. The pre-Marcan tradition may have gone from verse six smoothly to verse eight, the appearance of the angel and the fright of the women. It is difficult to know the precise motivation of the women. Did they come to see to the proper burial of Jesus (Mark, Luke) or simply to visit the tomb (Matthew)? Which women went to the tomb? The different accounts vary, but Mary Magdalene is included in all of them, and is named first. In John 20:1, Mary Magdalene is the only woman.

It is important to note that the tomb narratives do not give any information about the risen Jesus and the nature of the resurrection as such. The woman or women arrive and the tomb is empty. In Mark they leave frightened. The discovery that the tomb was empty does not lead to faith, but rather to fear and wonder.

2. Matthew 27:62-28:15. Our discussion of Matthew's narrative of the events which took place at the tomb of Jesus falls into three parts. (1) Matthew 28:1, 5-8 is the core of the narrative in which Matthew relies upon Mark. (2) Matthew 28:9-10 is a separable narrative of an appearance to the women. And (3), Matthew 27:62-66, 28:2-4, 11-15, reflect Christian apologetic or polemic against the Jews.

Vv. 28:1, 5-8. The relationship between Matthew's and Mark's resurrection narratives can be noted by means of a synopsis.[18] Matthew 28:1, 5-8 provide the core of his narrative which follows Mark. There are several variations from Mark as we have seen. The number of women in Matthew is two rather than three. They do not come to anoint Jesus but only to see the tomb. They do not leave and say nothing but rather in fear and joy rush to tell the disciples what has happened. These variations are minor and behind them is the Marcan narrative and the basic narrative about the tomb.

Vv. 28:9-10. These verses are somewhat intrusive. Matthew

---

[18]E.g., see *Synopsis of the Four Gospels*, ed. Kurt Aland (United Bible Societies, 1970).

28:8 could move directly to 28:16-20, the narrative of the appearance of Jesus to the disciples in Galilee. But, before continuing, Matthew inserts the narrative of an appearance to the women.

> [9]And behold, Jesus met them and said, "Hail!" And they came up and took hold of his feet and worshipped him. [10]Then Jesus said to them, "Do not be afraid; go and tell my brethren to go to Galilee, and there they will see me."
> (Mt 28:9-10)

This is a separate narrative representing another pre-Matthean tradition. Jesus, not an angel, appears to the women. It is an appearance narrative in the vicinity of the tomb. It is not easy to say whether it is an earlier or later tradition than the angelophany which has preceded it.

Vv. 27:61-66, 28:2-4, 11-15. These verses are singled out because they reflect the story of guards at the tomb. In 27:62-66, the chief priests and some of the Pharisees go to Pilate to secure guards for the tomb. In 28:4, the guards see the angel and are literally scared stiff. In 28:11-15 the guards report to the chief priests what happened and are bribed to tell people that the disciples stole the body. Matthew's Gospel is written in the context of tension within Judaism. By the time his Gospel is written, the tradition of the events at the tomb had developed, and there must have circulated among the Jews rebuttals to the story of how the tomb was empty. Both Jewish and Christian charges and rebuttals over the proclamation of the resurrection would have been strong. Evidently there was among the Jews the opinion or charge that the body had been stolen. Christian rebuttal developed, an example of which we find in the story of guards at the tomb. There is little likelihood that the story has any basis in fact. The Jewish leaders (Sadducean) would hardly have anticipated or feared a resurrection, much less the resurrection of an individual. The Christian apologetical story simply explains that the Jewish people were not accepting the Christian interpretation of Jesus' tomb being empty.

3. Luke 24:1-12. Luke's narrative differs significantly from Mark in those verses that parallel Mark. It appears throughout the narrative that he not only relies upon Mark but upon another source as well. Luke is also going to report appearances to disciples in Jerusalem. In Matthew the appearance to the Eleven had been in Galilee.

There are several details to note in Luke's narrative. The emptiness of the tomb is made very clear (v. 3). This, however, does not lead the women to believe in the resurrection of Jesus. Rather, they do not know what to think (v.4). What the two men say differs from the account in Mark and Matthew (vv. 5-7). As in Matthew, the women go to report what has happened. The disciples are still in Jerusalem. Verse 11 is significant:

> But these words seemed to them an idle tale, and they did not believe them. (Lk 24:11)

The discovery of the empty tomb did not lead to faith among the women. It took an appearance-experience of the two young men (vv. 4-7). The entire report of the women is not believed. It not only does not lead to faith among the disciples but is dismissed as nonsense. It is important to be aware that within the Scriptures and within the resurrection narratives themselves, the narratives associated with the tomb do not lead to faith. An appearance of some sort accomplishes that. The emptiness of the tomb or stories associated with the tomb lead to fear or amazement or disbelief or disregard.

4. John 20:1-18. As with the passion narrative, John and Luke share elements which reflect a common tradition. For both, the appearances occur in the area of Jerusalem. In the Johannine narrative concerning the tomb, we have two separable narratives probably reflecting two distinct traditions: the narrative about Mary Magdalene (20:1-2, 11-18)

and the narrative about Peter and another disciple (20:2-10). The Mary Magdalene tradition probably goes directly from verse 1 to verses 11-18. Verse 2 connects it with the second narrative concerning the two disciples.

In the Johannine narrative Mary Magdalene goes to the tomb alone (v. 1). She then looks into the tomb, sees two angels, and their dialogue follows (vv. 12-13). She turns around and Jesus appears to her but she does not recognize him. A similar dialogue ensues (vv. 14-15). Then comes a very moving verse, the moment of recognition:

> Jesus said to her, "Mary." She turned and said to him in Hebrew, "Rab-bo-ni!" (which means Teacher). (v. 16)

Jesus asks her not to hang on to him but to go to his brothers to whom she does go and reports what has happened (vv. 17-18). The account contains both an angelophany and christophany. It is an appearance narrative in its own way. Jesus presents himself to her but she does not recognize him until he pronounces her name. Verse 16 reflects what we have learned in the appearance narratives, that they are revelatory recognitions of the risen Jesus.

Verses 3-10 provide a separate narrative although they are linked together in the Johannine account by verse 2. It is an account of men visiting the tomb. There was a reference in Luke 24:24 of some men going to the tomb to check out the women's story. In Luke 24:12, Peter alone visited the tomb. In John 20:3-10 two disciples go to the tomb. The "other disciple" is not included in Mark 14:54 or in Luke 24:12. It is more reasonable to assume that the Fourth Gospel has added the reference to the other disciple (cf. John 18:15-16; 20: 2-10). The core of the text is then Peter's going to the tomb, finding it empty, and returning home. There is no link between finding the tomb empty and believing. How could this be? *Because* Peter did not yet understand the Scriptures (v. 9). (See Luke 24:31-32.) The core of the text, Peter's visit to the tomb, may be historical. It does not credit Peter as believing, and thus would not have been developed later.

Luke's account reflects the same tradition of a visit of Peter to the tomb.[19] The Fourth Gospel records, however, that "the other disciple" saw *and* believed (v. 8). This is the only instance of seeing the tomb empty which leads to faith. The historical core of the story, however, is reflected in verse 9, but it is Peter who sees and does not yet believe.

Observations on the Narratives Associated with the Tomb of Jesus

1. Any discussion of the resurrection must consider not only the Gospel narratives but also Paul who gives us our earliest written testimony in the New Testment. Paul lists the appearances of Jesus as testimony to the resurrection but Paul nowhere in his writings refers to the empty tomb. Thus the appearances of Jesus had a priority in Christian proclamation.

2. Although the tomb narratives may not have been at first part of the proclamation, they did become vehicles for the proclamation as well. In this, however, it is not the emptiness of the tomb which is the object of concern but the resurrection of Jesus. The tomb narratives are not concerned with proclaiming the revivification of Jesus' corpse. Their concern is that Jesus has been raised and the eschatological implications of this fact. Within the resurrection narrative this is made clear by the central statement of proclamation in Mark 16:6, "Do not be amazed; you seek Jesus of Nazareth, who was crucified. He has risen, he is not here; see the place where they laid him."

3. With regard to the male disciples of Jesus, neither a visit to the tomb nor the narratives of the tomb events brought

---

[19]The authenticity of Luke 24:12 is questioned. The RSV translation assigns it to a footnote. Cf., Fuller, *The Formation of the Resurrection Narratives*, 101-103. For a fuller discussion of the Lucan and Johannine narratives, see M.E. Boismard, "Saint Luc et la rédaction du Quatrième Évangile," *Revue biblique* 69 (1962), 185-211.

them to faith in the risen Jesus (one could argue that "the other disciple" is an exception although this is probably not historical fact). Faith is a consequence of the appearance-experiences. This is the testimony of the resurrection narratives themselves. Faith followed the personal encounter with the risen Jesus. In the Lucan/Johannine tradition in which Peter actually visits the tomb of Jesus, it is never proclaimed that Peter believes. In Luke 24:11, when the disciples hear the reports of what the women have experienced, they do not believe them. If the appearance to the Eleven took place in Galilee, the disciples may have come to believe in Jesus before the events at the tomb were even known to them. The tomb and narratives concerning it do not lead to faith. The tomb narratives were vehicles for the proclamation of the faith but not sources of faith.

The same fact seems true of the women. After experiencing the tomb, the women were afraid or astonished and go off to report to the disciples what they had heard. Matthew records not only the event of the women at the tomb, but also an actual appearance-experience of the women leaving the tomb. John also records not only the encounter of Mary Magdalene with the angels at the tomb, but an appearance of Jesus to her at the tomb itself. Thus both the appearance narratives and the tomb narratives associate faith with the appearance-experiences rather than with the experience of Jesus' tomb being empty.

4. The emptiness of the tomb neither proves nor disproves the Christian proclamation. It only proves that the corpse was missing. Yet the tomb narratives represent a very early tradition, even though absent from Paul. They were not the creation of the evangelists. The Marcan and Lucan/Johannine traditions have their own history. The story of the empty tomb was further elaborated and elaborated in distinctive ways. Matthew represents one direction of development. A pre-Lucan and pre-Johannine tradition was another, in which disciples remained in Jerusalem and in which Peter himself visited the tomb.

The story of the women, which may or may not have been only Mary Magdalene, was a very early Jerusalem tradition.

The appearance of Jesus to the Eleven, very possibly in Galilee, led to faith. As these believers went to Jerusalem (perhaps even for the next great Jewish feast of Pentecost) they encountered the tradition of what had happened at the tomb. Thus there is the Jerusalem-centered tradition focused on the tomb and associated with the women, and the Galilee-centered tradition focused on the appearances and associated with Peter and the Eleven.

A Possible Reconstruction of the Events Surrounding the Resurrection of Jesus

Given both the nature of the event and the nature of the materials which give us access to the event, there is no way in which one can historiographically reconstruct with certitude what took place in history between the death of Jesus and the proclamation of the earliest Christians. We operate on the basis of hypothesis only.

Jesus died a scandalous death. Not long thereafter he is proclaimed as having been raised from the dead. What led to this proclamation? The most immediate causes, as we have seen, were the appearance-experiences of the disciples and the gift of the Spirit to the disciples. Can anything further be said?

What actually happened to Jesus we cannot say. What the experience itself consisted in for him we do not know. What happened, however, was interpreted by others on the basis of their experiences to be not a question of the immortality of Jesus' soul but rather the rising of Jesus to life from the grave by God. The question is: in what did this event described as resurrection consist?

We have seen in our study of the Jewish background to the doctrine of the resurrection that there were a wide variety of ways in which future life and resurrection from the dead were conceptualized in the first century C.E. One cannot speak of *the* Jewish doctrine as such, but only of the varied and often inconsistent conceptions. These ranged from more physicalized to more spiritualized understandings. Resurrection itself was not a precise concept. It connoted resurrection of the corpse (revivification, resuscitation), or transformation of the corpse (a transformation in which the materiality of the corpse seems necessary but is changed), or transformation to a new mode of existence (in which the new life may be bodily but a bodily life for which the materiality of the corpse is unnecessary, perhaps akin to Murdach Dahl's somatic but not material identity), or even re-creation with the implication of greater discontinuity than the word transformation implies. We have then a variety of concepts which are not completely clear, and we must call to mind our eschatological skepticism wherever we discuss the *how* of the resurrection. We really do not know in what resurrection consists; we can only conjecture.

Since we do not know, a safe course is to follow Paul, who both cautions us and helps us. Paul believed that he himself experienced the resurrected Jesus (1 Cor 15:8). Paul considered the glorified, resurrected life of Jesus to be analogous to the glorified, resurrected life of Christians (1 Cor 15:12-13, Phil 3:20-21). Paul himself experienced the risen Jesus, and on the basis of his experience attempted to describe what resurrection is like. Paul realized that it was foolish to try to speak about how the dead are raised and what they would be like. At the same time he developed some understanding with his analogy of the seed, his concept of transformation, and his teaching about a spiritual body. Does Jesus' risen life correspond in some way to Paul's description?

But Paul's effort will not answer all our questions. Paul clearly does not see the resurrection as a revivification of a corpse: what is sown a physical body is raised a spiritual body. Yet Paul sees continuity with this earthly life, as with a seed. Yet flesh and blood as we know it cannot inherit the reign of heaven. Thus, in Jesus' resurrection, Jesus was transformed into a new mode of existence, but it was Jesus who was so transformed. On the basis of Paul, we can choose to describe Jesus' resurrection as a transformation event.

On the basis of Paul, however, we cannot clearly say whether that transformation was one in which the corpse

was involved or one for which the materiality of the corpse
was not necessary. We could hypothesize either. Let us
suggest for a moment that resurrection is a transformation
to a new mode of existence for which the materiality of the
corpse is unnecessary but a transformation which does
involve both personal identity and some form of embodiment. It is just not a transformation of the corpse. One of the
best efforts to explore this perspective along contemporary
and philosophical lines is that of John Hick and what he
calls the replica theory.[20]

Paul's seed analogy makes the point. An apple seed does
not become an orange. So X does not become Y. But if one
were to attempt to describe an apple or an apple tree, if one
had never seen one, simply on the basis of the seed, one
would have a hard time doing so. Thus there is continuity in
the resurrection from an apple seed to an apple (personal
identity), but there is also great discontinuity (the apple is
not the seed, the spiritual body not the physical body; flesh
and blood do not inherit the reign of heaven). Thus, on the
basis of Paul's description and on the basis of Paul's
experience, one could suggest that the resurrection of Jesus
was an event for which the materiality of the corpse was not
necessary.

For the moment we are only suggesting this as a possibility. It rests upon a particular interpretation of Paul and also
maintains that it is possible to conceptualize a bodily
resurrection (not simply an immortal soul, but an embodied,
transformed, personal being) for which the corpse, its
matter, is simply not necessary. Now Jesus' resurrection may
be conceptualized in other ways. We do not know for sure in
what it consisted. Yet it is possible to envision an event
which was real and bodily but for which the materiality of
the corpse was not necessary.

What can be stated with assurance about Jesus' resurrection is not its precise empirical character but its reality as an

---

[20]See John Hick. *Death and Eternal Life* (New York: Harper and Row, 1976),
278-96. Also see pp. 171-77 for his discussion of Jesus' resurrection.

act of God. It is God who raises the dead to life. It is God who likewise raised Jesus from the dead. The biblical vocabulary for the resurrection involves the verbs *egeirein* and *anistanai*.[21] *Egeirein* is the more frequent in the New Testament and is used with *ek tōn nekrōn* (from among the dead), with *apō nekrōn* (away from the dead), or simply by itself. The subject of *egeirein* is always God or else the verb is used in the passive with the meaning of "raised by God." Thus resurrection is understood to be God's act.

God is in fact the one who raised Jesus (Rom 4:24; 8:11; 2 Cor 4:14; Gal 1:1; Eph 1:20; Col 2:12; 1 Peter 1:21). The subject of *anistanai* is also God. Used intransitively it still has the sense of "raised by God" (1 Thes 4:14).

In the son of humanity predictions in Mark, however, *anistanai* has the sense of "he will arise by his own power" (Mk 8:31, 9:9, 9:31, 10:34); but this use reflects later understanding. The son of humanity parallels in Matthew retain *egeirein* and the sense of "raised by God." The fourth Gospel is an exception to this principle, but it reflects a more developed christology. In John, Jesus has the power to raise himself (2:19, 5:21, 6:39-54, 10:17-18, 11:25). The earliest tradition, however, saw Jesus' resurrection (as Jesus himself would have envisioned it) as God's act, an act of Jesus' heavenly Father. Jesus' resurrection then was an act in which God effected a transformation of Jesus into a new bodily life for which the materiality of the earthly body was unnecessary.

Another plausible suggestion within our hypothesis is that the event which we call resurrection occurs at death. This is true for all of us and thus equally true for Jesus. There are several reasons for this suggestion. Biblically, we can point to Paul. Paul's earliest teaching reflects that he associated the event of resurrection with the end days or the Parouisa of Jesus (1 Thes 4:15). Paul's later teaching, however, shows

---

[21]Evans, *Resurrection and the New Testament*, 20-27. Also see Raymond Brown in *The Jerome Biblical Commentary* (Englewood Cliffs, N.J.: Prentice-Hall Inc., 1968), vol. 2, 78: 158, pp. 794-95.

a shift in his thinking, as we have seen: the moment of death is the moment of resurrection (2 Cor 5). Thus we find in Paul himself two theological opinions about the time of resurrection. We have been saying that resurrection is a transformation event and an event in which the whole person is transformed as a body-soul unity. Resurrection is not resurrection of the body (in the sense of revivification) but resurrection from the dead (of the psychosomatic unity that a person is). Our basis here is both Paul and contemporary theologies of death, which have moved away from a more philosophically dualistic or Platonic approach and speak less of death as a separation of body and soul (an idea which has its roots in philosophical dualism) and speak of death rather as a transformation event.[22] The shift away from the body-soul dichotomy has a basis in Semitic or biblical anthropology, in Aristotelian philosophy, and in contemporary philosophy which perceives the human being as a whole.[23] This is not to say that body and soul (materiality and spirituality, corporeity and personality) are not distin-

---

[22]Modern Roman Catholic theologies of death include Ladislaus Boros, *The Mystery of Death* (New York: Herder and Herder, 1965); Karl Rahner, *On the Theology of Death* (New York: Herder and Herder, 1961); Roger Troisfontaines, *I Do Not Die* (New York: Desclée Co., 1963). Not all of these move away from speaking about death as a separation of body and soul; they simply move in that direction. Rahner still speaks of death as separation of body and soul but argues that the soul does not become acosmic at death. Boros and Troisfontaines use the language of transformation. For summaries of these varied views, see Robert Francoeur, *Perspectives in Evolution* (Baltimore: Helicon, 1965), 231-80; and John Hick, *Death and Eternal Life*, 228-41. For a discussion of Teilhard de Chardin's approach to death, see Henri de Lubac, *The Religion of Teilhard de Chardin* (New York: Desclée Co., 1967), 47-55.

[23]For further discussion of the biblical perspective on the human person as a body-soul unity, see Wulstan Mork, *The Biblical Meaning of Man* (Milwaukee: Bruce, 1967); Claude Tresmontant, *A Study of Hebrew Thought* (New York: Desclée Co., 1960). For some contemporary efforts see J.F. Donceel, *Philosophical Anthropology* (New York: Sheed and Ward, 1967), 410-63, and "Teilhard de Chardin and the Body-Soul Relation," *Thought* 40 (1965); Robert North, *Teilhard and the Creation of the Soul* (Milwaukee: Bruce, 1967), 188-202; Piet Schoonenberg, *God's World in the Making* (Techny, Ill.: Divine Word Publications, 1967), 46-48. For a modern effort to construct a view of resurrection based upon the psycho-physical unity of the person, see John Hick, *Death and Eternal Life*, 35-54.

guishable; they are simply not completely separable. Death in this anthropological perspective is not a separation but a transformation.

Resurrection is transformation, and death is transformation. Are we not talking about the same event? When we die, we are raised to a new mode of life. Death and resurrection are two aspects of the same event. Death is the word that describes the biological, empirical, and phenomenal side of the transformation event: the earthly, fleshly mode of existence ceases, comes to an end. But this does not mean that the person ceases. The person has died, has passed on to a new mode of existence or life, has been raised. Just as death is the empirically observable side of the event, so resurrection is the word used to describe the ontological side of the event. All that happens in this event is not empirical and observable.

To use Teilhard de Chardin's terms, the human person has a "without" and a "within." At the level of the without, the person has died. At the level of the within, the person has been raised. The death-resurrection event is a transformation.

What dies is not exactly what is raised; we shall be changed, but it is still we who endure through the change. Thus not only is there the biblical opinion of death being the moment of resurrection, but there also is the opinion of some philosophical theologies that death is resurrection. When we die, we shall be changed, transformed, raised.

But if the event and experience of death is also an event and experience of being raised up, what about the body (the corpse) that is placed in the grave? That is simply the materiality that is unnecessary to the risen body or glorified mode of existence. The person at death does not become disembodied (a soul) or naked but is rather newly clothed or re-embodied with a spiritual body and glory, and the materiality of the corpse is matter unnecessary to the new mode of embodiment. This lacks greater precision because some of our questions are unanswerable and because eye has not seen what God has in store for us. When we die, we are transformed into another mode of life: so likewise was Jesus. His death was the empirical side of his resurrection to new life.

Rather than saying that death is resurrection, it is more precise to say that death inaugurates resurrection. I do not want to suggest that all that we wait for is accomplished in a single event, a death-resurrection-transformation. There are further questions which we can only pursue later. After we die and are raised, is there nothing "more" to come? What about the event variously described and associated with the end of days, the final judgment, and the Parousia of Jesus? I suggest that death is the beginning of a new mode of existence but not the consummation of it. We do not know how to express the experience of this intermediate but risen life and often do so in temporal and metaphorical terms.

There is also the question of whether personal development continues after death. Although we are accustomed to think of one's fate being sealed at death and some theologies of death see death as the moment of final and irrevocable decision, the theological opinion which I prefer sees the possibility of personal development after death.[24] The word development is analogous. Development after death has an analogue in the Catholic understanding of purgatory.

There is a further question about the corporate dimension of the human person. Although the resurrection body spoken of by Paul is an individual body, it is still true to say that we are all one body in Christ. The final consummation—which even those already raised from the dead await—is not simply for individuals. What is the relationship between the individual and the community in the resurrection event as well?[25] As we set aside dualistic categories, so we must set aside individualistic ones. Thus the resurrection

---

[24]With respect to the question of the continuing development of the human person after death, see especially John Hick, *Death and Eternal Life*, 221-41, 272-76, 407-14, 455-58. Also, Edmund Guernl, *Evolution in the Afterlife* (Exposition).

[25]Concerning the relationship between individuality and community, see R.H. Charles, *Eschatology, The Doctrine of a Future Life* (New York: Schocken Books, [1899/1913] 1963), 305-6; Donald Goergen, *Personality-in-Process and Teilhard de Chardin* (Ann Arbor; Mi.: University Microfilms International, 1984), 7-35, 126-32, 327-72; John Hick, *Death and Eternal Life*, 455-64; and John A.T. Robinson,*The Body, A Study in Pauline Theology*, SBT 5 (London: SCM Press, 1966), 49-83.

that death inaugurates is not necessarily the whole story for an individual person. The person longs for the last days, continues to develop, and awaits the other members of the body of Christ. We cannot say more about these questions now. The resurrection that death inaugurates is real but not complete. Resurrection itself is a process.

If one interprets death itself to be the occasion which inaugurates resurrection, something needs to be said about the expression "on the third day" (1 Cor 15:4). Whether one accepts other aspects of the present hypothesis or not, exegetes today do not interpret this expression as reflecting historical chronology. It does not date the resurrection of Jesus, nor does it necessarily refer to the discovery of the empty tomb. Although one cannot be certain of its background, one explanation is that the expression has its roots in Hosea.

> Come, let us return to the Lord; for he has torn, that he may heal us; he has stricken, and he will bind us up. After two days he will revive us; on the third day he will raise us up, that we may live before him. (Hos 6:1-2)

The Jerusalem Bible notes with respect to Hosea 6:2 that the phrases "after a day or two ... on the third day" mean "before long." One cannot be certain that the Hosea passage is the basis for the New Testament image, but there is targumic evidence that the Hosea passage was interpreted as a prophecy about the resurrection. "The third day" became the day of the resurrection of the dead or the day of redemption. That Jesus was raised "on the third day" simply means that shortly after his death and burial he was raised, that the day of redemption had come, or that the resurrection of the dead had begun. It is a theological, not chronological statement.[26]

---

[26]H.C.C. Cavallin, *Life After Death, Paul's Argument for the Resurrection of the Dead in 1 Cor. 15, Part 1, An Enquiry into the Jewish Background* (Lund, Sweden: CWK Gleerup, 1974), 189, supports Hosea 6:2 as the basis for the New Testament usage and provides targumic interpretation of Hosea. Also see Cavallin, 192, notes 16-17 for further references. Also see Evans, *Resurrection and the New Testament*,

Jesus' resurrection, like ours, is not a question of a revivification of a corpse. The corpse is that which is unnecessary to resurrection. Jesus died, and at that time or shortly thereafter, was raised from the dead. The corpse was buried, but Jesus had been transformed into a new mode of existence. He continued to live as an embodied person - whatever glorified and pneumatic bodiliness may be. There is no necessary reason for the tomb of Jesus later to be empty. Even if the tomb had not been empty, Jesus would have been raised. An empty tomb is unnecessary for faith in the bodily resurrection of Jesus. Yet a serious historiographical problem remains. If no empty tomb was necessary for the resurrection of Jesus, and if the tomb was not empty, what gave rise to the empty-tomb tradition? We do not know for sure, and of course, there are several possibilities. Events may have happened at or in the vicinity of the tomb, but these events were appearances, such as an appearance to the women. The story then began to circulate about what happened to the women at the tomb.

Van Iersel has offered an hypothesis based on a tradition of pilgrimage to the tomb of Jewish saints and martyrs.[27] Early on, Jewish Christians would have visited the tomb of Jesus. Mark 16:6—"You seek Jesus of Nazareth, who was crucified. He has risen, he is not here; see the place where they laid him"—represents an account given by one who led Christians to the tomb of Jesus. It was not a question of whether the tomb was empty or not, but an announcement of the resurrection in accord with the appearance-experience-based faith of the followers.

47-50. Gerald O'Collins, *The Resurrection of Jesus Christ*, 10-15, sees the expression as more likely derived from the discovery of the empty tomb. Also see John M. Perry, "The Three Days in the Synoptic Passion Predictions," *Catholic Biblical Quarterly* 48 (1986), 637-54, for his own hypothesis and its relationship to Hosea 6:2. And for covenantal connections in the use of 'the third day,' see W. Brueggemann, "Amos 4:4-13 and Israel's Covenant Worship," *Vetus Testamentum* 15 (1965), 1-15.

[27]See Bas van Iersel, "The Resurrrection of Jesus-Information or Interpretation?" in *Immortality and Resurrection*, ed. by Benoit and Murphy, Concilium, vol. 50 (New York: Herder and Herder, 1970), 54-67, esp. 62-63. Also O'Collins, *The Resurrection of Jesus Christ*, 38-43.

Our hypothesis so far has suggested that the tomb of Jesus may not have been empty. Yet such a suggestion explains less well the data behind the empty-tomb narratives. Thus we must push our thinking further. Historiographical investigation must take into account the fact that there were a wide variety of options in first-century Judaism concerning life after death: there was no one Jewish doctrine nor even one Jewish conception of resurrection. In explaining their experiences of the risen Jesus, why did the disciples pick the category of resurrection? The concept of immortality of the soul was present in Judaism; it was not simply foreign or Hellenistic. Why did the disciples choose the category of resurrection rather than immortality—unless their experiences conformed or led to the category of resurrection? Even the early versions of the appearances imply that the disciples experienced Jesus in some bodily way, although the physicalness was not emphasized in the earliest accounts. Yet the category of bodily resurrection must have been more in accord with the actual experiences of Jesus' appearing to them. But there was also in the Judaism of Jesus' day a variety of conceptions of what resurrection consisted in— from very material to very spiritual conceptions. If the experiences of the risen Jesus were so spiritual, why did the disciples not explain them as such, in categories already available within Judaism? Why allow or create an unnecessary empty tomb tradition which implied a more bodily conception of resurrection—unless disciples actually experienced the tomb as empty and had to give an account of that fact? Given the variety of options available to Judaism, there was no need to assume or create an empty-tomb tradition— unless of course the tomb had been so experienced.

Jesus was experienced as alive. The Christians had a variety of ways in which they could express this. Yet they chose to speak of Jesus in terms of resurrection and in terms of an empty tomb. The more solid historiographical conclusion is that some people had actually witnessed the tomb as empty. The experiences of the women at and in the vicinity of the tomb ought not be dismissed as legend. If there were no factual basis to the tomb narratives, the stories of the women's experiences would not have been incorporated into the tradition. The account of Peter's visit to the tomb (Jn 20:3-10) with its basis in a Lucan/Johannine tradition cannot be simply labeled as late. As with the passion narratives, the Lucan and Johannine accounts provide historically reliable material. The earliest stages of the Johannine text give witness to a visit of Peter to the tomb; the best explanation for the tradition is the historicity of the event itself. There was no reason to invent the story; the faith of Peter is not linked to the experience; it is more probable to suggest that it happened. Some of the women (at least Mary Magdalene) and Peter knew that the tomb was empty. The empty tomb, however, still does not *prove* anything. There could be other explanations advanced for the absence of the corpse from the grave. Yet, historiographically, it is still more probable that the grave was empty. The corpse was not there.

After the series of events surrounding the execution of Jesus, Jesus died and was buried. Accompanying his death was the resurrection-transformation to a new and eschatological life. For this, the materiality of Jesus' corpse was in fact not necessary. Perhaps, however, in the case of Jesus, the materiality of the corpse was dematerialized and became a factor in the resurrection of Jesus. The risen Jesus (raised by God) could well have had the power (his own power) to materialize or dematerialize himself. This "miracle" was simply one more among the extraordinary events on earth which accompanied the resurrection of Jesus, such as the appearances and the experience at Pentecost.[28]

---

[28]I am attributing here the disappearance of the corpse to a miracle. In this sense, the resurrection of Jesus was a miracle. In a more profound sense, however, one can describe the entire resurrection event as a miracle. See Walter Künneth, *The Theology of the Resurrection*, trans. James W. Leitch (St. Louis, Mo.: Concordia Pub. House, 1965), 73-80. There is also the miracle of faith: "To the miracle of the resurrection there inevitably corresponds the miracle of faith" (Künneth, 99). On the miracle of faith, see Marxsen, *The Resurrection of Jesus of Nazareth,* 112-29. There are three ways in which miracle can be applied to the resurrection: the event itself; the accompanying phenomena, e.g., empty tomb; the birth of faith. Another whole approach to the historicity of the empty tomb and the fate of the corpse is that of J. Duncan M. Derrett, *The Anastasis: The Resurrection of Jesus as an*

After the sabbath, Mary Magdalene (perhaps alone, perhaps with other women) went to the tomb. In the vicinity of the tomb, Jesus appeared to her (or them). We don't know her reaction, but she goes to report her experience of the tomb and of Jesus to the other disciples. They, however, have left for Galilee, with the possible exception of Peter who may have lingered longer in Jerusalem. If so, Peter may have gone to the tomb where Jesus may also have appeared to him, or simply went to the tomb and then hurried to catch up with the others and Jesus appeared to him on the way. When Peter arrived in Galilee and caught up with the others, who had perhaps returned to their fishing, Jesus appeared to all Eleven gathered together. After the death of Jesus, these appearance-experiences were the next truly significant events.

If the tomb was empty, then Mary Magdalene, or the women, or Peter witnessed the tomb as empty. What still stirred them to faith, however, was not the witnessing of the

Historical Event (Shipston-on-Stour, Warwickshire, England: P. Drinkwater, 1982). He argues a fairly eccentric thesis but one based on extensive research and knowledge. The correct word describing what happened is *anastasis* (a getting up), from the verb *anastēnai* (to get up). The church adopted *egerthēnai* (to be awakened, raised up) as a second thought. The implication is that Jesus himself got up in the grave. In the ancient Western world there is sufficient evidence to suggest that persons declared dead did sometimes revive. Jews who spoke Greek used the word *anastasis* in two senses: (1) revival from death, and (2) revival to participate in the resurrection which was envisioned as a collective experience on the last day. Thus *anastasis* (1) and the resurrection (2) are not synonymous. What happened in Jesus' "resurrection," for Derrett, was *anastasis*. Jews visited graves for three days after burial to be sure that the body had *not* returned to life and been buried precipitously.

Even in modern times, recoveries after what used to be called clinical death and prior to brain death have occurred. Thus Jesus' *anastasis* may have been a genuine revival from reversible death. That Jesus revived in the tomb would not be a "miracle" outside the course of nature. Signs of death appeared which convinced bystanders that he was dead and thus he was taken down from the cross and placed in a tomb.

We cannot consider here the detailed analysis and hypotheses Derrett enters into, but Jesus revived, in an extremely enfeebled condition, able to give a message to a "young man" who acted as a messenger to the women or to Mary of Magdala. The message did not call for the disciples to come to meet Jesus in the vicinity of the tomb but rather that he would meet them in Galilee.

Jesus' post-anastasis life was short. There would not be a lengthy period of time between the revival and actual death. Eventually the disciples, after their meeting Jesus again in Galilee, would have to dispose of the body, after Jesus had actually

tomb but their own personal encounters with the risen Jesus in the appearance-experiences, whether at the tomb, in the vicinity of the tomb, or somewhere else, such as on the road to Galilee. If the tomb was in fact empty, one still cannot document the cause of that fact—whether the empty tomb was the result of some miracle or whether the corpse had in fact been removed or even stolen.

John Dominic Crossan argues that there was no empty-tomb tradition prior to Mark and that Mark himself created the tradition of the empty tomb.[29] Although the tradition lying behind Mark 16:1-8 is a subject for discussion, we cannot conclude convincingly that there was no prior tradition at all. The early preaching would have been affected if the tomb were not empty. Granted that the faith may have originated in Galilee and granted that it may have been impossible to verify the identity of a corpse by the time the preaching emerged in Jerusalem (say the feast of Pentecost), yet there is no evidence in the tradition for there being a

died. Derrett argues that the most plausible path for the disciples to take was that of cremation, a holocaust of a sort prefigured in the narrative of Isaac, perhaps even following upon instruction from the post-anastasis Jesus himself. What happened to Jesus' corpse was no longer relevant.

Between Jesus' *anastasis* or revival and his eventual death and cremation, Jesus visited his disciples and in some fashion commissioned them, perhaps transferring some of his charisma to them by the laying on of hands and the gift of the Spirit. Thus Jesus was actually seen physically by Peter, James, and others.

Although Derrett's conjectures are outside the mainstream of contemporary studies of the resurrection narratives, they ought not be simply dismissed. The major difference between his hypothesis and my own is that I suggest the appearance-experiences as the events which form the historical basis for the faith of the disciples in the resurrection of Jesus, whereas Derrett sees the appearance *narratives* as the *result* of the resurrection faith which had its basis in the actual physical revival of Jesus in the tomb and his going to meet the disciples in Galilee.

[29]John Dominic Crossan, "Empty Tomb and Absent Lord," *The Passion in Mark*, ed., by Werner Kelber (Philadelphia: Fortress Press, 1976), 135-52. Also see Werner Kelber, in the same collection of essays, 162-4, for his critique of Pannenberg. For a contrasting opinion, that the tomb traditon pre-dates the Gospels, see Brown, *The Virginal Conception and Bodily Resurrection of Jesus*, 126, point 4; Fuller, *The Formation of the Resurrection Narratives*, 50-780, esp. 170-82; O'Collins, *The Resurrection of Jesus Christ*, 38-43; Pannenberg, *Jesus-- God and Man*, 88-106; H. von Campenhausen, "The Events of Easter and the Empty Tomb," *Tradition and Life in the Church* (Philadelphia: Fortress, 1968), 42-89.

corpse in the tomb. A resurrection could have been interpreted in a variety of ways. Yet there is no evidence of any
interpretation of a resurrection that accords with the presence
of a corpse. No matter how difficult verification would be
(being able to identify the place of burial, being able to
locate where Jesus was placed in the tomb, being able to
identify the decomposing corpse), there is no evidence that
anyone used the presence of something in a grave somewhere
to argue against the preaching of the disciples. All evidence,
Jewish and Christian, suggests that the tomb was empty.
The question seems to be how or why—not whether.

The problem seems to be that the tomb was accepted as
empty. The challenge was not how to understand the
presence of a corpse but how to understand its absence. An
early response to the tomb affair was the suggestion that the
body had been taken or even stolen. Even the emptiness of
the tomb had to be explained; it did not lead anyone, even
disciples, to posit the resurrection of Jesus. Only the appearances did this. Yet the disciples had to face the fact of the
empty tomb, and it was not necessarily an argument in favor
of their proclamation. Granted the apologetic and polemical
character of the Matthean material in 27:61-66, 28:11-15, the
texts still suggest that the problem facing the disciples is how
to interpret the emptiness of the tomb, not the presence of a
corpse. The fact of an empty tomb better explains the
historiographical data.

We must keep in mind, however: (1) Belief in the empty
tomb is not a part of Christian faith. Christian faith is in the
risen Jesus. (2) The empty tomb itself is not historiographical
evidence for the resurrection of Jesus. There are other ways
of interpreting an empty tomb. (3) The empty tomb tradition
itself does not relate the discovery of the tomb to faith. Faith
is the effect of the appearance-experiences, and fear or
bewilderment or wonder the effect of the discovery of the
tomb. (4) The empty tomb does not say anything about the
nature of the resurrection or the risen body. The emptiness
of the tomb may have been an effect accomplished by Jesus
after raised rather than constitutive of the resurrection-
transformation. (5) The empty tomb is a historiographically

questioned as well as argued point. An empty tomb was not philosophically necesssary for the fact of the resurrection. In either case, what was experienced and proclaimed was the resurrection of Jesus from the dead.

With the appearance-experiences, the faith of Jesus' followers had been restored and even inaugurated on a new plane. We do not know the precise nature of those appearances, but after the gift of the Spirit and event of Pentecost, the preaching took shape. The movement had begun. After the beginning of the preaching, traditions developed. There was the passion story and the announcement of the resurrection. There were the growing collections of the sayings of Jesus. Eventually the announcement of the resurrection developed into narratives—narratives in which the appearance of Jesus was highly physicalized (as in Luke and John), narratives which reflected polemic with the Jews (as in Matthew), and narratives about the discovery of the tomb. But the basic facts seem to have been that Jesus died, was buried, was raised from the dead shortly thereafter, and then appeared or manifested or made his continuing presence known to the disciples. Discipleship which had been briefly interrupted was continued on a new plane.

The Historicity of Jesus' Resurrection

Having taken a look at the background for the language of resurrection in early Judaism, the concept of resurrection as articulated by Paul on the basis of both his Jewish traditions and his personal experience of the risen Jesus, the resurrection (appearance and tomb) narratives as present in our Gospels, and having made some hypotheses and suggestions toward an effort to understand the events that happened following upon the death of Jesus, we are now in a position to say something further about the event itself. Was it an historical event? An answer to this question does not give us information about the precise nature of the event itself, but it helps us to understand what we are talking about.

The answer to the question partially depends upon what we mean by history. There are two primary meanings. An event can be described as historical if it actually happened in the world of our earthly existence and human experience. Or describing an event as historical can mean that it is scientifically or historiographically accessible, verifiable. These two meanings are closely related; ordinarily we do not say that something happened if its actual occurrence is not verifiable. Yet the two meanings are distinguishable. The first meaning refers to the course of history, the actual events themselves. Many things have happened in history that remain unknown because they are not accessible to us or insufficient historiographical evidence remains. The second meaning refers to the discipline and methodology of the professional historian, the way he or she goes about "doing history." The first is history itself; the second is the study of it. When one studies history in schools, one is studying not only what happened but also how what happened has been reconstructed for us by the historians. Is an event historical because it happened or because it left its traces or because the historian can get at it?

There are three primary options which modern theologians have taken. (1) The resurrection did not happen as an actual event in history or in the life of Jesus himself. He was not "personally raised." The resurrection happened insofar as this refers to other phenomena—say the emergence of the faith of the disciples, or the continuation of the kerygma, or the significance of the crucifixion for authentic life (Bultmann, Marxsen).[30] (2) The resurrection did happen,

---

[30]Regarding Rudolf Bultmann, see *Kerygma and Myth I* (London: S.P.C.K., 1953), esp. 38-43. Regarding Marxsen, see his earlier (1964) article, "The Resurrection of Jesus as a Historical and Theological Problem," reprinted in *The Significance of the Message of the Resurrection for Faith in Jesus Christ*, ed. by C.F.D. Moule, 15-50; and his later (1968) *The Resurrection of Jesus of Nazareth*. Although one may disagree with Marxsen, as I do, about the adequacy of his interpretation of the resurrection, there is still much in his 1968 book that deserves attention, particularly his insight into faith, pp. 112-29, 149-54. For a critical review of Marxsen's book, see G. O'Collins, *The Heythrop Journal* 12 (1971), 207-11. For a survey of many of the issues involved in the contemporary discussion on the resurrection, see *The Significance of the Message of the Resurrection for Faith in*

was an event in the personal life of Jesus as well as much more, and it can also be verified historiographically as having happened (Pannenberg).[31] (3) The third option lies between the previous two and rests upon the distinction made above. The resurrection of Jesus was an historical event in the sense that it actually hapened in the course of human events and personally happened to Jesus, but it is not historical in the sense of being able to be conclusively verified by historical research and historiographical methods. I see the third option as the best description of the facts. (Moltmann and Fuller argue also for some form of this option.)[32]

We can say then that the resurrection is an historical fact in the sense that it happened. Our language is metaphorical, but the language still expresses a reality. Jesus himself was raised bodily from the dead (body here does not denote corpse). How can one know this? Both faith and historiography play a role.

We *believe* that Jesus was actually raised from the dead, that Jesus still lives. Otherwise, as Paul tells us, our faith is in vain. In other words, one can't prove as such that Jesus was raised but one's conviction by faith is that he was. One can no more prove this event as having happened than one can

Jesus Christ, ed. by C.F.D. Moule, the introduction, 1-11, and especially the article by Hans-Georg Geyer, "The Resurrection of Jesus Christ: A Survey of the Debate in Present Day Theology," 105-35, which gives particular attention to the positions of Barth, Bultmann, Marxsen, and Pannenberg. Also see Gerald O'Collins, *What Are They Saying About the Resurrection?* (New York: Paulist Press, 1978). For a critique of Bultmann, see Künneth, *The Theology of the Resurrection*, 40-47.

[31]For Pannenberg, see "Did Jesus Really Rise from the Dead?" *Dialog*, vol. 4 (1965), 128-35, a summary of views more fully developed in his *Jesus—God and Man*, 53-114, esp. 88-106. For further discussion of Pannenberg, see also *Theology as History*, vol. III of New Frontiers in Theology, ed. James Robinson and John Cobb (New York: Harper and Row, 1967), which contains an essay by Pannenberg and responses. For a critical response, also see Evans *Resurrection and the New Testament*, 177-83.

[32]For Moltmann, see "Resurrection as Hope," *Harvard Theological Review* 61 (1968), 129-47, esp. 135-41. For Fuller, see *The Formation of Resurrection Narratives*, 22-23. Fuller uses the expression "meta-historical" to describe the resurrection. In this same vein, see Künneth, *The Theology of the Resurrection*, 21-107 , esp. 23-33.

prove the faith itself. Faith cannnot be proved by reason alone. Yet one's faith contains belief in the reality of the event. And although the event is not scientifically provable as such, it is still verifiable in human experience in that the risen Jesus is accessible to our experience. We, too, can personally encounter him, and that experience can corroborate our faith. And there are many through the centuries who give testimony to their experience of the risen Jesus.

Although the actuality of Jesus' being raised cannot be proved as such, Pannenberg is correct in suggesting that the resurrection of Jesus is the most intelligible way of understanding the historiographically accessible facts. It is well founded and the most reasonable historiographical hypothesis. Yet, historiographically, it is hypothesis, but a hypothesis which accounts for the events: the resurrection of Jesus is what ultimately explains the faith of the disciples, the Christian movement, and the emergence of Christianity as a new fact in history. The empty tomb did not stir the people to faith, but the risen Jesus did. "Something happened" behind the events as we have them, and that "something" was "the resurrection of Jesus."

Although the resurrection of Jesus himself is the most plausible hypothesis for explaining history, yet we go too far if we describe the resurrection as a historiographically accessible datum of history. The nature of the event itself is such that history as we ordinarily know and experience it meets with the beyond that both permeates history and transcends it. One can interpret the effects of such an event that leave their mark on history as we know it, yet these effects are not definitive but suggestive. They are invitations to faith but not demonstrations of it. The nature of a resurrection event is meta-historiographical.

The resurrection was then an historical event in the sense that it actually happened and left its effects on history as we know it. It was not an historical event, however, in the sense that it is historiographically demonstrable at this point in history. It is, however, credible, reasonable, and plausible, but certain only to faith and personal experience, not to the science we call history. It is better described as a meta-historiographical historical event. In other words, "The assertion, which has been handed down in the form of a statement concerning reality, that 'Jesus has been raised from the dead,' is valid as a statement concerning reality"[33] (The resurrection of Jesus is an historical event). But the validity of the above statement is ultimately a statement of faith, not an historiographical judgment, although historiography itself points in that direction, but not conclusively so, given the very nature of the resurrection event (The resurrection of Jesus is a meta-historiographical judgment).

[33]See Hans-Georg Geyer, "The Resurrection of Jesus Christ: A Survey of the Debate in Present Day Theology," in *The Significance of the Message of the Resurrection for Faith in Jesus Christ*, ed. C.F.D., Moule, 133. See pp. 132-35 for Geyer's summary of options. I attempt here to place my opinion with those suggested by Geyer. I would agree with Barth and Pannenberg in B, 1, p. 133. I would not agree with Pannenberg, however, in B, 2, b. I also do not agree with A, 1, p. 132, if historical judgment means historiographical judgment.

5

The Servant Becomes Lord

We have put effort into interpreting the historical character of Jesus. As we noted in chapter three, however, a skepticism must prevail in any effort to speak of the nature of the resurrection and eschatological events. Likewise, we must avoid the temptation to harmonize the Gospel materials; such does a disservice to the nature of these materials.[1] Yet we can work with hypotheses.

Faith in Jesus implies the belief *that* Jesus has been raised from the dead, but it says little about *how* he was raised or what actually happened from an empirical or historiographical point of view. Yet there is a further question beyond the question of whether, how, and what happened. This is the question of "so what?" What difference did Jesus' resurrection make? What were its consequences? What is the significance?

These are not historiographical but theological questions —another level in terms of which the resurrection must be understood. Jesus rose. What does this mean, not in the sense of what happened, about which we must be suggestive

---

[1]On the futility of such harmonization see Gerald O-Collins, *The Resurrection of Jesus Christ* (Valley Forge: Judson Press, 1973), 18-28; Pheme Perkins, *Resurrection, New Testament Witness and Contemporary Reflection* (Garden City, New York: Doubleday and Co., 1984), 17-35.

and limited to hypotheses, but in the sense of what was its perduring significance? The resurrection of Jesus is meta-historiographical, yet historical. It is also rich with theological significance.[2]

The Significance of Jesus' Resurrection

1. In the resurrection, Jesus was vindicated by God. The death of Jesus was not to be the final fact about him. The death of Jesus was not God's judgment about Jesus. The resurrection reversed some of the implications of the cross and allowed the cross itself to be taken up into the workings of God in history. The resurrection thus says that there is more to the death of Jesus than appears on the surface. The resurrection permits the cross to be theologized. Thus the resurrection opens the door for a theology of the cross, a new interpretation of the death of Jesus. The death of Jesus did not mean abandonment by God.

Humankind crucified Jesus, but God raised him up. Ulrich Wilckens has written, "His shameful end during the Passover feast in Jerusalem was a disaster which cannot be overestimated for the discipleship of his disciples. Not only was the actual self-authentication of Jesus now absent—it was even called into question."[3] The resurrection counteracted the catastrophe of the cross. Jesus had been vindicated. His death did not mean rejection by God.

2. The resurrection said something about the death of

---

[2]For a theological understanding of the resurrection of Jesus, see C.F. Evans, *Resurrection and the New Testament*, SBT, Second Series, 12 (London: SCM, 1970), 132-83. A Protestant discussion which remains comprehensive and insightful is Walter Künneth, *The Theology of the Resurrection* (St. Louis: Concordia Pub., 1933/1951/1965), a discussion of both historical and theological questions. Also comprehensive is the Roman Catholic discussion, F.X. Durrwell, *The Resurrection* (New York: Sheed and Ward, 1960).

[3]See Ulrich Wilckens, "The Tradition-History of the Resurrection of Jesus," in *The Significance of the Message of the Resurrection for Faith in Jesus Christ*, ed. by C.F.D. Moule, SBT, Second Series, 8 (London: SCM, 1968), 64.

Jesus, but it also said something about his whole life and ministry—that Jesus was what he had said he was. The resurrection of Jesus was the vindication of Jesus in the face of the cross, but it was also the ratification of Jesus' life and teaching. The resurrection permitted a theologization of the cross. It also authenticated the message of Jesus and set the stage for its retention. Jesus was a true prophet, not a false one, and his words and deeds would not be lost. Gerhard Delling writes, "It is through the raising of Jesus that God once and for all identified the whole earthly ministry of Jesus as the work of him who inaugurates the kingdom of God by his preaching and actions, and by his words and acts redeems men and women and brings them into the kingdom of God; God confirms by raising Jesus that his actions were carried out under God's command, and were God's actions."[4]

The resurrection disclosed Jesus as God's chosen one, as a prophet of the Most High. The resurrection not only enabled the disciples to recover from the death of Jesus, but it also enlightened them in understanding the life of Jesus— who this man had been during his life with them on earth. The resurrection of Jesus was thus ultimately the cause of their new faith in Jesus.

The resurrection vindicated Jesus and permitted an understanding of his death. It also ratified the teaching of Jesus, authenticated his ministry, permitted his life to be understood, gave birth to faith in Jesus as "from God," and thus assured that Jesus' life was not lost and that his message was handed on. All these are consequences of the resurrection of Jesus which necessitates a theology of his death as well as a theology of his life and ministry.

3. The resurrection of Jesus not only vindicated, validated, and authenticated Jesus. It was also a source of salvation. There is no theology of redemption which can be complete

---

[4]Gerhard Delling, "The Significance of the Resurrection of Jesus for Faith in Jesus Christ," in *The Significance of the Message of the Resurrection for Faith in Jesus Christ*, 99. On this point, also see Pannenberg, *Jesus-God and Man*, trans. Wilkins and Priebe (Philadelphia: Westminster Press, 1964), 67-68, point b.

without including the theology of the resurrection.[5] Through being raised, Jesus became for us a mediator of salvation in a new way. It was necessary not only that Jesus die but that he be raised as well, and not only that his life and death might be revealed as having God's approval but that Jesus might continue to function in a new mode on our behalf, that he might continue to be for us and for our sake. Jesus' return to God, to his darling Abba, was a prerequisite for his further work. His mission was not accomplished with death on earth. Jesus continued to be son and servant in a new way. Fellowship with Jesus and the offer of salvation it brings was not only re-established but expanded. The raising of Jesus was part of the divine "must" (*dei*, as in Mark 8:31, 9:31, 10:34, as well as in John 20:9).

4. One of the direct consequences of Jesus' resurrection was that it reversed the impression left by the cross and thus allowed another interpretation of the death of Jesus, and that new understanding also meant a ratification of the life and ministry of Jesus as well. Jesus' ministry and death were, simply speaking, acts of God on behalf of Israel: Jesus' life, death, and resurrection were salvific acts, a part of the history of salvation, of the history of the acts of God.

The resurrection of Jesus had other consequences as well: Jesus himself was taken up into a new life with his heavenly Father. He was taken home to God. With the resurrection another stage in his life and ministry had begun. Jesus' new life is interpreted as an exaltation, as being at the right hand of the Father, as his having been made Lord of heaven and earth. With the resurrection-exaltation, Jesus becomes Lord. The resurrection is that event which lies behind the birth of faith in the disciples. It also leads to a new life for Jesus himself. The Lordship of Jesus has begun.

5. Still another consequence of the resurrection of Jesus is that it contributed to the birth of the church and its mission. Without the resurrection of Jesus, without his appearances,

---

[5]See Durrwell, *The Resurrection*, esp. 1-77; Künneth, *The Theology of the Resurrection*.

there would have been no Christians and no church. It was Jesus as raised who appeared to the disciples and brought them to believe in him and eventually to proclaim Jesus as Lord and Christ. Likewise, it was Jesus as raised who inaugurated a new institution on earth, the community of believers, the *ecclesia*, through the power of his Spirit.

Jesus in his earthly ministry had not founded a church. He had gathered together disciples, created a new consciousness, and precipitated a movement identified with him and his followers. After his death this movement could have collapsed and the disciples dispersed. But after the resurrection, this movement became church, for the sake of the word which had been issued by the Galilean prophet, that it might continue to be proclaimed. And accompanying his proclamation there was now also the proclamation of his resurrection as a witness to it. The disciples and believers became church for the sake of the gospel. By entering into a new stage of history themselves, they were commissioned to proclaim that message of God which Jesus had proclaimed and to proclaim Jesus as crucified and raised as well. "By seeing Jesus, probably there in Galilee, Peter and the twelve experienced the overcoming of this catastrophe by God himself, the reconstituting of the discipleship of Jesus, and the giving to them of a commision to carry on the preaching of Jesus themselves."[6] "If then, resurrection is the principal source of faith in the lordship and messiahship of Jesus, it follows that resurrection is also the source of the existence of the church, and its knowledge of itself as the community of the risen Lord and Messiah, the community of the last days."[7]

6. Another consequence of the resurrection is that it heightened eschatological expectation. For many Jews and Jewish Christians, the raising of Jesus could not be separated from the general resurrection of the dead.[8] Jesus was the

---

[6]Wilckens, "The Tradition - History of the Resurrection of Jesus," 65.

[7]Evans, *Resurrection and the New Testament*, 149.

[8]On this point, see Pannenberg, *Jesus-God and Man*, 66-73, esp. points a,c,e.

firstborn from the dead.[9] Would the resurrection of others soon follow? Does this not mean that the end has come? What would happen now? The heightened eschatological awareness led to the apocalypticization of Jesus' message, the expectation that he would soon return as king and judge in the Parousia, and that a new apocalyptic age had begun.

In some of these beliefs and expectations the early Christians were mistaken, but they could not be blamed for what seemed to them an obvious interpretation of the events. In fact, a new age had begun, but it was not necessarily to conform to their expectations of it. Jesus' resurrection was not only vindication, ratification, exaltation, salvation, and proclamation. It was also the beginning of something new in history. God had come. Paul and the Synoptic authors manifest this heightened eschatological consciousness.

7. Another consequence of the resurrection was the gift of the Spirit. The Spirit had special significance in the history of Israel. The gift of the Spirit implied the gift of prophecy. After the exile, the people had experienced a quenching of the Spirit which was to be reversed in the last days. The Spirit, however, was seen to be active again in Israel at the time of Jesus. John had the gift of the Spirit. Jesus was given the Spirit on the occasion of his baptism. Jesus gives the gift of his very own Spirit to all his disciples, to all who believe in him. Whether this Spirit was given on the occasion of the appearance-experiences or shortly thereafter at the feast of Pentecost, we cannot say.[10] There may have been many outbursts of the Spirit. But the sending of the Spirit followed

[9]Cf., Rom. 8:29; 1 Cor. 15:20, 23; Col. 1:18; Rev. 1:5. The expression, Jesus as firstborn from the dead, indicates the eschatological significance attached to Jesus' resurrection among early Christians. Even if Jesus were not literally the first human being to have been raised, say the patriarchs and martyrs before him had been raised, or that resurrection for all begins at death, Jesus' resurrection would still be considered by Christians as first in the order of eschatological significance. His resurrection has a pre-eminence.

[10]See James D.G. Dunn, *Jesus and the Spirit, A Study of the Religious and Charismatic Experience of Jesus and the First Christians as Reflected in the New Testament* (London: SCM Press, 1975), 95-156.

upon the resurrection of Jesus. And life with the Spirit led to a new type of fellowship with Jesus. In the Gospel of John, the resurrection of Jesus is a prerequisite for both his going to the Father and the sending of the Paraclete (16:7f, 20:17). John gives the impression that Jesus gave the gift of the Spirit on the occasion of his appearance to the Eleven (20:22-23). Yet he also gives the impression that he does not send the Advocate until after he goes to the Father (16:7f) and that he does not go to the Father until after the appearances (20:17). Luke in Acts provides us with the events that occurred at the celebration of Pentecost (Acts 2). Paul speaks about how fellowship with Jesus has followed upon the life of the Spirit. Through the power of the Spirit one is with Jesus even in this life. We saw this realizable eschatological dimension present more and more in Paul as he grew in his own understanding.

We can see the richness of the resurrection event—for Jesus and for the disciples, for history itself and for faith— immediate consequences as well as possibilities for new interpretations and understanding. The resurrrection of Jesus left its mark on history, to be further understood by theology. It was a historical, meta-historiographical, theo-logically pregnant event. There was and is no limit to probing its meaning and understanding it more fully. It may have had cosmic implications as well.[11]

C.F. Evans raises the question, "Was the resurrection creative, or was it simply probative?"[12] Our response must be that it was both. It enabled the disciples to probe further the meaning of the life and death of Jesus, to understand or see them more clearly, to see in the history of Jesus an event of salvation, to recognize in him the Messiah of God, to proclaim him Lord. At the same time it was creative of new realities: Jesus became Lord, faith in Christ and the mission of the church were born, and the Spirit had been given to the

[11]Cf., Künneth, *The Theology of the Resurrection*, 161-79.
[12]Evans, *Resurrection and the New Testament*, 147.

people. A new era had begun which could no longer be contained in the existing wineskins.

The Exaltation of Jesus

Jesus' earthly life came to a close with his death by crucifixion. This, however, was but one dimension of the event, an empirical and historiographically verifiable dimension in contrast to the personally experienced but meta-historiographical dimension of the resurrection of Jesus. Jesus died and was raised. Death inaugurated his resurrection. But there was a third dimension to this death-resurrection event in the life of Jesus, his exaltation. Jesus was not only raised; he was "given a place at the right hand of God." Jesus died, was raised to new life and also exalted. With the first two dimensions we can identify. Jesus is like us. We too die and are raised. In the third aspect of this event, however, Jesus is not like us. He has been exalted in a way that we are not. He is given a name that we are not given. He was made Lord and acknowledged to be the Christ.

What is meant by the exaltation of Jesus? What is the language of exaltation trying to convey? What is the relationship between exaltation and resurrection? Are these two distinct realities, two distinct events, two distinguishable aspects of a single event, or simply different words for the same thing?[13]

In the New Testament, resurrection and exaltation are variously related. (1) There are passages which refer to Jesus' exaltation which do not speak about any resurrection (Phil 2:9-11; 1 Tm 3:16; Heb 1:3-4, 8:1; Mk 14:62). This does not mean that the authors do not believe in the resurrection of Jesus, as if the exaltation is a complete alternative to the

[13]See C.F. Evans, *Resurrection and the New Testament*, 135-43; X. Léon-Dufour, *Resurrection and the Message of Easter*, trans. R.N. Wilson (New York: Holt, Rinehart and Winston, 1974), 55-75. Künneth, *The Theology of the Resurrection*, 129-49.

resurrection. Paul, Mark, the author of Hebrews all refer to resurrection elsewhere. Yet the language of exaltation is separable from the language of resurrection. (2) Sometimes the exalted status or lordship of Jesus appears side by side with references to the resurrection of Jesus (Rom 8:34; 1 Cor 15:20-28; Eph 1:19-20; Acts 2:32-33, 3:13-15, 5:30-31; 1 Pt 1:21). It is as if these are the same event or aspects of the same event. (3) Sometimes it appears as if Jesus' lordship actually follows upon his resurrection and that exaltation is a consequence of resurrection (Rom 1:4, 10:9). (4) Luke clearly distinguishes between the two, between the resurrection and ascension. Luke is the only author to give us an ascension as such, a physical way of connoting the exaltation (Lk 24:51, Acts 1:9). We can recall Luke's physicalization of the resurrection appearances as well. (5) In the Gospel of John exaltation is often expressed as glorification (7:39, 12:16, 13:31), or as the lifting up of the Son of Humanity (3:14, 8:28, 12:23-34), a lifting up which implies the crucifixion as well—the crucifixion resulting in the exaltation of Jesus.

The exaltation of Jesus denotes the conviction of the early Christians that he had been given a special status or prerogative, a name above other names, that Jesus had been made Lord. This status is not simply an inevitable consequence of resurrection and does not necessarily flow from it. Many, indeed all the righteous, will be raised from the dead. However, only one became Lord and was exalted to the position of "the right hand of the Father." This exaltation implies another aspect of God's act of raising Jesus. There are at least two aspects to God's act—Jesus' being raised and also being exalted. Both are God's act. Jesus neither raises nor exalts himself.[14]

Since exaltation ordinarily includes within it the concept of resurrection, at least in reference to the exaltation of Jesus, whereas resurrection need not imply exaltation, the

---

[14]See Künneth, *The Theology of the Resurrection*, 129-30.

concept and langauge of exaltation ought be taken as the more inclusive. Exaltation includes resurrection, but the converse is not true. Thus one can readily speak about Jesus' exaltation without any reference to resurrection, for it is implied (as in number 1 above).

Although resurrection and exaltation are distinguishable, they are still closely connected (numbers 2 and 3 above). Thus it is best to see them as distinguishable aspects, but not as separate events. Only Luke's language suggests a basis for distinguishing two events, resurrection and ascension. For John the exaltation or glorification is almost an immediate consequence of the cross. Thus the exaltation, or glorification or ascension, is another aspect of the mystery of the death and resurrection of Jesus, another action of God which went beyond simply raising Jesus from the dead, or at least a further understanding or interpretation of God's act of raising Jesus. We can thus speak of the death-resurrection-exaltation of Jesus, three dimensions of one historical event in the life of Jesus, the last two aspects of which are both meta-historiographical.[15]

Although exaltation and resurrection are not necessarily distinct, separable, distinguishable events for Jesus, but simply distinguishable aspects of an event, the language of exaltation for talking about the fate of Jesus is distinguisable from the language of resurrection. The language of exaltation may in fact have preceded the language of resurrection as a way of describing Jesus' destiny. Although it represents another dimension or fuller understanding of the resurrection of Jesus, in the consciousness and proclamation of the disciples it may have preceded an articulation of Jesus as raised. It may also have been the primary understanding.

[15]The New Testament distinguishes the resurrection and exaltation of Jesus. See H. Sasse, "Jesus Christ, the Lord," in G.K.A. Bell and A. Deissmann, eds., *Mysterium Christi* (London: Longmans, Green and Co., 1930), 93-120. This distinction, however, does not imply two separate events as suggested by Acts. See A.M. Ramsey, "What Was the Ascension?" *Historicity and Chronology in the New Testament* (London: SPCK, 1965), 135-44

But there is no way of knowing. Both aspects of Jesus' fate and the language to express them are present early in the preaching of the church.

Death-exaltation then is not simply a synonym for nor an independent alternative to death-resurrection. Exaltation and resurrection are distinguishable in meaning but not as events in history. Exaltation expresses the full significance of *Jesus'* resurrection. In this sense Jesus was exalted (ascended to heaven) directly from the cross. When he died he was raised from the dead and also given authority at the right hand of the Father.[16] The image of exaltation captures a further consequence or richer understanding of the resurrection of Jesus as distinct from the resurrection of others in general. Yet, as an event, it is part of his resurrection.

Ascension and Pentecost

We have already indicated that the theological content of ascension is the exaltation of Jesus to the status of Lord.[17] It means that Jesus ascended to the heavens, was exalted to the right hand of the Father, given God's glory. Only Luke, in Acts, speaks about the ascension in a physical and temporal way, as a distinct historical event. Yet we have suggested that we are not dealing here with two events, but with one event with several aspects to it. A.M. Ramsey writes, "Theolo-

---

[16]Evans, *Resurrection and the New Testament*, 137. Also G. Bertram,. "Die Himmelfahrt Jesu vom Kreuz aus und der Glaube an seine Auferstehung," *Festgabe für Adolf Deissmann* (1927), 187ff. In spite of critique, it is a valid way of describing the reality even if it may be a mixing of the metaphors. Jesus ascended to heaven from the cross, for the reality that ascension figuratively describes is the exaltation of Jesus.

[17]Concerning the ascension, see Benoit, "Ascension," *Revue biblique*, 61 (1949), 161-203, also in *Theology Digest* 8 (1960), 105-10; Benoit, *The Passion and Resurrection of Jesus*, trans. Benet Weatherhead (N.Y.: Herder and Herder, 1970), 334, 341-42; Joseph Fitzmyer, "The Ascension of Christ and Pentecost," *Theological Studies* 45 (1984), 409-40; A.M. Ramsey, "What Was the Ascension?" note 15 above; H. Sasse, "Jesus Christ the Lord," note 15 above. Also see Bruce Vawter, *The Four Gospels* (Garden City, New York: Doubleday, 1967), 410-11.

gically the two doctrines are distinct. As to an *event* of Ascension distinct from the event of the Resurrection, the allusions to the Ascension in the apostles' preaching and letters give almost no hint that it was a separate historical event."[18]

Matthew's account of the appearance to the Eleven presupposes that Jesus has already ascended to the heavens and entered into his glory. It is an appearance from the heavens.

> And Jesus came and said to them, "All authority in heaven and on earth has been given to me." (Mt 28:18)

John's Gospel also envisions Jesus' ascension as following shortly upon the resurrection (Jn 20:17). Even the Gospel of Luke suggests that the ascension took place on Easter Day or shortly thereafter. If not read in the light of the Acts, there is no interval in Luke between the appearance to the Eleven and Jesus' ascension to heaven (Lk 24:36-53). The Marcan appendix records the ascension and suggests it as an event following the appearances, but gives no precise date (Mk 16:19-20). Thus only the account in Acts suggests a visible ascension forty days after the resurrection (Acts 1:1-11). The forty days is symbolic, and various suggestions have been made with respect to the symbolism, for example, Moses on Sinai, the period of the disciples' preparation for ministry in relation to Jesus' own preparation in the wilderness, as an imitation of the rabbinic usage of forty as a norm for the disciples' learning and repetition of their masters' teachings.

The ascension or exaltation of Jesus took place on the same day and at the same time as the resurrection of Jesus. It was an aspect of that one event. Pierre Benoit writes, "The deepest meaning of the ascension is Jesus' entry into glory, and in this sense it took place on Easter Day itself, at the moment of the resurrection."[19] The earliest Christian theo-

---

[18]A.M. Ramsey, "What Was the Ascension?" 144.

[19]Benoit, *The Passion and Resurrection of Jesus*, 334.

logians placed the ascension on Easter Day.[20] Even now—
although we are accustomed to thinking of the ascension as
a feast forty days after Easter—the liturgical celebration is
within the Easter season, a celebration during the continuing
fifty-day celebration of Easter itself. It is a celebration of one
theologically distinguishable aspect of the Easter mystery.
Liturgically it is a celebration of Easter and not a feast or
event distinct from Easter.

At the time of the celebration of the feast of the Passover,
in 30 or 33 C.E., Jesus was executed by crucifixion outside
the walls of Jerusalem. On that day, as he died, he was raised
from the dead by his beloved and heavenly Father who also
exalted him and shared his Lordship with him. For a period
of time after this event Jesus made his presence known to
those whom he loved and who had followed him. Jesus had
become the Lord and Risen One. The faith and proclamation
were born. During this period Jesus also imparted to his
disciples the gift of his Spirit. Whereas the appearances seem
to have been the immediate source of faith, the gift of the
Spirit was the immediate source for the proclamation. Thus
Jesus who was crucified had been raised from the dead and
became both Lord and Christ. Faith emerged and the church
had been born. A decisive event for the history of the
church, however, came with the celebration of the feast of
Pentecost.

Although the celebration of the Feast of Weeks or
Pentecost was not as prominent a feast in the time of Jesus
as were Pesach (Passover) and Sukkot (the Feast of Taber-
nacles), it was nevertheless a feast which many pilgrims
would celebrate in Jerusalem, a festival celebrating the end
of the grain harvest. The feast had no fixed date but was
celebrated fifty days after the offering of the first sheaf of the
newly cut barley. Sadducees and Pharisees reckoned the day
for the first offering of the grain harvest differently, but both
did so in relation to the feast of Passover. Thus the

---

[20]See Benoit, "Ascension", note 17 of this chapter.

celebration of the Feast of Weeks or Pentecost was approximately fifty days after the feast of Passover.

Given the events of this one particular Passover for the disciples of Jesus—the execution of their teacher, their fear and disillusionment and sorrow, and later the appearance-experiences and their corresponding joy and faith, perhaps even the gift of the Spirit and the beginning of the proclamation that Jesus had already been raised from the dead—this was a Passover that would not be forgotten. Did some of the disciples who had returned to Galilee now go as devout Jews to celebrate joyfully the feast of Pentecost in Jerusalem? Had the disciples already received the gift of the Spirit (John 20:22-23), or did they receive it in Jerusalem on the occasion of the feast (Acts 2:1-13)? Was this the occasion when the stories of the events in Galilee met for the first time the stories of the events that had occurred in Jerusalem and its vicinity? Was the Pentecostal experience in Jerusalem an experience of the giving of the gift of the Spirit or an experience of the outpouring of that gift as many disciples of Jesus met for the first time since the calamity there at the preceding Passover celebration? Was it an experience of the strength of being back together and thus the first fruits of the gift of the Spirit? Did any of the disciples really return to Jerusalem at this time at all, or was this an event solely within the Jerusalem community? Was this experience at Pentecost the same as the appearance-experience related by Paul when he speaks of Jesus' having appeared to more than 500 at the same time?[21] Although we do not know the answers to these questions, the experience of Pentecost in that particular year was an event of historic significance in

[21]For the suggestion concerning the relationship of events to the Jewish festival, see C.F.D. Moule, "The Post-Resurrection Appearances in the Light of Festival Pilgrimages," *New Testament Studies*, 4 (1957-58), 58-61. For the suggestion of a relationship between Pentecost and the appearance to the 500, see Fuller, *The Formation of the Resurrection Narratives* (New York: The Macmillan Co., 1971), 36. For a thorough and critical commentary on the passages from Acts, see Ernst Haenchen, *The Acts of the Apostles* (Philadelphia: Westminster Press, 1971), esp. 135-96. Also see Fitzmyer, "The Ascension of Christ and Pentecost," note 17 above.

the life of what would be the Christian Church.

The event included the feast of Pentecost, manifestations of the gift and power of the Spirit, and truly public preaching. Following the description of the event, Luke presents an address, one of the sources for our knowledge of the earliest preaching of Jesus as Lord and Christ (Acts 2:36). This is followed by a report about converts and an idealized description of an early Jewish-Christian Jerusalem community.

What actually happened on this occasion is not our concern here. But the celebration of Pentecost brought to a close the Easter season. It was both end and beginning. It was the end of that period of history in which the disciples experienced the risen Jesus as recorded in the appearances and the end of the resurrection event itself as its consequences draw to a close. It was the beginning of a new period in the story of Jesus, the proclamation and the church. The concluding episode in Jesus' life on earth comes to a close as Jesus leaves with his disciples the gift of his very own Spirit. Jesus had died, was raised, exalted, appeared to his disciples, and gave the gift of the Spirit. The power of the Spirit had already begun to manifest itself. The events following upon the death-resurrection-exaltation of Jesus were coming to a close. The church had been born. Paul was to experience his own call within a couple of years.

Jesus is Lord

The efforts to trace the history of the titles which are applied to Jesus in the New Testament often lead to complex and hypothetical suggestions. There are three principles which will be of help to us, however. (1) It is necessary to be conscious of two phases or at least the possibility of two phases of development behind each New Testament expression—the pre-resurrection situation and the post-resurrection situation. The resurrection of Jesus had a significant impact on the understanding and expectations of Jesus' followers.

Faith in him, which was being expressed after the resurrection, the appearance-experiences, and the event of Pentecost, was no longer the same as the faith in him which the disciples had shown while he was with them in the flesh. Thus we have to ask the question, with respect to the expression "Lord" or any of the titles, what meaning it conveyed as applied to Jesus prior to the resurrection and what meaning it conveyed as applied to Jesus after the resurrection. Behind each expression there lies the possibility of at least two phases of development. (2) After the resurrection, within the development of early first-century Christian thought, one can also distinguish between the situations of Jewish Christianity and Gentile Christianity. Thus "Lord" as applied to Jesus within Jewish Christian communities may not have carried all the meaning or the same meaning that it carried within a Gentile Christian church. Caution must be expressed, however, with respect to another distinction which has almost become commonplace, that between Palestinian-Jewish and Hellenistic-Jewish Christianity. Given the pervasive effects of hellenization within Palestine, as we saw in Volume One of this series, this is no longer a valid way of speaking and ought not be presumed. Although one can validly speak about Jewish Christianity and Gentile Christianity, the distinction between Palestinian Judaism and Hellenistic Judaism is on tenuous grounds. (3) In the post-resurrection period, some of the expressions or titles are fluid and flexible, especially some of those which are more significant or frequent. In fact, those titles which were too fixed in their meaning were more likely to die out or be of less use to the church. The expressions which were of greater value to the church were those capable of carrying more and more meaning. Thus, those expressions which became particularly prominent were those about which one cannot be as precise with their meaning. The most valuable titles were flexible, such as Lord, Christ, Son of God.

In discussing here the Lordship of Jesus, we will focus on the first of these three principles. What did the title "Lord" mean and how was it applied to Jesus prior to the resurrection, and what did it mean as applied to Jesus after the resurrection?[22] The Greek word for Lord in the New Testament is *kyrios* (*ho kyrios* = the Lord, *kyrie* = Lord, as a form of address). The Greek *kyrios* translates two Semitic words: the Aramaic *mar*, lord (*mari* = my lord, *maran* = our lord); and the Hebrew '*adonai* = my lord); and the Hebrew '*adhon*, lord ('*adonai* = my lord). The Semitic words were used in Judaism in at least three ways.

1. "Lord" means God. In Aramaic literature there is evidence of God's being addressed as "my Lord," *mari*. In Hebrew, God was also addressed as '*adonai*, which was also the substitute for the proper name of God which was the unpronounced tetragrammaton. In the Greek Septuagint, the name of God was translated as *kyrios*. The Greek word itself, *kyrios*, entered the language of Galilean Aramaic as an Aramaic word borrowed from the Greek and used to refer to God.

2. In Aramaic, the word "Lord" (*mar*) was also commonly used as a form of address for human beings, as in addressing a ruler or father or husband. Here also there was an interchangeability between the Aramaic word (*mar*) and the Greek word (*kyrios*). *Kyrios* was sometimes used almost as an Aramaic word and *mar* as a Greek word. Thus *mar* and *kyrios* were practically interchangeable.

3. A variation of this second use was the relationship between "lord" and "teacher." Usage overlapped here, and yet *mari* was not a synonym for *rabbi*. "Lord" was used frequently as an address to teachers, yet the word *mar* connoted an even higher level of dignity or respect and may

---

[22]See Oscar Cullmann, *The Christology of the New Testament*, Revised Edition, trans. Shirley C. Guthrie and Charles A.M. Hall (Philadelphia: The Westminster Press, 1963), 195-237. Joseph Fitzmyer, "The Semitic Background of the New Testament *Kyrios* - Title," in *A Wandering Aramean: Collected Aramaic Essays* (Missoula, Montana: Scholars Press, 1979), 115-42. Reginald Fuller, *The Foundations of New Testament Christology* (New York: Charles Scribner's Sons, 1965), 184-88. Ferdinand Hahn, *The Titles of Jesus in Christology*, trans. Harold Knight and George Ogg (London: Lutterworth Press, 1969), 68-135. Geza Vermes, *Jesus the Jew, A Historian's Reading of the Gospels* (Philadelphia: Fortress Press, 1973), 103-28. The most up-to-date expositions of the issues are those of Fitzmyer and Vermes.

also have connoted the power to work miracles. The word "Lord" also came to be applicable to the expected Messiah.

Thus we can see that the Aramaic word for Lord had a variety of meanings or uses. It had a thoroughly Palestinian setting. It was practically interchangeable with the Greek *kyrios* which found its way as a Greek word into the Aramaic language. One cannot restrict the background for its meaning to the Hellenistic Gentile church. The word denoted authority in some form. The varied usage is reflected in Psalm 110:1, "The Lord said to my lord," where the first is the tetragrammaton (YHWH) and the second the king (*'adonai*), both translated into the Greek Septuagint as *kyrios*. Was Lord applied to Jesus in his lifetime, and, if so, in what sense?

There is sufficient New Testament evidence to suggest that Jesus was referred to as Lord, *mari* (e.g. Mk 7:28; Mt 8:2, 6-8, 21).[23] There is no reason to see this in contrast to ordinary Palestinian Aramaic usage. Jesus referred to as Lord, in the pre-resurrection phase, did not denote the divinity of Jesus, but rather was in accord with the way of addressing someone human with proper respect. We have already seen Jesus in Volume One as a teacher, for some *the* teacher. He was also a worker of wonders, healings and exorcisms. He spoke as one having authority. The title was not simply an equivalent to *rabbi* and could have carried several connotations in reference to his earthly ministry.

The post-resurrection use of *kyrios*, however, was different. The expression may have acquired increased meaning in Gentile churches, but there is no need to go outside Jewish Christianity for its origins. In the post-resurrection usage the expression acquired more significance than it had in reference to Jesus during his lifetime. It was based on the disciples' experience of Jesus as raised from the dead and exalted and their belief that he would come again. It expressed their new faith and understanding. Fitzmyer opts for a Palestinian

---

[23]See Fitzmyer, "The Semitic Background of the New Testament *Kyrios* - Title," 127-28; Vermes, *Jesus the Jew*, 122-28.

Jewish-Christian background for the post-Easter application of the title Lord to Jesus, a title already incipiently used by Jews for the tetragrammaton.[24] The expression *kyrios* had its post-Easter origins among the Jewish-Christian Hellenists. The "Hebrews" of the Jewish-Christian community applied to Jesus the expressions *mar* and *'adhon* and may have translated these by *kyrios* in their dealings with the Hellenists. Fitzmyer also suggests that "Lord," in its post-resurrection usage, was first applied to Jesus in reference to his future coming but then extended and retrojected to apply to the continuing present activity of Jesus, to the exalted Jesus, to Jesus as raised from the dead, and even to the earthly Jesus. The post-resurrection title as applied to the earthly Jesus was different from the way in which the expression was used of Jesus in his own lifetime.

Lordship contains the connotation of resurrection, exaltation, present activity, and future coming. Jesus is the one who is at the right hand of the Father and the one who is to come again. "Lord" expressed the newly born post-resurrection faith and commitment of the Galilean disciples. Thus we see a distinctiveness in the post-resurrection use as a proclamation of the new faith. We do not yet have here what later comes to be a statement on the divinity of Jesus. We have rather a statement of the earliest Jewish-Christian proclamation (Acts 2:36, 3:12). Jesus shares in the "transcendence" of God, is more than merely human, but is not yet identified as God. The New Testament seldom calls Jesus God and does so only in later writing (Heb 1:8, Jn 20:28).[25]

We see exemplified here our third principle above concerning the flexibility of some of the titles. The expression "Lord" was particularly useful and used because it was flexible enough to carry the increased meaning or understanding that would be demanded of it. An expression like

[24]See Fitzmyer, fn. 22 of this chapter.

[25]See Raymond Brown, "Does the New Testament Call Jesus God?" *Theological Studies*, 26 (1965), 545-73, reprinted in *Jesus-God and Man* (Milwaukee: Bruce, 1967), 1-38. Also see Fitzmyer, "The Semitic Background of the New Testament *Kyrios* - Title," 130-32.

rabbi or teacher was less able to carry the growing under-standing of the church. But "Lord" allowed the consciousness of the church to develop and, as a title, was able to carry more and more meaning. Jesus is Lord, which is to say not only was so on earth but still is, as raised from the dead, as exalted, as present to us, as one who is to come, as the Messiah for whom we had been waiting. "Lord" conveyed an understanding of both the pre-resurrection Jesus and post-resurrection Jesus. As Ferdinand Hahn writes, "What dis-tinguishes the use of *kyrie* and *ho kyrios* from *rabbi didaskale* and *ho didaskalos* is the fact that the latter remains confined in its use to the earthly Jesus, whereas the address 'Lord' was at a very early stage applied to Jesus whose return was expected."[26] Even in the pre-resurrection period, *rabbi* and *kyrie* were not synonyms, but Hahn is correct in observing that Lord/*kyrios* would be of greater use to the church. It could interpret both his pre-resurrection ministry and post-resurrection mission as well. Jesus was Risen Lord. The formula *maranatha* (1 Cor 16:22, "Our Lord, come") reflects the eschatological side of the post-resurrection Palestinian Jewish-Christian understanding of the Lordship of Jesus. This Lordship also includes an exalted status, as is apparent in the appearance narrative in Matthew. The expression "Lord" is flexible enough to carry the development in early christology.

Lord as a title was simply open to development, able to refer both to the earthly and the risen Jesus. It was able to carry eschatological, messianic, and cosmic connotations. It acquired even further significance in the Gentile Christian churches. In its earliest usage it expressed a risen, exalted, and soon-to-return Jesus. In its Palestinian Jewish setting it did not imply a divine nature. In the New Testament then, Lord (*kyrios*) can denote (1) God, (2) the earthly Jesus, and (3) the risen, exalted, and awaited Jesus. It is a flexible expression. And as applied to Jesus it has a different meaning in its pre-resurrection and post-resurrection usage.

[26] Hahn, *The Titles of Jesus in Christology*, 89.

Part Three

Toward an Understanding of Jesus

6

The Jesus of Historiography and the Jesus of Faith

In the Gospel of John, Pilate poses an unavoidable question. Jesus had just spoken about truth, how he saw his mission as bearing witness to that truth, and how anyone who is of the truth hears his voice. Pilate responded: "What is truth?" (Jn 18:37-38). Philosophers, saints, and ordinary people have struggled with that question. Universities are communities in search of truth. At times we talk about our true selves or being true to ourselves. Gandhi entitled his autobiography "The Story of My Experiments with Truth." Truth is associated with knowledge, light, enlightenment, wisdom, and even mystery. The question, "What is truth?," is, therefore, not a facile one.

Our concern here is not to explore this question itself, but rather to alert ourselves to the fact that there are different kinds of truth, different kinds of intellectual knowledge, different ways of knowing. It is a disservice to truth and to humankind to exalt one kind to the exclusion of the other. At this point in our discussion of Jesus, we need refer only to two kinds of knowledge. These will be two complementary ways of knowing Jesus.

The first kind of knowledge is objective and the second

personal.[1] I describe objective knowledge by one or several of the following adjectives: analytical, discursive, logical, scientific. It may be either rational or empirical. It seems to be publicly verifiable or demonstrable. It is often observable or factual. Logical deductions, scientific experiments, arithmetic equations, or historical facts all illustrate the search for objectivity.

I prefer to use the word "objective" to describe this kind of knowledge rather than one of the other adjectives because it points to a common quality. In this way of knowing, objectifying that which is known, considering it as an object outside oneself and putting some distance between it and the knower, is considered a value.

There is no such thing as purely objective knowledge.[2] Objective knowledge and personal knowledge are not in absolute opposition. Objective knowledge is not completely non-personal or impersonal, and personal knowledge is not completely non-objective. Thus objective knowledge is not accurately described as impersonal, nor is personal knowledge accurately described as subjective. Rather, the word objective points to a value, a personal value, within a particular method of inquiry. The value is in being able to put some distance between the inquirer and the object of inquiry. Complete objectification of this sort, however, is neither possible nor even an ideal. The assumption that it can be achieved is false. Yet, for some purposes, or in some methodologies, it is a value to try to do so to whatever degree possible. Scientific and historiographical research and behavioral studies seek to diminish the degree of

---

[1]In Volume Four, I will be discussing a third kind of knowledge or truth: symbolic knowledge or symbolic truth. But that is not necessary for our discussion here.

[2]See Michael Polanyi, *Personal Knowledge, Towards a Post-Critical Philosophy* (New York: Harper and Row, 1964). A briefer exposition of his basic tenets is *The Study of Man* (Chicago: University of Chicago Press, 1959). Also see Michael Polanyi and Harry Prosch, *Meaning* (Chicago: University of Chicago Press, 1975); and Richard Gelwick, *The Way of Discovery, An Introduction to the Thought of Michael Polanyi* (New York: Oxford University Press, 1977). In addition to Polanyi, Henri Bergson and Jacob Bronowski have been helpful in my effort to understand knowledge.

personal involvement. They see objectification as valuable to their goals.

One of the values in objective knowledge is that it has a public quality to it. It is capable of verification. Theoretically, it can be shown by someone else to be true or false. Hence, its objectivity does not flow simply from one inquirer's ability to achieve a distance from the object. Even if one is passionately personally involved, the results are open to verification by others who thus lend credence to the results. One can reflect upon such results critically. Objective knowledge is public property and open to critique.

I use the word "personal" to describe knowledge that is experiential, intuitive, or pre-reflective. This is not to say that it is subjective, private, or unrelated to the extramental world. It is personal because it involves more of the observer. This type of knowledge does not value distantiation between the knower and the known but rather values the fuller participation of the knower. The basis for this knowledge is one's experience, insight, or intuition. One suddenly sees something—mental sight, insight, synthetic awareness. It may be proverbial or practical wisdom which one cannot easily verify but which one knows to be true. It is less objective, but not subjective (not non-objective). It comes from deeper within and is apprehended by more than the discursive intellect alone.

Michael Polanyi also uses the expression "personal knowledge." I have not borrowed it from him and I am not using it in precisely the same way.[3] Yet his exposition helps to clarify what I mean by personal knowledge. *Personal*

---

[3]Polanyi has influenced my understanding, but I am not using the expression in precisely the same way as he. Polanyi uses it as a description of all knowledge and sees it as a value in all knowledge; purely objective knowledge is not only not possible, it is not desirable. I use the expression to refer to one of three types of knowledge. We will consider the third type in Volume Four of this series. The word "personal" for me describes the dominant characteristic of one kind of knowledge. Although I do not use the expression to mean exactly what Polanyi means, I agree with his expositon about knowledge in general. Yet it is important to be aware, even when I quote Polanyi, that I am not explicating his theory, but using his insights to explicate my own approach. Polanyi also distinguishes between explicit knowledge and tacit knowledge, and between focal awareness and subsidiary awareness. See note two of this chapter.

knowledge seeks understanding: it is a grasping of parts into a whole. "We cannnot comprehend a whole without seeing its parts, but we can see the parts without comprehending the whole."[4] Objective knowledge can give us facts, but personal knowledge gives meaning to those facts. To know something is not only to know it, but to know its significance. Personal knowledge focuses on the significance, the meaning, the whole, and is only subsidiarily aware of the particulars. It seeks understanding. Objective knowledge is focused on the particulars and unaware of the whole. In fact, an awareness of the whole or of its meaning can get in the way and is perceived as disadvantageous if one is seeking objectivity. Hence the focus of awareness in objective knowledge is distinct from that in personal knowledge. The goal of one is factuality or objectivity. The goal of the other is understanding. One can focus on a rose as a botanical or an aesthetic object. One can study its biological processes or admire its beauty. Both kinds of knowledge are valid and both are valuable.

An important aspect of these two kinds of knowledge is their complementarity. It is not a question of validating or valuing one or the other. They are not related to each other as either/or, but as both/and.[5] First, neither exists in pure form. I repeat that objective knowledge is not impersonal. There is no such thing as pure objectivity. Objective knowledge is also personal knowledge, but knowledge in which one chooses not to focus on the personal element, but in fact attempts to transcend it. And personal knowledge is not totally subjective. It is also objectified, communicated, articulated. It may not always be articulated or capable of articulation with "scientific" language; its mode of expression may be poetic, figurative, or even silence. The different ways of knowing express themselves in different kinds of lan-

---

[4]Polanyi, *The Study of Man*, 29.

[5]I reflected further on the need for thinking in terms of complementarity in *The Power of Love* (Chicago: Thomas More Press, 1979), 268-80.

guage.[6] In personal knowledge one does not choose to transcend the personal element, but to re-present it. If one objectifies what one attempts to articulate, one can use objective language (which can conceal the fact that the knowledge itself is not completely objective). But if one attempts to articulate what is personalized, scientific language is of no avail. It cannot do it. Yet personal knowledge can be formalized. Varied modes of expression are possible from art to philosophy.

A second aspect of the complementarity is that both modes of knowing and all different kinds of language are valuable. Our tendency, however, is to ask which is more important. The natural scientist is likely to say one and the novelist the other. But this is to perceive the relation between the two falsely. Which is more   important, inhaling or exhaling? Objective knowledge and personal knowledge are not opposed to each other. We need both. In the end, we cannot have one without the other because we need both the "facts" and the "significance." Some tasks may require objectification, others personalization. On one day I may wish to approach the rose objectively, as an object, and on another day personally, as conveying some personal meaning. I can see an apple as cells, as food, or as a gift. I can know another human being more objectively, as my client, or more personally, as my spouse. Both kinds of knowledge are valid, and both are valuable. The one who knows me more personally does not necessarily know me without objectivity.

Modern epistemology has struggled extensively with the problem of knowledge. Our only purpose here is to realize and recognize that there are different kinds of knowledge and different ways of knowing, and these need not be opposed to each other. I have spoken here of two: objective knowledge and personal knowledge. Associated with these

---

[6]See Edward Schillebeeckx, *Jesus, An Experiment in Christology*, trans. Hubert Hoskins (New York: The Seabury Press, 1979), 626-28.

two types of knowledge are two different mistakes, going so far in one direction as to deny the legitimacy or value of the other kind of knowledge. The mistake of the objectivist, rationalist, or empiricist can be to have positive or factual knowledge and thus to presume understanding. On the other hand, the mistake of the personalist, existentialist, or intuitionist can be to presume an understanding without its being based on something that is objectively real. Meaning becomes separated from the factuality of events. Both of these errors can be simply a manifestation of the fallacy of dogmatism (a mind unopen to truth perceived from another point of inquiry).[7]

Historiography and Faith

We are now conscious of two distinguishable types of knowledge, a more personal, experiential knowledge and a more objective, analytical knowledge. Historiography (the critical study of history) is an example of objective knowledge, and faith is an example of personal knowledge. Approaching Jesus in two ways enables us to talk about the Jesus of historiography and the Jesus of faith. But let us first say something further about historiography and faith themselves.

Methods of historical research and philosophies of history can vary. Yet modern efforts to lay open the past are more or less critical, exacting, and scientific in approach, with some objectivity a presumed goal. The word "history" can be used in different senses. It can refer to the past, that which is studied, what happened, and also to the study itself, the discipline, the research of the historian. History is what an historian does. It is also what he or she seeks to unfold. Ordinarily I will use the word *history* to refer to the past as an object of historical inquiry and I will use *historiography*

---

[7]See Alfred North Whitehead, *The Function of Reason* (Boston: Beacon Press, [1929] 1967), esp. 49-61.

for the academic and scientific study of that history.[8] Historiography is our means of access to history, but history cannot be equated with historiography. There is more to history than historiography has access to. Historiography is both aided and limited by its scientific critical methodology.

Much that has been said of objective knowledge can be said of historiographical knowledge as well. The historian seeks to objectify what is being studied, to eliminate personal bias. History is out there, to be observed, apart from me. Yet there is no such thing as purely objective historiography. Discussing this point, Polanyi writes,

> Napoleon's career forms a series of *actions*, while gravitation comprises merely *events*, not actions. Human action involves responsibiltiy, which raises the question of motive: such questions, for example, as how far Napoleon was responsible for the wars waged by France under his leadership. Professor Pieter Geyl has compared the views of twenty-seven French historians of Napoleon on these and similar questions. He gave his survey the title *Napoleon For and Against*, which shows that the historians' analysis of motives has resulted in the apportioning of praise and *blame*... Professor Geyl observes, accordingly, that the appreciation of Napoleon depends on the political views of the historian. He finds that these views have varied with the date of writing and the professional affiliations of the historian. Feelings of national pride or anti-clericalism favour Napoleon, while anti-militarism and religious feelings speak against him. We may recall how our own reactions to the Russian Revolution have recently caused historians to work out new interpretations of the French Revolution and of the Millenarian move-

[8]The distinction is comparable to the distinction between music and musicology. Or one may choose to speak of material history and formal history, material history as the past with its varying degrees of relevance to the present, and formal history or historiography as the academic, critical, and scientific discipline by which material history is interpreted and written.

ments that preceded it. Thus, the writing of history is itself
a process of history. . . .[9]

Even scientific historiography cannot completely separate
fact from interpretation. Even factual statements about
history can only be formulated by the use of some assumptions. Let us take as an example, "Christopher Columbus
discovered America in 1492."[10] Further reflection reveals
that Columbus did not in fact discover America. There were
already others there. We try to be more precise. Columbus
was the first European to discover America, and it was 1492.
This, however, disregards the prior Viking voyages. And
even so, what Columbus "discovered" was not America but
a land later to be named America. Thus we say that in 1492
Columbus, a European, came to a new land, which was only
new to Europe and not those people who were living in the
new land, a land which later was named America . How
different it would be if the textbooks said: "In 1492, a man,
Christopher Columbus, under the auspices of Spain, came
to a land inhabited by people hithertofore unknown in
Spain, which people they disregarded, and they began to
treat the land as their own, as land for colonization. This
land was later named America by the Europeans." Even this
statement contains interpretation. The date 1492 would be
perceived differently by Jewish, Christian, and Moslem
dating patterns. We see how difficult it is to separate the
"history" from the "interpretation" and frequently after
attempting to do so, we discover that the interpretation was
more important to us than the history was (historiography is
also personal). Yet, in spite of difficulty, modern historiography strives after an objectivity.

We ought not oppose historiography to personal knowledge. They complement each other. One tries to find the

[9]Polanyi, *The Study of Man*, 78-9.

[10]For example, for a different reading of the "facts," or of the ordinary
presentation of the facts, see Howard Zinn, *A People's History of the United States*
(New York: Harper and Row, Publishers, 1980), esp. 1-22.

facts while the other seeks to understand them. A bare fact by itself is of little interest. Hence the difficulty of separating it from interpretation.[11] Interpretation (a more personal knowledge) has already given some significance to the fact or it wouldn't be included in history books. Fact and interpretation, historiography and personal knowledge, go hand in hand. Yet the historiographer tries to achieve objectification, and that is the value of what he or she does. The search for factual accuracy is important. We can neither reduce truth to objective factuality, nor can we separate truth from it.

Now to turn for a moment to faith, which can be understood in several ways.[12] Faith primarily denotes trust in God, as when we speak of Abraham, Mary, and Jesus as examples of faith. In a Christian context, faith refers to the belief that Jesus is the Christ. And faith also refers to those beliefs which accompany Christian life.

Faith, as a kind of knowledge, is an example of personal knowledge. Faith, whether as trust or belief or a way of life, is grounded in experience, the experience of God. One trusts or follows or believes One whom one has experienced personally. This experiential knowledge of God or Jesus is the ground of faith. Hebrew, Israelite, and Jewish faith is deeply rooted in the experience of the people. The early Christian proclamation and faith were rooted in the experience of Jesus as raised from the dead. Throughout history

[11]See Van A. Harvey, *The Historian and the Believer, The Morality of Historical Knowledge and Christian Belief* (Philadelphia: the Westminster Press, 1966), esp. 214-21 on "facts" and "interpretation." Constructive insights on history and historiography can be found in John Marsh, *The Gospel of Saint John*, Pelican New Testament Commentary (New York: Penguin Books, 1968), 17-20; note especially his distinction between "what took place," and "what was going on." Also see R.G. Collingwood, *The Idea of History* (Oxford: Oxford University Press, [1946] 1967); Bernard Lonergan, *Method in Theology* (New York: Herder and Herder, 1972), 175-234; and T.A. Roberts, *History and Christian Apologetics* (London: S.P.C.K., 1960).

[12]See the article by Avery Dulles, "The Meaning of Faith Considered in Relationship to Justice," in *The Faith That Does Justice*, ed. John C. Haughey (New York: Paulist Press, 1977), 10-46.

many have given witness to their own personal experiences of God in Christ. Faith then is an experiential, personal knowledge.[13]

What we have said of personal knowledge above can be said of faith knowledge here. Faith is not subjective and private. It is personal because it involves all of me. In experiential knowledge I do not distance myself from the experience. I am the experience and it is constitutive of who I am. The experience of God can lead to faith, conviction, insight, or to a knowledge of some aspect of God such as God's love or mercy. This knowledge of God comes from within me. Faith seeks understanding, attempts coherence, formalizes itself for the sake of communication. Faith opens up the meaning of the life of Jesus, makes it significant and puts it in the context of a whole history of God's saving acts. One can know Jesus historiographically, but also experientially or personally by faith. We ought appreciate the complementarity of these two kinds of knowledge. They can be distinguished but not separated. Faith cannot be severed from historical events and an historical Jesus whom historiography (to some degree) can rescue from subjectivism, ideological distortion, and unguarded bias. Yet historigraphy can never give us the full story of Jesus. The Jesus of history can be submitted to scientific historiography but also transcends its domain. We need *both* historiography *and* faith in order to know Jesus.[14]

Historiographical knowledge is not without its biases.

---

[13]Bernard Lonergan provides a brief description of faith as knowledge. See *Method in Theology*, 115-18.

[14]Hence the importance of both distinguishing but not separating the "Jesus of historiography" and the "Jesus of faith." The earthly, historical Jesus cannot be reduced to the Jesus of historiography alone. Thus I agree with David Tracey that the Jesus of modern historical-critical exegesis cannot be the basis or norm for Christology (David Tracey, *The Analogical Imagination, Christian Theology and the Culture of Pluralism* [New York: Crossroad, 1981], 233-41; 242, n 5; 300, n 97; 334, n 15), but I do not think we can any longer terminologically identify the Jesus of history with the Jesus of historiography. See Volume One of this series, Donald Goergen, *The Mission and Ministry of Jesus* (Wilmington, Del.: Michael Glazier, 1986), 11-22 esp. n 1, pp. 11-12.

And faith is not completely non-objective. It rests upon testimony and experience. The language expressing historiographical truth and faith truth will not be the same. Nor can one say that either faith or historigraphy is the more important in our understanding of the historical Jesus. Neither historiography without faith, nor faith without historiography grasps the Jesus of history. Historiography and faith need not oppose each other; faith seeks understanding and is rooted in history; historiography welcomes interpretation that illuminates the facts.

By faith knowledge I do *not* mean accepting an historical fact as historically factual on the basis of faith. Faith and historiography must rightly be kept distinct. We cannot historiographically prove the content of faith. Nor can we argue by faith to something as historiographically accurate. Methodologically they must be kept distinct. What I am saying is that we do not come to a full knowledge of Jesus of Nazareth by either alone. We do not understand Jesus apart from faith, nor do we get more historical information as a result of faith. Faith knowledge neither confirms nor refutes the results of historiographical research, although it may lead us to question those results. Other historiographers help to confirm or refute the historiographical conclusions of another. We do not accept as fact something that falls short of some consensus.

Nor is faith knowledge primarily the acceptance of something on the basis of someone else's testimony. Faith, as I am using the expression here, is accepting something on the basis of personal experience. This is what ultimately grounds faith. It grounded the faith of the very first Christians. It is their faith knowledge which helped them to *see*—to understand and interpret who Jesus was. Only that experiential, personal knowledge helped them to know the Jesus of Nazareth whom they had known previously but not fully. For many later generations of Christians, faith has meant acceptance on the basis of someone else's experience. Yet, in theory, for us of later generations, a living faith still implies an experience of Jesus through the power of the Spirit. We come to our own, or to own that experience to which the disciples were the first witnesses. Christian initiation is careful lest this "conversion experience" be lacking. Adult faith still rests upon the experiential knowledge of Jesus as alive. It does not do what only historiography can do, but this experience-based faith enables one to understand better the historical events. Historiography can only arrive at facts and provide some possible interpretations. It cannot grasp fully the meaning because the event of the resurrection, the horizon within which they become meaningful, is meta-historiographical. The Jesus of history will always be an enigma to historiography, but that historiography is still significant for faith. It stands as critical inquiry over against distorted interpretations. Faith and historiography check and balance each other.

Historiographical research into the earthly, historical Jesus is insufficient by itself because not all the "facts" are accessible to historiographical investigation. We have seen in the earlier chapters that one of the most determinative facts about Jesus, namely his resurrection from the dead, is meta-historiographical. Yet no understanding of the earthly Jesus is complete apart from faith in the resurrection. Another element which escapes full historiographical investigation is the experience of the disciples. The experience is personal knowledge, not objective knowledge, and the articulation or formalization of it still does not make it capable of complete historiographical confirmation. The confirmation lies within the testimony that the disciples give it. Thus we cannot limit ourselves exclusively to those elements in the story of Jesus which are capable of historiographical verification lest we distort the Jesus for whom we search. Historiography's search for the real Jesus of Nazareth must thus at least be open to faith.

But Chistian faith, likewise, must also be open to secular historiographical research. For there is something very crucial to faith that is no longer under the control of faith, namely, Jesus who stands always as a challenge to the church's Jesus. There is an element of autonomy and autonomous rationality that is not subject to Christian faith, just as there is an element of history not subject to critical historiography, namely, the resurrection of Jesus.

Walter Künneth makes a similar point with respect to the resurrection. In our quest for the Jesus of history, we cannot dismiss "believing knowledge."[15] The knowledge of the resurrection is open only to faith. "Every method that is detached from faith must in principle lead to failure."[16] The resurrection narratives themselves are testimonies to the faith of the early Christians in the resurrection. One cannot set aside the character of these narratives: that they manifest and are intended to manifest faith knowledge. One cannot rightly face the narratives without personally being challenged by the question: do you believe? The resurrection narratives can be subjected to historiographical or literary analysis, but historiography alone will never be able to confirm or deny what those narratives testify to .

We are thus saying: (1) The Jesus of history is inaccessible by historiography alone. The Jesus of history is not the same as the Jesus of historiography. Since the expression "historical Jesus" is so widely used in the sense of the Jesus reconstructed by historical, literary and critical research, we should perhps use the expression "earthly Jesus." As christology eventually asserts, there is more to Jesus than the earthly Jesus alone, the earthly phase of Jesus' life and mission. But there is also more to the earthly Jesus than the historiographical Jesus. The Jesus of historiography is not synonymous with Jesus of Nazareth. (2) The Jesus of history is inaccessible by faith alone. One can have a personal experience of the risen Lord, but that experience has to be further grounded in the tradition that makes Jesus accessible. The earthly Jesus cannot necessarily be presumed to be the Jesus in whom one personally believes. Faith knowledge alone is insufficient. (3) The earthly Jesus then (to the degree accessible at all) is the Jesus of historiography and the Jesus of faith, or the Jesus whom we come to know both by

---

[15]Walter Künneth, *The Theology of the Resurrection*, trans. James W. Leitch (St. Louis: Concordia Publishing House, 1965), 102-7.

[16]*Ibid.*, 103.

objectification and personalization, or the Jesus whom we know as the result of dialogue between modern historiography and Christian tradition. The Jesus of history can only be known by faith, but not by faith divorced from historiography. Historiography can give us "parts" of Jesus but not the whole Jesus. Faith is concerned with the whole picture, but a whole which cannot be separated from the parts. Historiography attempts to provide accurate pieces to the puzzle. Faith tries to put the puzzle together. They need each other.

What we have just said also helps us to appreciate the distinction common in contemporary theology between *Historie* and *Geschichte*, both German words for history. *Historie* denotes what happened, factual occurrence, the record of the past, what we may often think of as history and to some degree the object of historiographical research. *Geschichte* implies the past as it impinges upon the present, history with a significance to it, history more existentially understood than positivistically researched. The contrast in meaning is sometimes conveyed in English by translating "historisch" as *historical*, and "geschichtlich" as *historic*. The kind of history we have in the New Testament is assumed to be *Geschichte*—not a record of the past for the sake of an accurate record, but events which changed and still change lives. Martin Kähler introduced the distinction into the modern study of Jesus, but Bultmann with a different emphasis popularized it. Bultmann tended not only to distinguish but to separate the two meanings. What is important from our perspective, however, is to see their complementarity. There can be no *Geschichte* that is not also in some sense *Historie*. In other words, the meaning of an event cannot be completely divorced from the actual occurrence of the event. Significance or meaning which not only transcends but in no way relies upon the events interpreted is vacuous, myth in the pejorative sense, subjective. *Geschichte* then implies an event that is not only "geschichtlich" but also "historisch" although it acknowledges that there is not *Historie* in the pure sense, no past events which have no significance whatever; or, if so, no one is interested in them. What the historiographer is interested in is a history which is "geschichtlich," at least to the historiographer. Yet he or she studies history under the formality of *Historie*. Faith, however, is concerned with history under the formality of *Geschichte*, but with the awareness that its character as *Historie* is vital to the assertions of faith. The earthly Jesus is both the "historisch" Jesus and the "geschichtlich" Jesus.

Schillebeeckx also indicates the need for a complementarity between historiographical inquiry and faith knowledge.[17] "Faith and historical criticism go hand in hand ... (they) have each their own proper competence and angle of approach."[18] There can, in fact, be no search for an historical Jesus apart from the confession of faith on the part of the Christians. For Schillebeeckx, the Christian movement is our access to Jesus, and there is no access to Jesus apart from it. Thus any approach to Jesus is inevitably bound to faith already—that of the proto-Christian movement. Historiography can only have access to "a part of the real past"; hence the Jesus of historiography is also only an image of Jesus, as is the so-called Christ of faith. One cannot deny reality to the non-historiographically accessible. Reality is bigger than what historiography can recover. Jesus of Nazareth is not accessible by historiography alone.

Schillebeeckx describes a valid approach to Jesus as requiring a "second innocence."[19] We can relate this to the

---

[17]Schillebeeckx uses the word historical to describe what I mean by historiographical. I use the word historiographical so that we can keep the varied meanings of "history" distinct. He also speaks about Jesus as experienced and interpreted by the proto-Christian movement; I use the expression faith knowledge to be consistent with my own exposition. Schillebeeckx's expression and mine are related but not co-terminus. For Schillebeeckx's discussion of the relation between historiography and faith, see *Jesus, an Experiment in Christology*, trans. Hubert Hoskins (New York: The Seabury Press, 1979), esp. 19-36, 43-80; and *Interim Report on the Books Jesus and Christ*, trans. John Bowden (New York: Crossroad, 1981), 27-49, 93-102. Hans Küng also points to the complementarity between historiographical research and faith. See *On Being a Christian*, trans. Edward Quinn (Garden City, N.Y.: Doubleday and Co., 1976), 119-65.

[18]Schillebeeckx, *Jesus*, 34.

[19]*Ibid.*, 79.

modern literary theme of innocence, innocence lost, innocence regained.[20] An approach to Jesus by faith alone manifests a naiveté, the naiveté and beauty of first innocence. But, with the dawn of the age of reason (for an individual or for human history), this first innocence is lost. It then believes that it must, and can, live by reason alone. But maturity and experience bring them together at a new and deeper level. One can never come to the third level without going through the second. The danger in faith is to try and bypass the second level of critical reason. But the two cannot ignore each other, and eventually a faith seeking understanding or a rationality seeking understanding incorporate within themselves their needed and complementary shadow, and a new innocence is reached from which true understanding can flow. The complementarity between historiography and faith is the modern version of the medieval debate on reason and revelation.[21] It is a question of both/and. Historiography neither produces faith, nor is it dependent upon a faith perspective. Neither is it an enemy of faith. Nor is faith dependent upon historiographical research or an enemy of it.

A word should be said about whether accurate historiographical knowledge of Jesus is possible. There is no need to detail here the history of the quest for the historical Jesus. This has already been sufficiently done. We know the cast of characters: Reimarus, Lessing, Bauer, Strauss, Weiss, Schweitzer, Bultmann, and then "the new quest."[22] But every theologian needs to be conscious of being either optimistic or pessimistic about the effort to know the earthly Jesus. There are two extremes to avoid. The first is to assume that anything like a biography of Jesus as understood in the

[20]Consider this theme, for example, as developed in the writings of Hermann Hesse. Also valuable are the reflections of Rollo May, *Power and Innocence* (New York: W.W. Norton and Co., 1972).

[21]See Etienne Gilson, *Reason and Revelation in the Middle Ages* (New York: Charles Scribner's Sons, [1938] 1966).

[22]See the bibliography of suggested readings pertinent to this chapter at the end of this volume.

modern sense is possible. Our recovery of Jesus material may give us "Jesus," but it does not give us a life of Jesus in modern terms. The other extreme is to assume that a recovery of authentic Jesus material is impossible. Although it is not an easy task, critical scholars have been able to assess a significant amount of material which gives us access to the earthly Jesus.[23]

It may be helpful to look at two opinions about the possibility of recovering accurate Jesus material. One, more pessimistic, is Norman Perrin, a biblical scholar. Another, more optimistic, is A.M. Sherwin-White, a secular historiographer or Roman historian. Perrin's research into the teaching of Jesus has done us a great service.[24] Yet, his approach leaves one more skeptical about the Jesus material than we need be. The issue depends upon how one perceives the nature of the Gospel material. Perrin writes, "So far as we can tell today, there is no single pericope anywhere in the gospels, the present purpose of which is to preserve a historical reminiscence of the earthly Jesus, although there may be some which do in fact come near to doing so . . . "[25] If Perrin means no pericope whose purpose is *exclusively* to preserve a historical reminiscence, we must agree. But if he means that historical reminiscences as historical were unimportant to early faith and proclamation, we must disagree. Once Jesus was raised from the dead and experienced as raised, there was great interest in the *memoriae Jesu*. This does not deny the freedom of the evangelists in the construction of the Gospels. But the evangelists were *both* theologically *and* historically motivated. Theological moti-

---

[23]One can note here the ongoing work of The Historical Jesus Section of the Society of Biblical Literature as well as The Jesus Seminar of the Westar Institute and its journal, *Forum*.

[24]Especially valuable are Norman Perrin's clarity of expression and exposition of four stages of biblical hermeneutics (textual, historical, literary criticism, and hermeneutics proper). See *Jesus and the Language of the Kingdom* (Philadelphia: Fortress Press, 1976), 1-14.

[25]Norman Perrin, *Rediscovering the Teaching of Jesus* (New York: Harper and Row, 1967), 16.

vation does not exclude historical sensitivity. The evangelists saw their proclamation as the true understanding of the events that had come to pass, for whom the events were important as well as the understanding.

Perrin also makes a major point about the identity in the early church between the risen Lord and the earthly Jesus, and vice versa. He writes, "The early Church made no attempt to distinguish between the words the earthly Jesus had spoken and those spoken by the risen Lord through a prophet in the community... The early Church absolutely and completely identified the risen Lord of her experience with the earthly Jesus of Nazareth and created for her purposes, which she conceived to be his, the literary form of the gospel, in which words and deeds ascribed in her consciousness to both the earthly Jesus and the risen Lord were set down in terms of the former."[26] The early church did not distinguish between Jesus and the Christ in the way that modern historical scholarship does. The Risen Lord was the selfsame Jesus. And the early church was right.[27] Modern critical historiography, however, has an interest which was not important to the early church, namely to distinguish the teachings of the pre-resurrection Jesus from the post-resurrection community of believers. And we have seen the importance of this historiographical pursuit *for the faith*. In the Gospels, sayings whose origins were most probably post-resurrection are attributed to the earthly Jesus. Yet this does not negate the fact that this early church also respected some of the sayings and deeds of Jesus because they were sayings and deeds of the historical, earthly Jesus whom they had known. Although they could readily attribute a saying to Jesus since the Risen Lord after all was Jesus, they also remembered and collected sayings which were "earthly Jesus" material. Their lack of distinction between the pre-resurrection and post-resurrection Jesus

---

[26]*Ibid.*, 15; also see 15-53.

[27]Is this not the primary purpose of Mark's Gospel? See H.C. Kee, *Community of the New Age: Studies in Mark's Gospel* (Philadelphia: Westminster Press, 1977), 9.

makes our modern historiographical task more difficult. However, it goes too far to imply that the church had no regard for Jesus' words and deeds qua historical.

Perrin distinguishes three different kinds of knowledge in the current discussion on the historical Jesus: (1) descriptive historical knowledge, or *Historie*, which I have called historiographical knowledge; (2) significant historical knowledge, or *Geschichte*; and (3) faith knowledge, knowledge of Jesus which is significant only in the specific context of Christian faith.[28] Although Perrin's distinctions are helpful, he makes the mistake of separating what he distinguishes. We have to distinguish different ways of knowing Jesus. But, as we have seen, we cannot separate completely *Historie* and *Geschichte*. Otherwise, one has a false picture of the situation. *Historie* without some interpretation or some significance exists only in the abstract. Likewise significant historical knowledge is still historical (historiographical) knowledge. It cannot be severed from it roots in history as it was for Bultmann. Faith knowledge is also knowledge based upon the experience of Jesus as raised from the dead, experiential and valid knowledge of Jesus. It is in the area of faith-knowledge that I disagree most with Perrin. He writes, "'Faith knowledge' depends upon special worth being attributed to the person concerned."[29] Faith knowledge does not derive from attributing special significance to Jesus. Rather, attributing special significance to Jesus derives from knowing him by faith, that is, having personally experienced him as having been raised. Faith knowledge does not derive from some abstract significance. It is derived from the experiences of those who knew Jesus and of one (Paul) who did not know him in the flesh but still experienced him as raised. Perrin's approach makes faith knowledge useless in the search for the Jesus of history. He then tends to equate the Jesus of historiography with the real Jesus of Nazareth. Rather we must see that the real Jesus of history is accessible

28 Perrin, *Rediscovering the Teaching of Jesus*, 234-44.
29 *Ibid.*, 237.

only through both historiography *and* faith.

Perrin writes, "True, this Jesus of the kerygma, this Jesus of faith-knowledge, encounters us in our historic situation, but he is not the historic Jesus, he is the Christ, the eschatological Jesus."[30] But such a (common) distinction between Jesus and the Christ is one which we can no longer accept. We can and must distinguish the two phases in the life of Jesus—pre-resurrection and post-resurrection. However, we cannot identify our access to the pre-resurrection Jesus with historiography and access to the post-resurrection Jesus with faith and church, and sever the two. The Jesus of historiography is not adequate to give us the earthly Jesus of history. And faith not only gives us a "Christ of faith" but a Jesus of faith, but in the end faith is also necessary for the goal of historiography in its pursuit of the real Jesus of Nazareth. I grant with Perrin the necessity of the distinctions. I disagree that the three kinds of knowledge all have different objects. While they may have different formal objects, they do not have different material objects. Both faith and historiography are necessary if we are to reach Jesus.

In contrast to Perrin, Sherwin-White, the Graeco-Roman historiographer, has more confidence in the historiographical nature of the Gospel materials than form critics. "It is astonishing that while Graeco-Roman historians have been growing in confidence, the twentieth century study of the Gospel narratives, starting from no less promising material, has taken so gloomy a turn in the development of form criticism that the more advanced exponents of it apparently maintain—so far as an amateur can understand the matter— that the historical Christ is unknowable and the history of his mission cannot be written."[31]

Sherwin-White questions whether the tendency of myth to prevail over historical fact is likely within the period of time

[30] *Ibid.*, 238.

[31] A.M. Sherwin - White, *Roman Society and Roman Law in the New Testament* (Oxford: Clarendon Press, 1963), 187.

within which the Gospels came to be written, a space of three generations. He also questions, on historiographical grounds, the tendency to exaggerate the Gospels' lack of concern for history. In other words, on historiographical grounds, skepticism with respect to historical material within the Gospels is unjustified. "What to an ancient historian is most surprising in the basic assumptions of form-criticism of the extremer sort, is the presumed tempo of the development of the didactic myths... The agnostic type of the form-criticism would be much more credible if the compilation of the Gospels were much later in time, much more remote from the events themselves, than can be the case. Certainly a deal of distortion can affect a story that is given literary form a generation or two after the event, whether for national glorification or political spite, or for the didactic or symbolic expositon of ideas. But in the material of ancient history the historical content is not hopelessly lost... Herodotus enables us to test the tempo of myth-making, and the tests suggest that even two generations are too short a span to allow the mythical tendency to prevail over the hard historic core of the oral tradition... It can be maintained that those who had a passionate interest in the story of Christ, even if their interest in events was parabolical and didactic rather than historical, would not be led by that very fact to pervert and utterly destroy the historical kernel of their material."[32]

Thus, we ought not be uncritically optimistic or skeptical in our historiograhical quest for Jesus; nor ought we assume that historiography alone is the only access to Jesus and that faith is an access to some other Christ but not at all to the earthly Jesus.

The Jesus of History and the Church's Jesus

Roman Catholic biblical scholars, as well as biblical scholars in general, recognize a process of transmission

[32] *Ibid.*, 189-91.

behind the canonical Gospels as we have them. Although theories concerning the process of transmitting the Jesus material, the development of the Jesus tradition, and the formation of the Gospels differ, three stages are recognized by Roman Catholic scholars: (1) the Jesus Material, (2) the Oral Tradition and the Apostolic Preaching, and (3) the Written Tradition and the Christian Scriptures.[33]

The first stage contains material which comes from the earthly Jesus himself. It is the pre-resurrection stage in the history of Christianity and its central character is the earthly Jesus. Today we have access to this stage only by going back through stages three and two. The Jesus material is the object of contemporary Jesus research and was a primary concern in the first volume of this series.

If the first is the Jesus stage, the second is the post-resurrection or apostolic stage. In this stage Jesus is proclaimed as having been raised from the dead. This is the formulation of the kerygma and of the apostolic preaching. The central character is still Jesus, but Jesus as he comes to us through apostolic preaching, Jesus as understood in the light of the resurrection and the gift of the Spirit, the Jesus of a tradition passed on orally. This stage in the formation and transmission of the Jesus tradition spans several decades, from the death of Jesus in 30 or 33 C.E. to the stage of the tradition being submitted to writing. Although Paul's first letter was written around 50 C.E., our first Gospel, Mark, dates from shortly before or after 70 C.E., or perhaps the mid sixties. This second stage is the pre-literary oral tradition within which the Jesus material is preserved. Modern exegetical methods have given us some understanding of both the creative and the retentive dynamics of this stage in the

---

[33]For a concise discussion of these three stages, see Joseph A. Fitzmyer, *A Christological Catechism* (New York: Paulist Press, 1982), 7-23, 97-140. Also see "The Biblical Commission's Instruction on the Historical Truth of the Gospels," *Theological Studies* 25 (1964), 386-408, esp. pars. 6-9 of the text, reprinted in Fitzmyer above; and "The Biblical Commission and Christology," *Theological Studies*, 46 (1985), 407-79, esp. pp. 477-79.

life of the church.[34]

The Jesus tradition is in part submitted to writing, under the continuing influence of the Spirit, and the Christian Scriptures are born, a third significant stage in the life of the Christian Church. The written tradition, namely the New Testament, is our primary access to the oral tradition and apostolic preaching of stage two, as well as to the Jesus material of stage one. The third stage, the first literary stage in the history of the church, which gave rise to the most significant of all Christian literature, continued for decades. The stage of Gospel formation extended from the composition of the Gospel of Mark through the end of the first century. The Gospel of John gives access to a second and third generation of Christian believers. Sifting the Christian writings and recognizing which ones constituted Scripture was a second century task.[35] In any study of this process, we realize that the Gospels do not give us direct access to Jesus or the Jesus material. The Gospels are not Jesus' writings or preaching but the church's writings and preaching about him.[36] Our access to Jesus is through them, but stage three cannot simply be identified with stage one, as if the New Testament were the teaching of the earthly Jesus. The Holy Spirit acted in the life of the church between the gift of the Holy Spirit after the resurrection of Jesus through the formation of the Christian biblical literature as we now have it and beyond. We will now look more closely at these three stages of church history. No period in the history of

---

[34]For a very readable summary of the methods of contemporary exegesis, see Daniel Harrington, *Interpreting the New Testament*, vol. 1 of New Testament Message series (Wilmington, Delaware: Michael Glazier, 1979). Also Raymond F. Collins, *Introduction to the New Testament* (Garden City, N.Y.: Doubleday and Co., 1983).

[35]On the formation of the canon, see Raymond F. Collins, *Introduction to the New Testament*, 1-40. Also see James Barr, *Holy Scripture: Canon, Authority, Criticism* (Philadelphia: Westminster Press, 1983).

[36]Note the appropriate title of John Reumann's study, *Jesus in the Church's Gospels* (Philadelphia: Fortress Press, 1968). Pp. 18-43 give a succinct summary of the formation of the Gospels as understood in contemporary research.

Christianity is more important. History creatively but conscientiously moved with divine guidance from Jesus to the church.

A. The Jesus Material. The earthly Jesus, the Jesus of history, demands both historiographical research and faith knowledge. No one *knows* Jesus who does not acknowledge or believe that he was raised from the dead. This "knowledge" of Jesus comes through faith. Yet this belief that Jesus was raised does not give us knowledge of the mission and ministry of Jesus. We only have access to that through the Scriptures, our understanding of which requires critical, historiographical reflection.

How do we determine the authentic teaching of Jesus? How does one determine whether a particular saying of Jesus is really an "authentic saying" of the historical Jesus, the *ipsissima verba Jesu*? The task involves both science and art, both critical reason and prudential judgment. While there are no universally agreed upon criteria, critical exegesis has given rise to principles which are very helpful.[37]

Before looking at some of the principles, however, we must keep in mind several facts lest we wrongly apply the principles. First, to refuse to call a saying authentic does not imply its inauthenticity. A saying judged to be authentic is a saying about which we can make a critical historiographical judgment. There are sayings, however, for which we do not have a sufficient basis to clearly judge them to be authentic; this is not then a judgment in favor of inauthenticity. It simply means we do not have sufficient basis, given our present methods, for an affirmative judgment. In other words, the principles we use cannot be used negatively, but can validly be used only positively to make a judgment in favor of a saying's authenticity. The "authentic sayings" give

---

[37] A helpful article which is clear, constructive, and critical is D.G.A. Calvert, "An Examination of the Criteria for Distinguishing the Authentic Words of Jesus," *New Testament Studies*, 18 (1971-72), 209-19. The article has influenced Schillebeeckx's treatment of this material. For Schillebeeckx's discussion, see *Jesus*, 36-40, 81-102, esp. 88-100. Also see Joachim Jeremias, *New Testament Theology, The Proclamation of Jesus*, trans. John Bowden (New York: Charles Scribner's Sons, 1971), 1-41; and E.P. Sanders, *Jesus and Judaism* (Philadelphia: Fortress Press, 1985), 3-22.

us reliable material but not the whole Jesus.

Second, granted that the valid application of criteria implies making a positive judgment or refraining from doing so for insufficient evidence, valid application also implies making a positive judgment on the basis of several criteria. It is only by putting a saying to the test of several principles that an exegete or theologian can wisely make the prudential judgment about a saying. None of the principles are absolutes; they only function in conjuction with one or more of the other principles.

Third, in many situations it may be a question of a part of a saying, or of a substratum behind a saying. The questions we ask are important, and the right question is not simply: can we judge this saying or parable as it stands to be authentic? But rather: what about this saying or what part of it can we judge to be authentic?

In what we are doing then, we are not dividing the material, as is commonly assumed or mistakenly done, into authentic and inauthentic sayings but rather into material which we can reasonably judge to be authentic and material about which we can make no such judgment. Let us now look at some of the principles on which exegetes rely.

1. The principle of multiple attestation.[38] If a saying is found in more than one form or in more than one tradition in the Gospels, this multiple attestation is an argument in favor of authenticity. As indicated above, however, this principle cannot be applied negatively. If a saying is found in only one tradition, this says nothing about its authenticity or inauthenticity. It simply does not fulfill the requirement of this criterion and thus lacks an argument in favor of authenticity. If a saying is found in more than one form (as a proverbial saying, in a parable, in a miracle story), or in more than one source or literary tradition (say in Mark and

---

[38]See F.C. Burkitt, *The Gospel History and Its Transmission*, third edition, (Edinburgh: T. & T. Clark, 1911), 147-68; D.G.A Calvert, note 37 above; C.H. Dodd, *History and the Gospel* (London: Nisbet and Co., [1938] 1947), 91-101, and *The Parables of the Kingdom*, revised edition (New York: Charles Scribner's Sons, [1935] 1961), 24; Schillebeeckx, *Jesus*, 95.

in Q, although here we are sometimes on precarious grounds not always being sure of the interrelationships among the literary traditions and how dependent or independent they may be), authenticity is indicated, though not proven.

2. The principle of redactional cross purposes.[39] Redaction criticism gives us a knowledge of the theological perspective of an evangelist and the motifs in a Gospel as a whole. The study of redaction can also help us in our search for Jesus material. "If each of the gospel writers is expressing his own point of view through the stories he selects and the way his material is presented, the inclusion of material which does not especially serve his purpose may well be taken as a testimony to the authenticity of that material, or at least to the inclusion of it in the tradition of the Church in such a clear and consistent way that the evangelist was loath to omit it. The material asserts itself even though it does not particularly suit the purpose of the storyteller."[40] Material which works at cross-purposes with the overall perspective of a Gospel has a claim to authenticity. An example is Jesus' scolding of Peter at Caesarea Philippi as recorded by Matthew. Matthew's version places Peter as the rock of the church. Yet Matthew does not exclude Jesus' rebuke of Peter even though it does not immediately support his purpose. Its version in Mark will be more original, but Matthew's inclusion of it in spite of his own theological purpose supports its having a basis in fact.

3. The principle of dissimilarity or distinctiveness.[41] This is

---

[39]There is no generally agreed upon name for this principle. Redaction criticism is more recent than either source criticism or form criticism. I am indebted to Calvert, note 37 above, 219, for his tentative suggestion in this direction. Also see Schillebeeckx, *Jesus*, 91-92.

[40]Calvert, 210

[41]Norman Perrin is articulate with respect to the principle of dissimilarity. See *Rediscovering the Teaching of Jesus*, 15-49. Perrin gives us the history of this principle which is associated with form criticism. Perrin is also careful in his attentiveness to the limitations of the principle: "By definition it will exclude all teaching in which Jesus may have been at one with Judaism or the early Church at one with him. But the brutal fact of the matter is that we 'have no choice'" (43). Yet he oversteps the caution when he writes, "If we are to seek that which is most

perhaps the best known of the criteria. A saying or deed or parable is authentic if it could not have been derived from the Judaism contemporary with Jesus nor from the early church. Hence it must come from Jesus. The principle is very solid as an argument in favor of authenticity when properly applied. It is easily abused, however, by applying it negatively and asserting the inauthenticity of a saying on its basis. Using the principle to argue inauthenticity, however, assumes a discontinuity between Jesus and Judaism when much of the teaching of Jesus was Jewish. A negative application of the principle thus distorts the teaching of Jesus. The principle can also force a discontinuity between Jesus and church which cannot be assumed methodologically. A saying which finds a *Sitz im Leben* in the life of the early Christian communities may still have been a saying with a *Sitz im Leben* in the life of Jesus as well, but one which found a (new) home in the church or Jesus tradition also.

4. The principle of the Aramaic character of a saying and the peculiarities of Jesus' way of speaking. This principle is concerned with the language and style of Jesus. Jesus' native tongue was Aramaic, specifically a Galilean version of western Aramaic. Thus, how "Aramaic" is a saying? The sayings as they come to us are in the *koine* Greek of the Gospels. In some sayings, original Aramaic expressions have been preserved.[42] Joachim Jeremias has drawn up a list of Aramaic words which occur on the lips of Jesus.[43] Or a saying may reflect an Aramaism, being based on something

---

characteristic of Jesus, it will be found not in the things which he shares with his contemporaries, but in the things wherein he differs from them" (39). What it comes down to is that the principle is valid if applied positively (as a support for authenticity) but invalid if applied negatively (as an argument against authenticity). Helpful critiques of the principle which make us aware of its limitations are Bruce Chilton, *A Galilean Rabbi and His Bible* (Wilmington, Del.: Michael Glazier, 1984), 86-90; Morna D. Hooker, "Christology and Methodology," *New Testament Studies*, 16-17 (1969-71), 480-87; Leander Keck, *A Future for the Historical Jesus* (Nashville: Abingdon Press, 1971), esp. 33-35, also 18-39.

[42]E.g., Mk. 5:41; 14:36; 15:34.

[43]See Jeremias, *New Testament Theology*, 5-6, for the list of Aramaic words, and 3-8 for his discussion of the principle of the Aramaic character of sayings.

idiomatic in Aramaic which does not readily translate to Hebrew or Greek.

Jeremias has also called attention to the peculiarities of Jesus' way of speaking. Some of these characteristics of Jesus' speech are not unique to him but are simply manifested with great frequency. They are very common for Jesus and relatively uncommon in other Jewish circles. Other characteristics appear pratically unique in the speech of Jesus. A speech pattern characteristic of Jesus although not unique is his use of circumlocutions for God. From the prohibition against pronouncing the tetragrammaton, the proper name for God (YHWH, Yahweh) there also arose the custom of avoiding direct talk about God, speaking of God periphrastically or by circumlocution. Jesus did not necessarily avoid the word God, but he seems to have preferred to do so. Especially notable in the language of Jesus is his use of "the divine passive," avoiding direct reference to God by use of the passive: "Your sins are forgiven you (by God)."[44] Another distinctive characteristic of Jesus' use of language is his parables. We have examples of parables in the Hebrew Scriptures, but they are relatively few. For Jesus, however, the parables were distinctive of the way he taught.

These are not the only principles which have been formulated and used, but they represent the task involved, and are from my perspective the most helpful and valid ones. What we see is that the earliest stage or stratum is Jesus material. It is the earliest and therefore also the most difficult to retrieve. Yet the task is by no means impossible. Historiography can give a fairly accurate picture of many aspects of Jesus' life, and makes Jesus material which was central to the kerygma accessible.

B. The Oral Traditon and Apostolic Preaching. The Christian proclamation had its roots or origins in Jesus of Nazareth himself, in the preaching and teaching of Jesus, and even moreso in the life and death of Jesus. It was Jesus,

[44]See Jeremias, *New Testament Theology*, 1. In Mark alone 2:5, 2:9, 2:20, 3:28, 4:11, 4:12, 4:24, 4:25, 8:12, 8:17, 9:31, 9:45, 9:47, 9:49, 10:40, 12:10, 13:11, 13:13, 14:41.

this same Jesus, in whom the first Christians believed. At the same time there can be no underestimating the significance of Jesus' resurrection for his disciples and for the earliest preaching. It was *Jesus of Nazareth raised from the dead* who was proclaimed. There was and could have been no proclamation apart from the resurrection. Both sides of the proclamation were essential: Jesus of Nazareth (the pre-resurrection, earthly Jesus, and his life, mission, ministry, and teaching) , and the fact of this Jesus' having been raised from the dead after having been scandalously executed as a criminal. Both the power of Jesus' life as well as the impact of the resurrection helped to forge the post-resurrection faith, understanding, and proclamation.

Faith in Jesus prior to his resurrection (confidence, hope trust) was not exactly the same thing as faith in Jesus after the resurrection when faith also meant the belief that God had raised Jesus from the dead and had vindicated Jesus who was thus truly God's prophet, servant, and son. Post-resurrection faith in Jesus meant "more," not that the "more" contradicted or conflicted with the pre-resurrection faith. The "more" was an assurance, a clarification, an insight and a deeper understanding. In the light of the resurrection the disciples *saw* and *understood* the Jesus whom they had known. In this sense we can say that the resurrection of Jesus (and the accompanying appearance-experiences and the gift of the Spirit) gave rise to Christian faith. Their lord was acknowledged as Lord at a deeper level of understanding. The resurrection gave birth to a new faith in Jesus and there could be no understanding or interpre-tation of Jesus except from the conviction that God had raised this Jesus whom they knew from the dead and vindicated him as God's very own prophet, sage, and servant.

The birth of faith in Jesus (in the sense of what is considered truly Christain faith) led to the emergence of an explicit christology, the articulation of some statement about Jesus in the light of the new post-resurrection under-standing. Faith *in* Jesus, the deepened understanding *of* Jesus, led naturally to some statement *about* Jesus. In this way the proclaimer became the proclaimed. The one who had preached now became the one who was preached. Just as the resurrection led to faith, so faith led to christology. Faith articulated itself, its understanding, and sought to deepen its understanding.

Prior to the resurrection of Jesus one cannot properly speak about christology, not in the sense of an articulated faith in Jesus or doctrine about him, nor in the sense of Jesus' teaching about himself. As we saw in Volume One, Jesus' instruction about himself was never a primary part of his teaching. Jesus' preaching was about God, not himself. This is not to say that one cannot speak of an implicit christology, in the sense of intimations in the preaching of Jesus or implications in the life of Jesus; but we can speak of christology proper only in the light of the resurrection of Jesus. Christology, strictly speaking, is an understanding of the person and mission of Jesus articulated in the light of faith in the resurrection. Christology emerges as articulated Christian faith after the death and resurrection of Jesus.

Prior to this, in Judaism or during the life of Jesus, christology was simply eschatology. We thus speak about Jesus' eschatology, but not his christology. Christology would simply have been some doctrine or teaching about the Christ, the Messiah to come, but any doctrine about a messiah or messiahs is a part of eschatology. We can speak about Jewish eschatology, or Jesus' eschatology, but we do not speak about a christology until we make some identification between someone and the expected Messiah, until we proclaim someone to be the Messiah or Christ, until we believe in the Christ not as an eschatological possibility but as an historical reality. Thus Christian eschatology became christology. Any doctrine about the one to come was tied up with the doctrine about Jesus, who had come, who suffered and died, who had been raised from the dead, and who would come again. The history of Christian eschatology would be inseparable and almost indistinguishable from the history of Christian christology—both were concerned about the person of Jesus and the proclamation that this Jesus was the Christ. Because of what happened to Jesus and because of the new understanding of Jesus, christology gradually replaced eschatology as the horizon for understanding God's actions and promises. The doctrine of God had become christological and not only eschatological.

This is not the place to examine theories about the developments which took place during the first stages of Christian history associated with the first generation of Christian disciples, the formulation and development of the kerygma, the solidification, identification and self-understanding of the Christian movement, at first a Jewish sect, and the validation of the Gentile misson. Let it suffice to say that the first two to three decades of Christian history, from the resurrection of Jesus to the writing of the Gospels, was a period of both tremendous creativity and also conscientious attentiveness to the memory of Jesus. As Schillebeeckx has written, this was a time of both *anamnesis* and *pneuma*.[45] The oral development of the Jesus tradition was guided or governed by both Jesus (the historical Jesus) and the *facta, verba,* and *memoriae Jesu,* and the Spirit (the Spirit of Jesus), the gift of Jesus as Risen Lord. Both the historical Jesus and the meta-historical Spirit helped lay the foundations for Christian development. The Christian movement was both retentive of Jesus and attentive to Jesus (making Jesus historiographically accessible) and also creatively insightful in understanding and articulating the meaning of this Jesus phenomenon (Jesus being fully comprehensible only pneumatologically). The quest for Jesus is now also interwoven with the quest for the early Christian proclamation about Jesus. Who was Jesus as he had come to be known and understood? This new understanding was not an addition to the Jesus material, or something other than Jesus material (if we can use that expression in a second sense), but rather an understanding of Jesus which emerged and deepened.

C.F.D. Moule prefers the word "development" as an

---

[45]Schillebeeckx, *Jesus*, 44-48.

appropriate analogy for the genesis of christology. He writes:

> The tendency which I am advocating as closer to the evidence, and which I call 'developmental', is to explain all the various estimates of Jesus reflected in the New Testament as, in essence, only attempts to describe what was already there from the beginning.
>
> They are not successive additions of something new, but only the drawing out and articulating of what is there. They represent various stages in the development of perception, but they do not represent the accretion of any alien factors that were not inherent from the beginning... When once one assumes that the changes are, in the main, *changes only in perception* (the italics mine) one is at the same time acknowledging that it may not be possible, *a priori*, to arrange such changes in any firm chronological order... Degrees of perception will depend upon individual persons and upon circumstances which may be impossible to identify in any intelligibly chronological sequence.

He continues:

> My main point is not that all Christological expressions in the New Testament are adequate for modern statements of Christology, but that they are all more successfully accounted for as insights, of varying depth, into what was there in Jesus, than as the result of increasing distance from him.

And:

> My point is only that the evidence does not support the assumption that a 'high' Christology evolved from a 'low' Christology by a process of borrowing from extraneous

sources, and that these Christologies may be arranged in an evolutionary sequence from 'low' to 'high.'[46]

The Scriptures (the Written Tradition) are our access to the Jesus material (the Synoptic Gospels being particularly important in this regard), and also our access to the oral tradition, or the pre-literary and pre-Pauline apostolic preaching, creedal formulations, and kerygma. Yet we must be careful about being naively optimistic in our search for Jesus and pre-literary material. Recently, and strongly, Werner Kelber has argued the case for a new hermeneutic of the pre-synoptic oral tradition, urging principles more in accord with what we know of orality and spoken language rather than imposing literary standards that assume an easy continuity between orality and textuality.[47] Some of his conclusions remain to be further assessed, but he has at least called our attention to the distinctive character of oral cultures and the spoken word and then also called into question assumptions about the nature of the pre-literary Gospel traditions. We may have to admit at least as significant a break in history between the oral tradition and the written as between the earthly Jesus and the post-resurrection communities of faith. The Gospel of Mark and the submission of the gospel to a textual medium may be as significant in the history of the synoptic tradition as Easter itself!

---

[46]C.F.D. Moule, *The Origin of Christology* (Cambridge University Press, 1977), 3-6. The word "development" may be less misleading than the word "evolution," although it depends upon what one understands by these two words. Moule's insights, however, are well taken. The "development of Christology" is a growth in understanding. Such development is *not necessarily* evoluntionary, and thus not necessarily capable of chronological arrangement. The more complex or "higher" does not necessarily come later. See *The Origin of Christology*, esp. 1-10, 22-23, 135-37. Moule's is an effort to ground Christology in the Jesus of history (not necessarily Jesus' words but the whole Jesus phenomenon), to see the continuity between Jesus and the Tradition, and at the same time recognize growth, and development, but the increase is increased perception, or as I have said, understanding.

[47]Werner H. Kelber, *The Oral and the Written Gospel* (Philadelphia: Fortress Press, 1983).

Interpretation of materials that are primarily oral in character (and that would include both Jesus material and the process of oral transmission) involves a respect for the social character of such material, the influence of audience and social circumstances, and the fact that one cannot legitimately speak about the original form of such material. Each spoken language event is equally original and social. The loss of materials and the abbreviation of materials are laws of oral life. Discontinuity and unpredictability as much as continuity and stability enter in. The social character of speech differs from the established character of a text.

Nevertheless, contained within the biblical literature, there are fairly clear examples of the early proclamation about Jesus that would have been formulated, circulated, and transmitted during this earliest stage of Christian history. Our concern here will not be to date them (all will be pre-Pauline and thus fall well within the period of our concern), nor to order them chronologically (Moule's suggestions above ought to make us cautious about being able to so order them). We cannot say which may have been the earliest "profession of faith." Yet they do manifest the early Christian preaching about Jesus during the first decades after his death.

Our sources are primarily two, Paul's letters and the Acts of the Apostles. Since Paul's letters are the earliest Christian writings we have (pre-dating the Gospels and Acts), we shall turn to Paul first. Here we shall look at three texts from Paul—1 Thessalonians 1:9b-10; 1 Corinthians 15:3-4; Romans 1:3b-4—and two texts from Acts—2:36; and 3:12-16.

> 1. For they themselves report concerning us what a welcome we had among you, and how you turned to God from idols, to serve a living and true God, and to wait for his Son from heaven, whom he had raised from the dead, Jesus who delivers us from the wrath to come.
>
> (1 Thes 1:9-10)

This is a succinct statement of the apostolic preaching.

Those whom Paul had evangelised, many of whom had evidently been pagans or Gentiles, had been converted to monotheism and the one true God. This faith in the one God is central to Christian faith as well. Verse 10 has both christological and eschatological implications. The Thessalonians have been converted not only to God, but to Christ Jesus as well. Jesus is God's Son who had been raised from the dead. We have an affirmation of Jesus as God's Son and the proclamation of the resurrection. We note the early way of announcing the resurrection: Jesus was raised by God. This christology of Jesus as God's Son raised from the dead is supplemented by an eschatology. We wait for this Son to come from heaven, to come again from God at whose side he now is. Jesus will come to deliver us from the wrath to come (see also 1 Thes 5:9; Rom 2:5, 5:9). The text shows an understanding of who Jesus is: God's Son. The sonship here is not an incarnational sonship. Yet Jesus was son while on earth. It was God's Son whom God raised. The text also proclaims the good news: Jesus will come and save us from the wrath to come. The tone is that of a future eschatology. Jesus, God's son, was raised and will come to save us. This is the proclamation. Those who did not believe in the one God and his Son, Jesus, evidently could only expect the wrath of God. Jesus saves from God's wrath.

> 2. For I delivered to you as of first importance what I also received, that Christ died for our sins in accordance with the scriptures, that he was buried, that he was raised on the third day in accordance with the scriptures.
>
> (1 Cor 15:3-4)

We have already seen this text in our discussion of Paul's understanding of the resurrection in chapter three. It is followed by the list of six appearances:

> and that he appeared to Cephas, then to the twelve. Then he appeared to more than five hundred brethren at one time, most of whom are still alive, though some have fallen asleep. Then he appeared to James, then to all the

apostles. Last of all, as to one untimely born, he appeared
also to me. (1 Cor 15:5-8)

The kerygma contained herein contains *at least* a threefold
reference to the death, burial and resurrection of Jesus. The
appearance formula as originally a part of the pre-Pauline
tradition is debated. We seem to have here the core of the
tradition. Paul presents himself here as the recipient of a
tradition; he did not compose this summary of the preaching
himself. Thus it well represents the period of oral tradition.
This is what Paul must have preached to the Corinthians
when he first came to them around 50 C.E. Therefore, the
pre-Pauline kerygma antedates that date.

The preaching understood Jesus' death and resurrection
to be in accord with the Hebrew Scriptures. This interpretation in the light of the Scriptures manifests early Christian
exegesis. The early disciples were concerned that the God of
Israel had vindicated Jesus and naturally assumed that he
was truly therefore a fulfillment of the Scriptures. As a
result, the Hebrew Scriptures give witness to Jesus as well.

The first statement of the kerygmatic summary states that
(a) Jesus died, (b) that he died for our sins, and (c) that he
died in accord with the Scriptures. The objective fact (a) has
already been interpreted (b). The "according to the Scriptures" need not go with "for our sins" but may rather go
simply with "he died." The Christians saw the necessity of
Jesus' death contained in the Scriptures. They had also
associated a meaning with his death: it was for our sake.

The second statement in the summary is the assertion that
Jesus was buried; this is an objective fact. There is no
particular theological interpretation of it.

The third statement is the proclamation of the resurrection. The resurrection is also seen as contained in the
Scriptures. We spoke previously about the "third day" as not
being a literal reference to a chronological event but rather a
part of interpreting the event according to the Scriptures,
with Hosea 6:2 as a possible basis. The earliest preaching
does not seem to have contained resurrection narratives as
much as a resurrection proclamation (see 1Thes 1:10 above).

These three statements form a unit and may be the kerygma which Paul received and passed on. It is difficult to know where the pre-Pauline material stops. It certainly included verses 3-4 above. It certainly did not include the last of the appearances, the one to Paul himself. Some include the reference to appearances as part of the pre-Pauline formula. Suggestions include (a) the threefold summary with no reference to appearances, (b) a simple reference to appearances, and thus the tradition ended with a fourth statement, "and that he appeared," (c) the ending included one appearance, the core of the appearance tradition, "and that he appeared to Cephas," and (d) the ending was "that he appeared to Cephas, then to the Twelve." This problem cannot be resolved. The appearance tradition is certainly early and the information pre-Pauline. The kerygmatic summary which Paul has received, however, may simply be the threefold affirmation.

> 3. The gospel concerning his Son, who was descended from David according to the flesh and designated Son of God in power according to the Spirit of holiness by his resurrection from the dead, Jesus Christ our Lord.
>
> (Rom 1:3b-4)

Here in Romans we have another pre-Pauline formula.[48] God's Son, (a) was descended from David, (b) according to the flesh, and (c) designated Son of God in power, (d) according to the Spirit of holiness, (e) by his resurrection from the dead. This Son is Jesus Christ, our Lord.

As in the text from 1 Thessalonians above, Jesus is seen as God's Son, and as God's Son raised from the dead. But God's Son, Jesus Christ, was descended from David. He was son of David, according to the flesh, that is during his earthly life and ministry. We have a theology of Jesus which

---

[48]Concerning some of the difficulites in this text, see James D.G. Dunn, *Christology in the Making* (Philadelphia: Westminster Press, 1980), 33-35; Ernst Käsemann, *Commentary on Romans,* trans. Geoffrey W. Bromsley (Grand Rapids, Mich.: William B. Eerdmans Pub. Co., 1980), 4-16; M.E. Boismard, "Constitué Fils de Dieu," *Revue biblique* 60 (1953), 5-17.

sees his life in two stages with the resurrection as the transition. Jesus was son of David on earth, according to the flesh, and by way of contrast, Son of God, according to the Spirit, as a consequence of the resurrection.

Jesus was "designated" or "appointed" or "installed" as "Son of God in power." This is not an incarnational or two-nature christology. Jesus does not become what he was from the beginning. The sonship here is not pre-existent. Rather Jesus enters upon a new stage of his life in which he is now properly designated Son of God.

There is question about whether the "in power" is part of the pre-Pauline tradition. Did Jesus' designation as Son begin with the resurrection? At the resurrection the son of David became, was installed as, Son of God. Or had Jesus already been Son of God in his earthly ministry and with the resurrection was installed as Son of God *in power*? His sonship becomes effective as of the resurrection. Either after the resurrection or on the basis of the resurrection Jesus was so designated. He was exalted. The new status was inaugurated by the resurrection and the Greek text implies that this is the general resurrection, which of course had already begun with Jesus' resurrection.

We have in this formula a two-stage christology: the earthly stage when Jesus was son of David, and perhaps also son of God (in 1 Thessalonians, Jesus was son of God already on earth), but not Son of God in power, and the post-resurrection stage in the life of Jesus who was appointed as Son of God in a much fuller sense. There are two stages of divine sonship manifested here. The second stage has eschatological implications. The resurrection of Jesus is also the general resurrection. There is no major disparity between two points, Jesus' resurrection and the parousia. There is Jesus' earthly life and misson, and the resurrection of the dead, whose time had come, and which had inaugurated Jesus as God's Son. Jesus became God's Son (in power) as of the resurrection. We have here a very early christology. The closing phrase, "Jesus Christ our Lord," may be Pauline rather than part of the received formula.

We have seen in Paul the early Christian interpretation of

Jesus and the designation of Jesus as Son, Christ, Lord, as well as the proclamation of the resurrection.

We now turn to two texts from Acts.[49] The book of Acts contains samples of early Christian preaching, portions of which may pre-date some of the Pauline formulae.

> 4. Let all the house of Israel therefore know assuredly that God has made him both Lord and Christ, this Jesus whom you crucified. (Acts 2:36)

This early and succinct christology is contained within the context of Peter's speech on the occasion of Pentecost (Acts 2:14-41). This does not mean that either the speech as a whole (2:14-41) or the christological statement (2:36) go back to a Jerusalem-based community. The speech is a Lucan composition placed in the mouth of Peter on the occasion of the feast of Pentecost. Yet the Lucan speech contains units of pre-Lucan tradition. Verse 36 is of this sort. Verses 33-36 contain the kerygma and reflect an early Christian interpretation of Psalm 110 as applying to Jesus. The confession of faith in verse 36 (that God has made Jesus Lord) flows from the dual meaning of Lord in Psalm 110:1. The God of Israel is Lord, and Jesus is Lord, and the Lord (God) said to David's Lord (Jesus) that he would make Jesus' enemies God's footstool.

The succinct summary—God had made Jesus both Lord and Christ with the resurrection-exaltation of Jesus. This is at variance with Luke's own christological tendency to attribute the titles of Lord and Christ to the earthly Jesus, hence the implication that Luke is including pre-Lucan tradition.

We find here an early expression of the Christian faith. "This Jesus God raised up" (v. 32), "God had made him both Lord and Christ" (v. 36). This is the proclamation of the resurrection. But this Jesus is also one "whom you crucified."

---

[49]For further discussion, see Ernst Haenchen, *The Acts of the Apostles, A Commentary* (Philadelphia: Westminster Press, 1971), 176-89, 203-12.

Two "titles" express the early faith: Jesus is Lord and Christ. As in Romans 1:3-4, Acts 2 reflects a two-stage christology, the stage of Jesus' life on earth, this Jesus who was crucified and raised, and the stage inaugurated by Jesus' exaltation, Jesus as Lord and Christ. Jesus (whom they knew) had been made Lord and Christ.

> 5. [12]And when Peter saw it he addressed the people, "Men of Israel, why do you wonder at this, or why do you stare at us, as though by our own power or piety we had made him walk? [13]The God of Abraham and of Isaac and of Jacob, the God of our fathers, glorified his servant Jesus, whom you delivered up and denied in the presence of Pilate, when he had decided to release him. [14]But you denied the Holy and Righteous One, and asked for a murderer to be granted to you, [15]and killed the Author of life, whom God raised from the dead. To this we are witnesses. [16]And his name, by faith in his name, has made this man strong whom you see and know; and the faith which is through Jesus has given the man this perfect health in the presence of you all. [17]"And now, brethren, I know that you acted in ignorance, as did also your rulers. [18]But what God foretold by the mouth of all the prophets, that his Christ should suffer, he thus fulfilled. [19]Repent therefore, and turn again, that your sins may be blotted out, that times of refreshing may come from the presence of the Lord, [20]And that he may send the Christ appointed for you, Jesus, [21]whom heaven must receive until the time for establishing all that God spoke by mouth of his holy prophets from of old. [22]Moses said, 'The Lord God will raise up for you a prophet from your brethren as he raised me up. You shall listen to him in whatever he tells you. [23]And it shall be that every soul that does not listen to that prophet shall be destroyed from the people.' [24]And all the prophets who have spoken, from Samuel and those who came afterwards, also proclaimed these days. [25]You are the sons of the prophets and of the covenant which God gave to your fathers, saying to Abraham, 'And in your posterity shall all the families of the earth be blessed.'

[26]God, having raised up his servant, sent him to you first, to bless you in turning every one of you from your wickedness." (Acts 3:12-26)

Here we have another of Peter's speeches, again a Lucan composition with strands of pre-Lucan tradition which are not easily distinguished. Verse 13b introduces a proclamation of the death of Jesus "whom you delivered up," and verse 15 proclaims the resurrection. Jesus is the one "whom God raised from the dead." These two elements are central to the preaching about Jesus, his death and resurrection. Jesus in all our formulae is always "the one whom God raised from the dead." Verse 18 indicates an early Christian perspective that the Messiah would have to suffer. Verse 20 indicates a very early interpretation of Jesus as the Christ. Verses 20-21 have an eschatological character. The eschatological character of Acts 3 led J.A.T. Robinson to conclude that it contains a christological tradition which antedates that of Acts 2.[50] As we have seen in 1 Thessalonians, it is difficult to distinguish early christology and eschatology. Jesus is the one to come. Verse 22 continues this tone with the interpretation of Jesus as the eschatological prophet like Moses of Deuteronomy 18:15, 18. The speech as a whole is Luke's. Our concern here is not to locate these early christologies more precisely in the history of the tradition or to suggest which may be the earliest. The early christologies may reflect either two poles (christology and eschatology, Jesus as God's servant and son on earth and as one to come again, 1 Thes 1; Acts 3) or two stages (the earthly Jesus and post-resurrection Jesus, Rom 1; Acts 2).

We see the proclamation of Jesus as Son, Lord, and Christ early in the tradition. Of course, these "titles" raise the question asked in chapter five about how they may have been understood and applied to Jesus in his lifetime and how

---

[50]J.A.T. Robinson argues not only that Acts 3 is more primitive than Acts 2, but that it may be the most primitive christology of all. "The Most Primitive Christology of All?" in *Twelve New Testament Studies* (London: SCM Press, 1962), 139-53; also in *Journal of Theological Studies* 7 (1956), 177-89.

they may have been understood and applied to Jesus after the resurrection. After the resurrection, given the perception of two stages to Jesus' life, we can also distinguish between what a title may have meant after the resurrection when it was applied to the earthly Jesus and when it was applied to Jesus raised and exalted. Yet Jesus was proclaimed as Son, Lord, and Christ, and these expressions were flexible enough to bear the growth in consciousness of the early church. The titles were not foreign assertions but rather carriers of ever deepening meaning. The flexible but traditional expressions permitted a growth in consciousness and understanding. That is why they were useful. The church's creativity was not unfaithful to the Jesus material but rather expressive of its own growth in perception and understanding. Christians understood Jesus better at that point than they did during his lifetime. The resurrection of Jesus and gift of the Spirit enabled them to be faithful to the Jesus whom they knew.

A two-stage christology is not so much interpretation as it is understanding—an understanding of Jesus based upon the realization that the Jesus who was crucified had in fact been raised from the dead. Jesus, in fact, lives, although in a new mode of existence. Jesus' "life" is not over. To understand Jesus is to realize that there are these two phases or stages to his life, both of which are significant, neither one of which can be understood apart from the other. Any "life of Jesus" or true understanding of him must take both of these stages into account.

The first stage of Jesus' life culminated in his death, and death on a cross. The second stage in his life was inaugurated by his resurrection. We thus speak of his pre-resurrection and post-resurrection existence, or his earthly and post-earthly existence. And the death which draws one stage to a close is also a resurrection which inaugurates the new stage.

Jesus' resurrection is not only an event for him; it has implications for the rest of us too. Although it will take clarification and refinement, Jesus represents not only a mission on earth but also a mission from heaven as well. This "eschatological mission" cannot be separated from who Jesus is and from who he had been all along. Eschatology became christology, partly because christology at this stage was still eschatology. They cannot be separated. The resurrection of this Jesus was not only a personal but also an eschatological event. A two-stage christology thus deals with a man whose life is lived in two stages—that of his earthly existence and that of his eschatological existence—and both of these stages are Jesus. Jesus is not another person after the resurrection. He is rather this Jesus whom we knew and whom we crucified, but this same Jesus as now raised from the dead and exalted to God's right hand.

Jesus is not only a man whose human life is lived in two stages. He is a man whose life reveals that our lives are lived in two stages as well. At this crucial point in his life (the death-resurrection event), Jesus' humanity does not suddenly become completely dissimilar to ours. Rather his resurrection clarifies what is elsewhere true. Our lives too comprise two stages. Our earthly existence will culminate in death, but a death which inaugurates resurrection into eschatological existence. Jesus' death-resurrection is in one sense the beginning of resurrection and eschatological existence for all of us, even for those who died and were raised prior to Jesus. No one other than Jesus had so clearly revealed the resurrection and the reality of how personal histories culminate in eschatological life.

The Lordship of Jesus is a Lordship of two stages. Jesus was referred to as lord while on earth, and referred to as Lord after the resurrection. His post-resurrection, eschatological Lordship, however, carried with it deeper, fuller, and richer implications. With his resurrection, Jesus had also been exalted. In this "growth of consciousness" we can see the flexible function of a title like Lord. Its sacredness in Christian tradition resides in the fact that it was able to serve this function. It permitted the growth in understanding through which the church would have to go before it could fully answer its Lord's question: And who do you say that I am? You, Jesus, are Lord. That title can never be fixed. It is as expansive as Jesus himself. And Jesus' life comprises *both* heaven *and* earth.

C. The Written Tradition. We have no written records

which as such go back to Jesus' own lifetime; all the Jesus material has reached us via the Christian movement. From 30 to 50 C.E., and beyond, the gospel was developed and handed on by word of mouth. The period of oral tradition was both creative and retentive; it handed on *memoriae* and *verba*; it was subject to the action of the Spirit; material assumed shape and definite forms. Between 50 and 70 C.E., our written sources began to appear. Not all of these written sources are extant today; nor are they to be limited to our canonical New Testament writings. But a literary phase in the history of the Christian movement had begun. Among our presently available sources, Paul's letters were the first to appear.[51]

The formation of the Gospels presents a complex problem. We recognize today two groups of Gospels: the Synoptic Gospels and the Gospel of John. The histories behind Matthew, Mark and Luke are closely woven together, and their interrelationships have become known as "the Synoptic problem." Although the Gospel of John is clearly distinctive, and its history distinguishable from that of the Synoptics, it cannot be dismissed as historiographically irrelevant. All the Gospels weave together history and theology as a means of proclamation.

The Synoptic problem has stimulated extensive critical research. Some variation of the two-source theory is the most comon explanation today. According to this theory, Mark was the first of the Gospels to have been written. Although efforts have been made to refute this position, Marcan priority still stands in the scholarly world.[52] Thus one of the two major sources of the Synoptic tradition is the

---

[51]On Paul, see Robert Jewett, *A Chronology of Paul's Life* (Philadelphia: Fortress Press, 1979).

[52]W.R. Farmer, *The Synoptic Problem: A Critical Analysis* (Dillsboro, N.C.: Western North Carolina Press, 1976); and "A Response to Robert Morgenthaler's *Statistische Synopse*," Biblica 54 (1973), 425-30, still argues for the priority of Matthew's Gospel, but the majority opinion supports the evidence for Mark. See Howard Clark Kee, *Community of the New Age—Studies in Mark's Gospel* (Philadelphia: Westminster Press, 1977), 14-17.

Marcan source. The second major source is Q (from the German word for source, *Quelle*), a sayings source or collection of Jesus material which explains the material both Matthew and Luke have in common but which they do not have in common with Mark. Thus, source one, Mark, explains the material common to all three; source two, Q, the material common to Matthew and Luke. In addition, there are two special sources containing material peculiar to Matthew or to Luke. All these sources—Mark, Q, special Matthew, special Luke—have their distinctive characteristics. The obvious importance of Q has led to much discussion about its particular character, whether it was at one time a written document or not, thus whether it is only a source or also a document, whether it reflects a particular community setting behind it.[53]

The period of Gospel formation began around 60 C.E. and continued through the close of the first century. It may be of benefit to look briefly at one Gospel as an exemplification of this first literary stage in the life of the church, and we can readily choose Mark.[54] It is difficult to date any of the Gospels with complete precision and certitude. Mark may have been written in the late sixties, perhaps after the outbreak of the revolt of 66-70 C.E., or in the early seventies. H.C. Kee argues that the lack of precision accompanying the fate of Jerusalem as described in Mark 13 inclines one toward a date prior to 70 C.E., but that the sense of urgency within the entire Gospel suggests a date quite close to that

[53]See Richard A. Edwards, *A Theology of Q: Eschatology, Prophecy, and Wisdom* (Philadelphia: Fortress Press, 1976); and *A Concordance to Q* (Missoula, Montana: Scholars Press and Society of Biblical Literature, 1975). A recent synthesis of research is Ivan Havener's *Q, The Sayings of Jesus*, with a reconstruction of Q by Athanasius Polag (Wilmington, Del.: Michael Glazier, 1987).

[54]See Paul Achtmeier, *Mark* (Philadelphia: Fortress Press, 1975); Wilfrid Harrington, *Mark* (Wilmington, Delaware: Michael Glazier, Inc. 1979); Sean Kealy, *Mark's Gospel, A History of Its Interpretation* (New York: Paulist Press, 1982); H.C. Kee, *Community of the New Age: Studies in Mark's Gospel* (Philadelphia: Westminster, 1977); Jack Dean Kingsbury, *The Christology of Mark's Gospel* (Philadelphia: Fortress Press, 1983); D.E. Nineham, *Saint Mark* (London: Penguin Books, 1963), along with many other studies.

disaster.[55] John Reumann dates Mark around 67 C.E.[56] On the other hand, others interpret the Gospel as having been composed in the aftermath of the 70 C.E. disaster.[57]

It is also difficult to be certain about the place where the Gospel was written. Evidence today suggests Palestine or an area thereabouts (rather than Rome which at one time was the commonly held opinion). Two plausible suggestions for the setting are those of Galilee (Marxsen)[58] or a small rural community of southern Syria (Kee).[59]

Our present ending, Mark 16:9-20, was not originally the ending of the Gospel. Either the Gospel ended at Mark 16:8, or the original ending has been lost. Mark 16:9-20 is not present in the older Greek manuscripts of Mark.

For Werner Kelber,[60] the pre-Marcan mode of language was that of oral discourse best exemplified in storytelling— such as Mark's heroic, polarization, didactic, and parabolic stories. Jesus' mode of parabolic discourse is not confined to those stories technically called parables, yet the parables help to exemplify oral discourse. Parables have a metaphorical quality, are never self-explanatory, are hermeneutically un-

---

[55] H.C. Kee, *Community of the New Age*, 100.

[56] John Reumann, *Jesus in the Church's Gospels* (Philadelphia: Fortress Press, 1968), 25-36.

[57] E.g., Wilfrid Harrington, *Mark,* xi-xii; Werner Kelber, "From Passion Narrative to Gospel," in *The Passion in Mark*, ed. Werner Kelber (Philadelphia: Fortress Press, 1976), 164; Schillebeeckx, *Christ, The Experience of Jesus as Lord*, trans. John Bowden (New York: Seabury Press, 1980), 571.

[58] Willi Marxsen, *Mark the Evangelist* (Nashville: Abingdon Press, 1969), 54-95, 102-16, 207-16. Marxsen's research also concludes that the community addressed by Mark is one awaiting the imminent parousia with the expectation that it will take place in Galilee. See pp. 93, 107, 209. Geography has theological significance for Mark—it is the locale of the awaited parousia. Galilee is not to be understood, according to Marxsen, in a narrow and precise sense (106-8). Marxsen writes, "The orientation to Galilee and the imminent Parousia awaited there provide the motive for the Gospel's formation" (209).

[59] H.C. Kee, *Community of the New Age*, 100, 176-77. Kee argues that cultural and linguistic features in the Gospel suggest the Eastern Mediteranean area rather than Rome. Mark's lack of accurate knowledge of some aspects of Galilean topography, however, suggests a location other than Galilee proper, therefore, southern Syria. Mark's anti-city and pro-village stance suggests a rural setting.

[60] Werner H. Kelber, *The Oral and The Written Gospel*, 44-139.

finished products, unite multiple hearings depending on social context, and are essentially an oral form of speech not meant to be frozen by writing.

Jesus' own way of speaking was oral and parabolic, and Jesus could not remain a living option without submitting his mission and message to language and a linguistic destiny. Both oral and written forms, however, exert specific controls; the medium will inevitably help to shape the message. Jesus is first preserved by the medium of orality, and with the Gospel of Mark submitted to the medium of textuality. Both facts are significant.

For Kelber, the written gospel is not simply the logical outcome of oral development. Mark owes much to oral tradition, yet textuality is a distinctive medium that involves a decontextualization of words from their oral matrix and a linearization of oral pluralism and recontextualization of the spoken forms. An oral form is not simply submitted to the written medium without further ado. The Gospel of Mark shows this tension between orality and textuality. A writer shapes and arranges words differently from a speaker. Parables by nature are more so forms of oral discourse than they are literary forms.

Yet the literary form or genre of the Gospel of Mark as a whole is that of a written parable, Kelber suggests, following a lead from John Dominic Crossan. The parables become the parable.

Whereas Kelber emphasizes the oral character of the tradition and hermeneutical principles distinctive of orality, Thomas Brodie[61] emphasizes the literary character of the

---

[61] Brodie argues that the historiographical use of the Gospels ought to be put on hold until further research can be done into the literary sources of the Gospels. A weakness in the present stage of Brodie's research is that thus far it has concentrated on the Gospel of Luke and it remains to be seen whether his method is equally fruitful for Marcan studies. See the following by Brodie: "A New Temple and New Law, The Unity and Chronicles-based Nature of Luke 1:1-4:22a," *Journal for the Study of the New Testament*, 5 (1979), 21-45; "The Accusing and Stoning of Naboth (1 Kgs. 21:8-23) as One Component of the Stephen Text (Acts 6:9-14, 7:58a)," *Catholic Biblical Quarterly* 45 (1983), 417-32; "Luke 7, 36-50 as an Internalization of 2 Kings 4, 1-37: A Study in Luke's Use of Rhetorical Imitation," *Biblica* 64 (1983), 457-85; "Graeco-Roman Imitation of Texts as a Partial Guide to

Gospels and sees the focus on orality as a misplaced emphasis for understanding the background and sources of Gospel formation. The Gospels are primarily literary works, composed by literary artists, indebted to literary sources, namely the Hebrew Bible.

The foundational dynamic behind the Gospels is not that of the relationship of textuality to orality however the relationship between those two be perceived, but rather the relationship of a text to a text, namely, a literary relationship in which classical biblical texts are imitated, adapted, and christianized. The search for sources is not a search for oral forms or even for hints of orality as such, but a search for (OT) biblical texts.

One can find the evidence for this literary method of Gospel composition in the later Hellenistic, Graeco-Roman world where such reshaping of classical texts was a dominant literary practice which provided both a sense of continuity and development. This fundamentally literary character of Gospel composition does not deny the oral (or better, aural) character of the Gospels. They were written with an ear to being heard. Yet it was a literary, textual process, one aspect of which was this aural purpose, not a fundamentally oral process of transmission. We rather have to do with a literary method or art and not the transformation of orality as such. The Old Testament, or Hebrew Scriptures, or Septuagint are being reworked and transformed into the New Testament message and interpretations of Jesus. The evangelists are literary artists christianizing ancient narratives, although this does not exclude elements which cannot be explained on the basis of the older narratives.

Mark, being aware of the suffering discipleship to which

Luke's Use of Sources," in *Luke - Acts: New Perspectives from the Society of Biblical Literature* (C.H. Talbert, ed.; New York: Crossroad, 1984), 17-46; review of Werner Kelber's *Orality and Textuality in the Gospels* in *Catholic Biblical Quarterly* 46 (1984), 574-75; "Towards Unravelling Luke's Use of the Old Testament: Luke 7, 11-17 As an *Imitatio* of 1 Kings 17, 17-24," *New Testament Studies* 32 (1986), 247-67; "Towards Unraveling the Rhetorical Imitation of Sources in Acts: 2 Kings 5 as One Component of Acts 8, 9-40," *Biblica* 67 (1986), 41-67.

his community was being called as they awaited the return of the Lord, wrote his Gospel to put before his community an example of suffering servanthood. He wanted to confirm disciples in their faith and to bring others to the faith by enabling them to recognize Jesus and proclaim him as the Christ of God. Three messianic designations play a prominent role in the Gospel: Christ, Son of God, Son of Humanity. Who is this Jesus? The first words of the first verse already make it clear: Jesus is the Christ, the Son of God (Mark 1:1).[62] The motif of Jesus as the Christ, as we have already seen, is central to Peter's profession at Caesarea Philippi and to the trial of Jesus. But this Christ is also Son of God, a fact which the demons in the narrative readily recognize. At the heart of the Gospel, according to Marxsen, is the expulsion of spirits who cry out *the* confession, "You are the Son of God" (3:11, 5:7).[63] Peter recognizes Jesus as the Christ. The demons recognize him as the Son of God. And Jesus so often speaks of himself as Son of Humanity. In this Gospel, "Son of Humanity" occurs on the lips of Jesus fourteen times.[64]

With Mark we see the process of fusing different titles together and applying them to Jesus for the sake of the church's self-understanding. The Gospels are part of the process of redefining, combining, and christianizing these titles so that they may answer the question of who Jesus is for the communities of Jesus' disciples. By the time we get to Mark, the expression "Son of Humanity" is clearly a title.[65] The expression was used by Jesus (his usage helps to embed it in the tradition) but not used as an apocalyptic messianic titular self-designation. Rather it was a simple, indirect way of referring to people like himself. By the time we get to

[62] The phrase "Son of God" in verse one is widely supported in the manuscripts although not found in all of them.

[63] Marxsen, *Mark the Evangelist*, 63.

[64] These are 2:10, 2:28, 8:31, 8:38, 9:9, 9:12, 9:31, 10:33, 10:45, 13:26, 14:21 (twice); 14:41, 14:62.

[65] H.C. Kee, *Community of the New Age*, 138.

Mark, however, the expression has come to carry more meaning and now connotes for the Marcan community "the one who is to come."

Norman Perrrin speaks of Mark's christology as a Son of Humanity christology.[66] In Mark 14:61, Jesus is addressed as the Christ and as Son of God, accepts the designation, but interprets it by means of the Son of Humanity concept. The same situation occurred at Caesarea Philippi. Jesus is confessed as the Christ but goes on to interpret his understanding by speaking of the Son of Humanity. In other words Mark is giving theological development to the titles of Christ and Son of God. He sees Jesus as the Christ, but he sees the Christ as being one like the Son of Humanity. Mark began to bring the titles together and fused them in order to interpret Jesus. According to Perrin, Mark's theology is christological, correcting false christologies, and giving a true one. He presents the disciples as voicing the opinions (the false opinions) present in Mark's church and then has Jesus teach a true understanding by using the Son of Humanity concept. Peter (like so many in Mark's church) confesses Jesus as the Christ but misunderstands this in a nationalistic sense and so has to be rebuked by Jesus into a proper understanding. Mark presents Jesus as teaching the Son of Humanity christology which in fact Mark himself is teaching. Mark's Gospel is to lead people into confessing that Jesus is the Messiah, the Christ, and that the Christ is in fact one like the Son of Humanity. Mark not only wants to teach that Jesus is the Christ but to correct the understanding that people have of Christ. In other words Mark represents theological development of the concept of Christ.   Mark not only presents Jesus as "the one who is to come," but also as one who suffered and died. Mark's is a passion-oriented christology. Jesus scandalized people by teaching that the

---

[66]Especially see Norman Perrin, "The Christology of Mark: A Study in Methodology," *Journal of Religion* 51 (1971), 173-87, the basis for my summary of Perrin's position. Also see "The Creative Use of the Son of Man Traditions by Mark," *Union Seminary Quarterly Review* 23 (1967/1968), 257-265; and *Rediscovering the Teaching of Jesus.*

Son of Humanity must suffer. Perrin sees this emphasis on passion as pointing to another element in Mark's theology— his concept of discipleship as servanthood. Jesus suffered and died and so will we if we follow him. Suffering became a part of Mark's theology, part of the new teaching on the Son of Humanity found in Mark. Thus there are two emphases in Mark's christology for Perrin: Jesus' suffering role and Jesus as Son of Humanity (the Christ). These two can be identified.

For Mark, Jesus is obviously the Christ, the Son of God, and Son of Humanity. And the Son of Humanity is one who spoke with authority on earth, who had to suffer and die, and who is coming again soon, in Galilee. Another important question, however, besides who Jesus is for Mark, is the question of what "the gospel," *euaggelion*, means for Mark, a question important both for Marcan studies and for christology. Mark uses it in the very first verse: "The beginning of the gospel of Jesus Christ, the Son of God" (1:1). In addition there are six other significant references[67] to "the gospel" in Mark: "Now after John was arrested, Jesus came into Galilee, preaching the gospel of God," (1:14); "and saying, 'the time is fulfilled, and the reign of God is at hand; repent, and believe in the gospel'" (1:15); "for whoever would save his life will lose it; and whoever loses his life for my sake and the gospel's will save it" (8:35); "Truly, I say to you, there is no one who has left house or brothers or sisters or mother or father or children or lands, for my sake and for the gospel, who will not receive a hundredfold ... " (10:29-30); "And the gospel must first be preached to all nations" (13:10); "And truly, I say to you, wherever the gospel is preached in the whole world, what she has done will be told in memory of her" (14:9).

There are three ways in which the word "gospel" is understood in a Christian context. First, gospel refers to the gospel of Jesus Christ in which "of Jesus Christ" is taken as an objective genitive in the Greek. This means that Jesus is

---

[67]Mk. 16:15 is an eighth reference but is in the later ending of Mark

the object, the content, of the gospel. The gospel is a proclamation of the life, death, resurrection, identity, and salvific significance of Jesus, the Christ. Jesus is the one proclaimed, the good news. Second, gospel refers to the gospel of Jesus Christ in which "of Jesus Christ" is taken as a subjective genitive. It is Jesus' gospel. He is the subject, the proclaimer. It is his proclamation of the good news of salvation and God's coming reign. In this use the object or content is the reign of God. Third, gospel has come to refer to writings, a literary genre, the four Gospels in which we find the gospel of Jesus Christ. This last sense, although so common, is the most derived. These writings are Gospels because they contain or bear witness to the gospel. In its primary sense the gospel is always the gospel of Jesus Christ and not the Gospels according to Matthew, Mark, Luke or John. The first two meanings are the primary analogates for the word gospel. Yet gospel is also a literary form, the first example of which is Mark's Gospel. Mark's innovation is this literary genre.[68]

The question emerges, however, whether "the gospel of Jesus Christ" in Mark is to be taken primarily as an objective genitive or as a subjective genitive. Marxsen's redactional study has helped to clarify Mark's usage.[69] Mark is the author who introduces the noun *euaggelion* into the synoptic tradition.[70] Except for 1:1 and 1:14, Mark uses the noun without further modification. (This is not true of Matthew who speaks of the good news "of the kingdom.") For Mark Jesus is *both* the subject *and* the object of the gospel. He is the subject most precisely as Risen Lord. He is the object

---

[68] Wilfrid Harrington, *Mark*, x. Willi Marxsen, *Mark the Evangelist*, 123-33, 149-50. Amos Wilder, *Early Christian Rhetoric, The Language of the Gospel* (Cambridge: Harvard University Press, 1971), 36. For Schillebeeckx's discussion of the word "gospel," see *Jesus*, 107-14.

[69] Marxsen, *Mark the Evangelist*, 117-50.

[70] Paul, of course, had already used the word "gospel." Werner Kelber, *The Oral and the Written Gospel*, 140-83, esp. 144-48, considers it Paul's master metaphor, a word Paul uses approximately fifty times, more than any other New Testament author. For Paul, the gospel is "the power of God" (Rom 1:16; 1 Thes 1:5; 1 Cor 2:4-5; 2 Cor 6:7). The gospel is inseparable from power.

most precisely as the one who is coming. "The material as a whole becomes a gospel which Christ, the Risen Lord, proclaims *and* which proclaims Christ, the Risen Lord."[71] Mark's usage in this twofold way is very much the same as Paul's. For Marxsen, then, the gospel is, "I am coming soon."[72] "Believe in the gospel (= the returning Lord) because of the gospel (= *his* proclamation of his return)."[73] Because Mark perceives his work as the gospel of Jesus Christ in both senses, he "entitles" it in 1:1 as *the* gospel, which then becomes a term which can be applied to the other "Gospels" as well. "Gospel" then becomes a reference to a book. But Mark's major use is that of the *one* gospel of Jesus Christ, who is *both* its proclaimer *and* its proclamation, an expression, following upon the use in 1:1, which lends itself toward application to the four Gospels. We can therefore see Mark's Gospel as both "the gospel of Jesus Christ" and as the first of those Christian literary testimonies which we call Gospels. But there is a fundamental unity within all three ways of understanding Mark. For it is in the literary work of his, the Gospel, that we encounter the gospel of the life, death and resurrection of Jesus, of Jesus' proclamation of God's dawning reign, and of the call to discipleship. It is in both the Gospel itself and in the good news it records that we encounter the proclaimer of the gospel and the ultimate author of the Gospel—the man Jesus raised from the dead and exalted. In other words the Gospel is both a literary form and a proclamation in which we are called upon or enabled to recognize Jesus and profess our faith, that this Jesus is the Christ, the Son of God. The word "euaggelion" in all three senses is an invitation to recognize Jesus. Jesus, the Risen Lord, the Son of God, the Proclaimer is inviting us to recognize him through both the proclaimed kerygmatic word and the written testimony of the Gospel.

The Gospel contains a christology which includes a call to

---

[71]Marxsen, *Mark the Evangelist,* 149.

[72]*Ibid.,* 134.

[73]*Ibid.,* 135.

discipleship. But the Gospel is also structured in such a way that we are enabled to "see for ourselves" what the Gospel proclaims. The Gospel does not simply teach christology (theologically speaking) but rather presents it (pedagogically speaking) in such a way that we "come to believe." In the hearing or reading of the Gospel we come to recognize who Jesus is as the Son of God, in such a way that we now know for ourselves, profess the faith, and respond to Jesus in *the only way possible to respond to him once we recognize who he truly is*—by becoming his disciples. In the Gospel then we come to encounter personally the Risen Lord and to say "yes" to his invitation to us to be his disciples. Central to this Gospel is this "act of recognition." It must precede the profession of faith and the response of discipleship. Apart from this recognition, the Gospel remains only an objective statement of someone else's faith, an inspiring religious testimony on someone's part, or a source for historiographical research, but never a gospel in its fullest sense. The Gospel form is structured for the purpose of recognition.

We can now "see" the connectedness between the earthly Jesus and the risen Jesus—the selfsame Jesus Christ, and that there is "more" to this Jesus Christ than the Jesus of historiography, although this "Jesus of historiography" remains necessary to our contemporary re-appropriation of the Christ. But, in the Gospels, we "see" or are at least called or challenged to recognize Jesus as the Christ, the one raised from the dead who still comes to be with us. Not to "see" this is to not yet know Jesus. This is why, for a Christian, the Jesus of historiography, albeit necessary, is never sufficient. The Jesus of historiography by itself is a construct, not the living Jesus of Nazareth, not even the earthly Jesus of history. The resurrection, faith, and the gospel all make us conscious that the Jesus of history *is* the Jesus of faith, and vice-versa. According to the Gospels, not to be a follower of Jesus in some sense is to not yet know who Jesus is. We are back to "And who do you say that I am?" (Mk. 8:29). And the Gospels insist in the end that this question can only be answered by faith alone. Hence, for the Gospels, no need for the modern distinction between "Jesus (of history)" and

"The Christ (of faith)." Such a distinction is to have already misunderstood Jesus.

We need not here detail further the development of christology in the Synoptic material, but it is probably advantageous for us to look at Synoptic christology in its most advanced form—the infancy narratives of Matthew and Luke.

The Infancy Narratives

The prologues to the Gospels of Matthew and Luke, the infancy narratives, make clear that Jesus was of God and from God from the moment of his conception. Although we refer to these prologues as infancy narratives, they do not actually give us information about Jesus' infancy and childhood. Rather, they answer the question, "Who is Jesus of Nazareth?" that he is a man of God, God's Son. As Joseph Fitzmyer writes of the Lucan infancy narrative, "Its obvious purpose is to introduce and identify these two children [John and Jesus], especially Jesus, as agents of God's salvation-history: both come from God."[74]

The Gospel of Matthew. The theology in Matthew was influenced by the Christian community for which he wrote, which consisted of both Jews and Gentiles. In contrast, Luke's Gospel was written primarily for Gentiles. According to Matthew, Jesus directed his ministry to Israel (10:5-6; 15:24), but the risen Lord sent his disciples to the Gentiles (28:18). This missionary emphasis reflects Matthew's ecclesial and pastoral situation.[75]

The effort to appeal to both Jewish Christians and Gentile Christians is reflected in the first verse of Matthew's Gospel. Jesus, the Christ, is both son of David (which ties Jesus into

---

[74]Joseph Fitzmyer, *The Gospel According to Luke I-IX*, Anchor Bible 28 (Garden City: Doubleday and Co., 1981), 309.

[75]Raymond Brown, *The Birth of the Messiah* (Garden City: Doubleday and Co., 1977), 47, 90. Also see Benedict Viviano, "Where Was the Gospel According to Matthew Written?" *The Catholic Biblical Quarterly*, 41 (1979), 533-546, who also points to the mixed character of the setting for Matthew's Gospel.

Jewish history) and son of Abraham (which ties Jesus into
an even broader plan of salvation). This relation of Jesus to
both David and Abraham predates Matthew (e.g., Rom 1:3;
Gal 3:16) but nevertheles is important to Matthew's situation
and theology.[76] Matthew's infancy story identifies Jesus not
only as being of David and of Abraham, but also as being of
God and another Moses.

Another important theological aspect of the infancy narrative is its perception of "the christological moment." At
what point in time did Jesus become the Christ, the Messiah?
The understanding and response of the early church to this
question was the moment of the resurrection. Later reflection
then maintained that the christological moment was at the
time of the baptism. Jesus is thus already the Messiah or
Christ during his life and in his ministry. This is the
conviction of Matthew's Gospel (16:16). Further reflection
understood the moment to be Jesus' conception. This is the
opinion of the infancy narratives. Thus, there was no time in
his life when Jesus was not already the Messiah. This means
that the church grew in its awareness that Jesus had already
been what they, his followers, came to perceive only after the
resurrection. Fitzmyer describes it thus:

> What is involved here is the growing understanding of the
> early church about the identity of Jesus. Though at first
> such titles as Son of God became attached to him
> primarily as of the resurrection (besides Rom. 1:4, see
> Acts 13:33), the time came when early Christians began to
> realize that he had to have been such even earlier in his
> career, even though it had not been recognized. It is not so
> much that the 'christological moment' . . . was pushed
> back as that there was a growth in awareness as time
> passed among early Christians that what Jesus was
> recognized to be after the resurrection he must have been
> still earlier.[77]

---

[76]Brown, *The Birth of the Messiah*, 66-69.

[77]Fitzmyer, *Luke I-IX*, 340. See Brown, *The Birth of the Messiah*, 29-32, 133-43,
179-83, 311-16, and Raymond Brown, "Gospel Infancy Narrative Research From
1976 to 1986: Part II (Luke) ," *Catholic Biblical Quarterly* 48 (1986), 677-78.

Matthew's intent in his genealogy (1:1-17) was to point to Jesus as a son of Abraham but especially to demostrate that he was of David. Matthew's genealogy begins with Abraham. Jesus was not only of Abraham but also of David through Joseph, though Joseph is not the biological father of Jesus. Luke's genealogy goes back to Adam, but his genealogy serves a different purpose. It lies outside his infancy narrative and intends to show that Jesus is Son of God. There are not only differences but disagreements between Matthew's and Luke's genealogies.

The presence of the four women in Matthew's genealogy is unusual. But all four have this in common: there is something irregular in their union with their partners and yet all have played an important role in God's plan. In Jewish piety these irregularities were seen as the workings of the Spirit in helping to bring about salvation. For Matthew these four women foreshadowed the role of Mary which Matthew will have to deal with shortly. Already in the genealogy Matthew implies that Joseph is not the biological father of Jesus. Note the phraseological shift in verse 16: Abraham was the father of Isaac, Amos the father of Josiah, etc. But not: Joseph was the father of Jesus. Rather, "Joseph, the husband of Mary, of whom Jesus was born."

In the section 1:18-25, Matthew indicates that Jesus was not only the son of David but also Son of God. He does this by pointing to the *how* of Jesus' conception—namely one effected through the power of the Holy Spirit without a human father. This irregular conception which strengthens the "Son of God" motif does not prevent Jesus from being son of David through the ancestry of Joseph since Joseph accepted Jesus as his own.

"Son of David" is a more important title to Matthew as an evangelist than for any of the other evangelists. John never uses it. Mark and Luke use it four times; Matthew ten times. Yet the title "son of David" is not adequate for Matthew. The only adequate answer is—Son of God (Mt 22:41-46; 16:1-17). The fact that Jesus is Emmanuel, however, God-with-us, does not follow from the genealogy but from the message made by an angel of the Lord to Joseph (1:20-21).

Jesus became God's Son through the power of the Holy

Spirit. Matthew disallows a human father who plays a sexual role in the begetting of Jesus. This divine begetting is not sexual. The Holy Spirit is not a sexual partner. The conception through the creative activity of the Holy Spirit is the begetting, the becoming, the coming-to-be of God's Son, the Messiah. It is not an incarnation but a new creation. We see here "the christological moment" of Matthew's infancy narrative. Raymond Brown writes:

> Conception christology and pre-existence christology were two different answers to adoptionism. In the former, God's creative action in the conception of Jesus (attested negatively by the absence of human fatherhood) begets Jesus as God's Son. Clearly here divine sonship is not adoptive sonship, but there is no suggestion of an incarnation whereby a figure who was previously with God takes on flesh. Incarnational thought is indicative of pre-existence christology ("emptied himself taking on the form of a servant"; "the Word became flesh"); and works reflecting that christology show no awareness of or interest in the manner of Jesus' conception.[78]

Jesus is not the biological son of Joseph (1:18-23) and yet his Davidic ancestry is traced through Joseph (1:16). In accepting the son as his own, Joseph gives Jesus a Davidic genealogy (1:24-25).[79] Although Joseph is the source of Davidic descent, this descent was not handed on via normal sexual relations between husband and wife. Davidic descent comes, not through natural paternity, but through legal paternity. Joseph, in exercising the father's right to name the child, becomes the legal father, the legitimate father, according to Jewish law. Both Mary and Joseph have their role to play. Through Joseph, Jesus is of Davidic descent. Through Mary, he is begotten as Son of God.

Scholars generally agree that the Matthean and Lucan

---

[78] Brown, *The Birth of the Messiah*, 141, also 160-61, 517-33.
[79] *Ibid.*, 132.

infancy narratives are independent of each other. Yet similarities between them indicate pre-Gospel traditions that each writer used in his own way. Raymond Brown places the virginal conception within this pre-Gospel tradition. Matthew and Luke did not create it.[80]

In chapter two there is a geographical motif (Bethlehem, Egypt, Nazareth) as well as further theological development. Matthew has presented Jesus in chapter one as Messiah, son of David, Emmanuel. This theme continues within the geography of chapter two. Jesus was born in Bethlehem and thus fulfilled messianic expectation. Matthew's use of Micah 5:1 and 2 Samuel 5:2 which both mention Bethlehem reinforce his theme. (For Matthew, Jesus seems to have been born in Bethlehem because that was where his parents lived. There is no journey to Bethlehem as in Luke. For Matthew the problem is to get Jesus to Nazareth, which he accomplishes by the flight into Egypt. For Luke the problem is to get Jesus to Bethlehem.) The flight into Egypt further identifies Jesus with the history of the Jews. In this journey he symbolically relives both the Exile (the massacre of the children is lamented by words Jeremiah used to describe the exiled northern tribe) and the Exodus (passing over from Egypt to settling in Nazareth), the two most significant events in Jewish history.

Yet Matthew's concern for Jesus as the son of David is secondary in the first part of chapter two. Chapter 2:1-12 is a focus on the coming of the magi, a focus that will develop the other side of Matthew's theology, that Jesus has also come to save the Gentiles, which was hinted at in 1:1 by reference to him as son of Abraham. The first to pay homage to Jesus are the Gentiles from the East. Jesus has come to the Gentiles as well.

Matthew 2:13-23 then goes on to narrate Herod's failure to kill the child because of the move of Joseph, Mary and Jesus to Egypt. He concludes the infancy story with the family's settling in Nazareth. The geographical motif in

---

[80]*Ibid*., 161, 521-31. Also Fitzmyer, *Luke I-IX*, 341-42.

chapter two mentions Bethlehem, the city of David, Egypt, the land of the Exodus, and Ramah, the mourning place of the Exile. Just as Jesus summed up the history of his people in chapter one (genealogy), so he does here. The massacre of the children in Bethlehem parallels Pharaoh's slaughter of male children in Egypt. Moses, however, escaped. So did Jesus. The angel's words to Joseph in 2:20 almost repeat the Lord's words to Moses in Exodus 4:19 which pertain to the pharaoh's death. The pharaoh's death allowed Moses to lead his people from Egypt. Herod's death allowed Jesus to return to the Promised Land.

In the fourth and final section of the infancy narratives (2:13-23), Jesus recapitulates the experience of Moses.[81] The infancy narrative patterns the birth of Jesus on the birth of Moses and there are five episodes in the infancy narrative centered around five scriptural citations which Jesus fulfills. These are Matthew 1:22-23 (citing Is 7:14); 2:5-6 (citing Mic 5:1 and 2 Sam 5:2); 2:15 (citing Hos 11:1); 2:17-18 (citing Jer 31:15); and 2:23 (citing perhaps Is 4:3 and Jud 16:17).[82]

Matthew cites the Hebrew Scriptures to portray Jesus as their fulfillment: "All this took place to fulfill what the Lord had spoken by the prophet" (1:22). The fulfillment formula indicates Matthew's intention and theology—the new events fulfill that which was anticipated.[83] In his use of Scripture, Matthew does not attempt to convey the previous meanings

---

[81]See W.D. Davies, *The Sermon on the Mount* (Cambridge: Cambridge University Press, (1977), 10-18.

[82]For Matthew's use of the biblical citations in the infancy narrative, see George M. Soares Prabhu, *Formula Quotations in the Infancy Narrative of Matthew* (Rome: Biblical Institute Press, 1976). Soares Prabhu indicates that the infancy narrative is not midrash (14-16), that the ten formula quotations in the Gospel are clearly Matthean redaction (104-6), that Matthean redaction is more interpretative than creative (135), and that the Matthean versions of the biblical citations are a deliberate, *ad hoc*, targumizing translation, with Matthew selecting passages relevant to Christ and "targumizing" these passages in order to make their christological relevance clear (157-61).

[83]In Matthew there are ten of these fulfillment or formula citations (Soares Prabhu, 40-49; Brown, *The Birth of the Messiah*, 98). If one includes Mt. 2:5-6 of the infancy narrative, there are eleven. Soares Prabhu considers this citation "a formula quotation by adoption" (36-40).

of the text but rather the way in which there is resemblance to Jesus as fulfillment. George M. Soares Prabhu speaks of Matthew's targumizing translations that make the christological relevance of the texts plain.[84] Matthew seems to be continuing a practice begun in early Christian preaching and influenced by Christian liturgy. Yet his use of these citations is his own. As we have seen, Matthew frequently uses preexisting narratives or traditions (e.g., pre-Matthean genealogies, pre-Matthean annunciation stories). Yet the final product becomes his own.

Neither the Hebrew text of Isaiah 7:14, for example, nor the Septuagint version imply a virginal conception.[85] The text refers to an imminent birth of a child whose birth will manifest that the Lord is still with God's people and is still their God. The Septuagint translation implies (in contrast to the Hebrew text) that the young woman to give birth would be a virgin but not that there would be a virginal conception. Emmanuel would simply be the firstborn of this virgin. Not the manner of conception but the presence of the Lord to the people lies behind Isaiah 7:14. Thus early Christian reflection on Isaiah 7:14 by itself would not have given rise to the idea of a virginal conception.

Although the Isaian text did not give rise to the notion of a virginal conception, which was pre-Matthean, it was an important text for Matthew. It helped him to articulate Jesus' identity and his divine origin. Matthew has adapted the passage to his purpose. He reads more into the text than had been understood in it previously and sees in it that which has now come to fulfillment in Jesus.

It is better to see chapters one and two of Matthew as a theological prologue to his Gospel than as an historical narrative. This interpretation does not imply that there is no

---

[84]Soares Prabhu, 157-61.

[85]See Brown, *The Birth of the Messiah*, 145-53. Also Sigmund Mowinckel, *He That Cometh, The Messiah Concept in the Old Testament and Later Judaism*, trans. G.W. Anderson (Nashville: Abingdon Press, 1954), 110-22. Also fn. 91 below. The word in the Hebrew text is *'almah* (young girl) and in the Septuagint *parthenos* (virgin), but neither word suggests a virginal conception.

factual history in the infancy narrative but rather that such history is not Matthew's primary intention. The history contained therein is not intentional history. His intention is to identify Jesus as the Messiah, the son of David, the son of Abraham, the Son of God, another Moses. Matthew points out carefully that Jesus fulfills Jewish history and at the same time has a mission to the Gentiles. Therefore all are called and can legitimately respond to Jesus. This is already Matthew's Gospel in miniature. The infancy narrative is a well constructed theological story in which many pre-Matthean elements are given the stamp of Matthew's theology.

The Gospel of Luke. Many scholars maintain that Luke's audience was more or less contemporary with that of Matthew's, the Gospel probably being written in the 70's or 80's. Luke's audience, however, seems to have been primarily Gentile Christian. The Gospel is only one part of Luke's work as the Gospel and the Acts of the Apostles really form one whole. For Luke, the mission to the Gentiles is as determinative of his theology as Matthew's audience was for his. The "revelation to the Gentiles" was part of God's plan from the beginning.[86]

Matthew seems to have begun his Gospel with chapter one, verse one, and composed the Gospel as it has come to us. Both Raymond Brown and Joseph Fitzmyer maintain that chapter three, verse one, was probably the original opening of Luke's Gospel and that the infancy narrative was added later, perhaps even after the Book of Acts was completed.[87] Mathew's and Luke's infancy narratives are distinct. Neither was a source for the other. Brown postulates two stages in the development of Luke's infancy narrative. In the second stage Luke added four canticles and the story about the boy Jesus in the Temple. Luke himself composed the narrative from beginning to end.

---

[86]Brown, *The Birth of the Messiah*, 235-39. For introductory background to Luke, see Fitzmyer, *Luke I-IX*, 3-283.

[87]Brown, *The Birth of the Messiah*, 239-43. Fitzmyer, *Luke I-IX*, 290, 310-11.

Brown maintains that some traditions were pre-Lucan, e.g., the names of John the Baptist's parents, the tendency to compare the conception of Jesus to the conception of previous salvific figures by use of the annunciation pattern, a virginal conception which took place while Mary was betrothed to Joseph but had not yet come to live with him. Luke combined and developed these traditions, incorporated portraits of John the Baptist and Mary, and constructed an annunciation of John's conception to parallel the annunciation of Jesus. Later Luke added four canticles and the story of Jesus in the Temple in a second stage of composition drawing upon Jewish Christian sources for the canticles (the *Magnificat, Benedictus, Gloria,* and *Nunc Dimittis*).[88]

The annunciation of the birth of John the Baptist comes first in Luke's narrative (1:5-25). In verses 5-7 he gives four items of information: the setting was the reign of Herod; the names of John's parents were Zechariah and Elizabeth; the parents were advanced in age and Elizabeth was barren. The Herodian dating, found also in Matthew, is probably historical and pre-Lucan. The names of the parents and their priestly lineage is probably also a pre-Lucan tradition, and more difficult to determine whether historical or not. There is no other confirmation of this elsewhere in the New Testament, yet Luke seems to convey fairly precise knowledge. Fitzmyer favors their reliability as historical. That Elizabeth was barren probably reflects, however, Lucan theology more than history. The motif of barrenness is common in biblical annunciations of birth, and Luke is placing the parents of John within this history. The paral-

---

[88] Brown, *The Birth of the Messiah,* 244-53, 397-99. Fitzmyer is less insistent on a two-stage composition for the infancy narratives. He writes, "The absence of a tight connection between the Magnificat and its context, and the Benedictus and its context might suggest that at least these passages were added at a later date than the rest. Whether other verses should be put in that category must remain questionable." *Luke I-IX,* 311. Fitzmyer does, however, agree with Brown that the infancy narrative in Luke was composed after the Gospel as a whole was written (290, 310-11). The question is whether there were two stages in the composition of just the infancy narrative itself. For the differences and similarities between Matthew's and Luke's infancy narratives, see Fitzmyer, *Luke I-IX,* 306-8. Also Brown, *The Birth of the Messiah,* 33-37.

lelism with Elkanah and Hannah (Samuel's parents) and Abraham and Sarah is present and links Zechariah and Elizabeth to God's acts in Israel.

The appearance of the angel Gabriel links Luke's message to the prophet Daniel (Dan 8:16 ff. and 9:21 ff.). In Daniel 9:20-21 Gabriel appears at a time of liturgical prayer, in 10:12 Gabriel tells the visionary not to fear, and in 10:15 the visionary is struck mute. The theme of the seventy weeks, as interpreted by Gabriel in Daniel 9:24-27, is in the background of the annunciation to Zechariah. The end of the seventy weeks is a time of fullness in Daniel; this time of fulfillment has come.

Luke portrays John as an ascetic, a Nazarite from his infancy (1:15). "Being filled with the Holy Spirit" (1:15) indicates his prophetic vocation, and specifically a vocation like Elijah's (1:17).[89] What Luke says here of John is consonant with what he says of him later in 3:1-20 and 7:18-35. The reason for introducing John is to provide a contrast with Jesus, not only to provide the background for the ministry of Jesus.

Historically, Jesus was baptized by John and may have been temporarily a disciple of John's, later receiving some of John's disciples as his own after the death of John. Because the historical parallels between Jesus and John are strong, John's career became the object of Christian interpretation in which he is represented as the forerunner of Jesus. John and Jesus are brought into harmony but John remains subordinate to Jesus. The miracle of Jesus' birth (virginal conception) is also greater than that of John's birth (barren parents). Further, when Elizabeth and Mary meet, Elizabeth praises Mary.

[89]The Elijah role in Luke is not clear. In the infancy narrative, and perhaps in 7:27, it is associated with John. Yet such association seems lacking elsewhere in the Gospel. Brown suggests (274-75) the possibility of two different Christian views of the Elijah role, one associating it with Jesus and another with John. The Gospel of John, 1:21, does not associate it with the Baptizer. Mark and Matthew do. Perhaps the earlier stage of Luke identified Jesus and Elijah and the later stage attributed the Elijah role to John after stressing Jesus as God's Son. See Fitzmyer, *Luke I-IX*, 318-20 and note on verse 15 on pp. 325-26.

At the annunciation of the birth of Jesus (1:26-38), Luke's christology is not unlike Matthew's. Neither is speaking in terms of an incarnation of a pre-existent Son of God. Luke seems unaware of the kind of christology we have in John's Prologue; for Luke and Matthew, the virginal conception and divine sonship are causally related.[90] The annunciation of John's birth and Jesus' are in many respects parallel. Contrast verses 5 and 26, 11 and 28, 13 and 31, 15 and 32, 18 and 34. The annunciation of Jesus' birth fits the pattern of angelic annunciations of birth. There are several peculiarities in the composition of the annunciation of Jesus' birth narrative, however, especially the virginal conception, the future accomplishments (32-33, 35), the portrait of Mary (34, 38).

Raymond Brown posits for Luke as he does with Matthew a pre-Gospel annunciation tradition upon which both Matthew and Luke drew. Matthew, however, developed an annunciation to Joseph while Luke developed an annunciation to Mary. It would appear that the tradition of a virginal conception was a pre-Gospel tradition as well. Yet the virginal conception in Luke plays a different role where it completes the contrast between Jesus and John and the emphasis on the superiority of Jesus. According to Brown, the entire annunciation including the virginal conception was composed by Luke who gave it the stamp of his theology.[91] The strangeness of Mary's question in verses 34-35, part of the original Lucan composition, enables Luke to tell the reader how Jesus was conceived and thus who he is: Jesus is the Son of God begotten through the creative power of the Holy Spirit. This relationship is even more stressed in Luke than in Matthew (v. 35). In response to Mary's question, Luke has Gabriel explicitly tell us who Jesus is, the

---

[90] Brown, *The Birth of the Messiah*, 290-91. Fitzmyer agrees, *Luke I-IX*, 340.

[91] Brown, *The Birth of the Messiah*, 301-3. Fitzmyer, *Luke I-IX*, 336, makes clear that the Lucan announcement story is not derived from Is. 7:14. Matthew, not Luke, is the one to relate Mary's condition to a Greek form of Is. 7:14. "That Matthean theologoumenon should not be imported from the interpretation of the Lucan account" (Fitzmyer, 336). Also see fn. 85 in this chapter.

Son of God. Luke's christology, as Matthew's, is not an adoption; it is the begetting of God's Son in the womb of Mary through the creative action of the Spirit. The christological moment is the moment of conception.

Fitzmyer points out the two stages in the announcement made to Mary in verses 28-37. The first stage indicates the "extraordinary character of the child" and the second stage indicates the "divine involvement in his origin." The passage shows "that he comes from humanity, just as he comes from God." The two stages and the careful parallelisms between John and Jesus indicate Luke's acceptance of the virginal conception.[92]

Already we have gained insight into Luke's christology—Jesus as Messiah and Son of God, a new creation at the moment of conception, greater than John, with a mission to the Gentiles. Next Mary visits Elizabeth (1:38-56). Without the *Magnificat*, which we will discuss later and which Brown considers part of the second stage of composition, the visitation (vv. 39-45, 56) is not so much a separate section of the narative as much as it is an epilogue to the previous annunciation. As the main characters of the two previous annunciation scenes meet, Mary and Elizabeth, the superiority of Jesus to John is made even more explicit by Elizabeth's praise and John's "leaping in the womb."

As the two annunciation scenes provide a contrast and parallel, so likewise do the next two scenes. Again, setting aside for the moment the *Benedictus* and the *Nunc Dimittis* since they may well represent a second stage in the composition, the major portion of the next section (1:57-80) concerns the naming of John. Without knowing what the angel had said, Elizabeth picks the name John. To everyone's surprise, Zechariah agrees to the name. Immediately his speech returns. This is followed by an account of the birth and naming of Jesus (2:1-21).

Both Brown and Fitzmyer reject the historicity of Luke's census. The only census conducted while Quirinius was

---

[92]Fitzmyer, *Luke I-IX,* 337-39.

legate in Syria affected only Judea, not Galilee, and took place in 6-7 C.E., a good ten years after the death of Herod the Great. Luke was able to use the census, based on a confused memory, to explain Joseph and Mary's presence in Bethlehem, something necessary to explain since Luke (unlike Matthew) assumed that Joseph and Mary lived in Nazareth before Jesus was born.[93]

The core message in this section, and indeed in the whole infancy narrative, is 2:11, "For to you is born this day in the city of David a Savior, who is Christ the Lord." The background for this is Isaiah 9:6—"To us a child is born; to us a son is given." In Isaiah further royal titles follow: Wonderful Counselor, Mighty God, Everlasting Father, Prince of Peace. Luke substitutes three Christian titles: Savior, Christ (Messiah), Lord. These same titles, in different christologies, were applied to Jesus either at his resurrection or his baptism and Luke's christology applies these now to Jesus at his birth. Philippians 3:20 applies all three to Jesus at the Parousia.

Although it may appear that there is duplication in the proclamation made by the angels to the shepherds and the one made by Simeon (2:22-40), both scenes are important. The earlier one to the shepherds, following upon the birth of Jesus, identified Jesus in continuity with the hope of Israel (2:10-11). Simeon's proclamation places Jesus in the context of his role for the Gentiles (vv. 30-32). Brown again suggests that the canticle in verses 29-32 is a later addition and part of the second stage of composition.[94]

Two different customs, which Luke has confused, are the background for Luke's setting in the Temple. First, there is the *presentation* of the firstborn child to the Lord (Ex 13:1

---

[93]Brown, *The Birth of the Messiah*, 412-20, 513-16, 547-55. Also Fitzmyer, *Luke I-IX*, 315, 393-96, 401-6.

[94]Brown, *The Birth of the Messiah*, 446. A difficulty I have with Brown's interpretation of the *Gloria* as being pre-Lucan and added later is that this would relegate to the second stage in the composition of the infancy narrative a very important element in Luke's theology, the revelation to the Gentiles. Fitzmyer offers another reason for viewing the Gloria as part of the first and Lucan stage.

and 13:11 ff.). Second is the *purification* of the mother forty days after the birth (Lev 12:1-6). Verses 22-24 reflect primarily the second custom, but Luke seems to imply that the reason for going to the Temple was the presentation of Jesus (v. 27) which did not require a trip to the Temple. Only the purification of the mother required this. Luke's inaccurate knowledge of the details of Judaism may reflect his background. The need to explain the practice may also reflect his Gentile audience. A biblical background for the story, however, can be found in 1 Samuel. Elkanah and Hannah brought Samuel to the sanctuary at Shiloh (1 Sam 1:24-28) where they encountered the aged priest Eli who blessed them (1 Sam 2:20) in the presence of women ministers (2:22). That story concludes (2:21, 26): "The young child Samuel grew in the presence of the Lord ... Samuel continued to grow both in stature and in favor with the Lord and with men." The conception of John the Baptist had been patterned on that of Samuel; now the conception of Jesus is so patterned. Verse 40 concludes the infancy narrative in its first stage.

Brown maintains that the story of the boy Jesus in the Temple (2:41-52) was not part of the original version of the narrative which ended with verse 40. It was added later and is reflective of "hidden life" stories. These stories may reflect another stage in christological development. Just as the christological moment varies from resurrection to baptism to conception, these "hidden life" stories show that Jesus was God's Son even in his youth, but not, however, that Jesus knew as a boy that he was Son of God. Jesus' changing water into wine at Cana in John's Gospel may be similarly interpreted, that is as a part of an older tradition recorded later by the evangelist—a pre-Johannine hidden life story.[95] Verses 51-52 is Luke's second conclusion. When the story of Jesus in the temple was added, Luke, rather than moving the previous conclusion, added a second conclusion which was comparable.

---

[95] Brown, *The Birth of the Messiah*, 378-95. As Fitzmyer points out, the *Infancy Story of Thomas* reports what Jesus did at ages five (2:1), six (11:1), eight (12:2), and twelve (19:1-5). For Fitzmyer's discussion of the episode of Jesus in the Temple, see *Luke I-IX*, 434-39.

There is little support for the view that the canticles were composed by Mary, Zechariah, or Simeon themselves. Nor is there strong support for Lucan authorship. It appears more probable that they were composed in a non-Lucan circle and were praises of God's salvific acts without reference as such to the events with which Luke associates them. Many scholars have proposed a Jewish setting. The tone of a salvation accomplished, however, leads other scholars, including Brown, to postulate a Jewish Christian setting, and more specifically that of the Jewish Christian Anawim. [96]The *Magnificat* (1:46-55) resembles the psalm type known as a hymn of praise. Brown proposes that it originally referred to a general salvation in Jesus given to Jews who had become Christians. The Psalm begins with the motives for praise (vv. 48-50). The poverty of the Anawim is both spiritual and physical (vv. 51-53). They see themselves as the remnant of Israel, as the suffering servant (vv. 54-55). The *Benedictus* (1:67-79) also reflects this Jewish Christian Anawim mentality. It is a christological hymn. The Lord is blessed because of what God has done (or is about to do) in Jesus as God fulfills the promises to Israel.

In concluding our discussion of these two prologues, and not without risking repetition, the following points can be made:

1. The infancy narratives are not historical narratives in our historiographical sense of the word. They are not primarily motivated to provide us with factual data concerning a sequence of events. This does not mean, however, that they do not contain some history in this sense. Nor does it mean that something which cannot be asserted as historical (historiographically) is then necessarily unhistorical (did not happen). It may be that something is factually true, but that we are not able to determine historiographically or scien-

---

[96]Brown, *The Birth of the Messiah*, 346-55. Brown holds that all four canticles are pre-Lucan and part of the second stage of the composition of the infancy narrative of Luke. Fitzmyer, however, considers only two, the Magnificat and Benedictus, and possibly a third, the Nunc Dimittis, to be pre-Lucan. The Angel's Song or Gloria in 2:13-14 is Lucan for Fitzmyer. See *Luke I-IX*, 358-59. See fn. 94 in this chapter.

tifically whether or not it is. There are: (a) factual history which is historiographically ascertainable and capable of being judged as probably true, (b) material which is capable of being judged historiographically as probably not true, and (c) material which is not capable of being judged historiographically with respect to its factuality or not—this may be true or may not be. That Jesus was born during the reign of Herod the Great and that he was baptized by John are facts (category a). That Joseph and Mary were prompted to go to Bethlehem because of a census is not factually accurate (category b). The names and priestly character of John's family may be factually accurate or may not be; we cannot speak with probability one way or the other (category c above). Something is wrongly described as unhistorical when what is really meant is that it is not historiographically verifiable.

The genealogies, the virginal conception (although very early pre-Gospel tradition), the annunciation stories, birth in Bethlehem, the flight into Egypt, the massacre of the children, the barrenness of Elizabeth, that Jesus and John were relatives, and the story of the boy Jesus in the Temple are not historiographically verifiable (category c). This does not necessarily mean that they are not based on fact or some historical memory. These items vary with respect to their historical probability. Although we cannot determine the historical factuality of these events, they can be nuanced further. We can be historiographically quite sure that Jesus was born during the reign of Herod the Great (category a, practical certainty favoring historicity).

We can also be sure historiographically that there was no census under Quirinius at this time (category b, practical certainty arguing against historicity). But between these two, although we cannot be certain historiographically (category c, incertitude), there may be something to incline one more in one direction or the other. For example, with respect to the masacre under Herod, although it may have happened, I am inclined to see it as not based on fact even granted Herod's evident tyranny and cruelty (category c 1, incertitude but probability argues against historicity). I am inclined to see the flight into Egypt, however, more neutrally. It may have happened, indeed could well have happened, but may not have happened and could well express only Matthew's theology of the relation between Jesus and Moses (category c 2, simple incertitude). The birth in Bethlehem, however, although we cannot be sure about it, I am inclined to see it as more likely true than not (category c 3, incertitude but probability favors historicity). I would argue in favor of the birth in Bethlehem (also Davidic descent and virginal conception of Jesus) as reflecting category c 3.

The birth in Bethlehem is attested by both Matthew and Luke whose infancy narratives are independent of each other. Even though the context for birth at Bethlehem in each infancy narrative differs, this is no argument against the possible historical nucleus of the birth at Bethlehem itself. Certainly it is a tradition that pre-dates both Matthew and Luke. There is no other reasonable way to account for the origins of such a tradition. It was not a strongly attested Jewish opinion that the Messiah would be born in Bethlehem.[97] Matthew brings Micah in as a witness, but Matthew's targumlike translations of biblical texts are more interpretative than creative. If there had been no historical basis for birth at Bethlehem, there would have been insufficient reason for Luke to bring Joseph and Mary there. The different contexts surrounding birth at Bethlehem in Matthew and Luke argue as much in favor of it as against it. Those who reject the historicity of birth at Bethlehem generally opt for birth at Nazareth.[98]

[97] Brown, *The Birth of the Messiah*, 513-14. Many Jews of Jesus' time probably expected the Messiah to be born at Bethlehem, but the evidence for this in Jewish writings is late. Granted the expectation of the Messiah being born at Bethlehem, we cannot prove that it was strong enough to create the story of Jesus' birth at Bethlehem. There were varied messianic expectations, e.g., the hidden messiah, which Christians could have utilized as well. Thus it is difficult to say that the opinion that the Messiah would be born in Bethlehem was so strong that Christians would have invented Jesus' birth at Bethlehem once they proclaimed him to be the Messiah.

[98] Raymond Brown points out that there is no basis suggested which accounts for the origin of the tradition of birth at Bethlehem. Yet he is cautious about affirming birth at Bethlehem. (I read Brown as placing birth at Bethlehem in my category c 2; I prefer to place it in c 3. I read Brown as placing Davidic descent, however, in c 3.)

With respect to the virginal conception, we also encounter difficulties. [99]Both Matthew and Luke seem to have regarded the virginal conception as historical although the primary importance of it was not its historical factuality but its christological significance. There is no other explicit or implicit reference to the virginal conception in the Scriptures outside the infancy narratives. This does not mean no other authors of the New Testament accepted a virginal conception. Most probably the belief in virginal conception pre-dated Matthew and Luke, yet there is no way of knowing how widespread a belief it was. Although there is much evidence which resists its historicity, there is much to support historicity as well. There is no reason to maintain that the Septuagint translation of Isaiah 7:14 was interpreted as necessitating a virginal conception. There is no evidence for the idea of a virginal conception present in Judaism which

He gives two objections to birth at Bethlehem. Neither of these hold up, however. First, he argues that the only two witnesses, Matthew and Luke, do not agree in their presentation. Matthew implies that the parents of Jesus lived in Bethlehem (2:11) and were natives of Judaea (2:22). For Luke, Mary and Joseph are natives of Nazareth and Galilee and come to Bethlehem where they have no house (2:7). These conflicting contexts as to why Jesus was born in Bethlehem do not invite re-assurance. On the other hand, however, they do not argue against birth at Bethlehem either. With different theological contexts and different presuppositions about family background, *both* still affirm birth at Bethlehem. The fact that both do have different presuppositions argues equally in favor of and not against birth at Bethlehem. At least it points in the direction of an old tradition that both retain.

And how does one explain the origins of this tradition? I would suggest by the fact of Jesus' birth there, unless there is a more cogent and rational explanation. Even Brown, however, has shown that its origin is not in the expectation that the Davidic Messiah would necessarily come from David's city of Bethlehem. The most reasonable explanation for the fact that two independent sources affirm a birth in Bethlehem is because Jesus was in fact born there (although I would agree that we cannot be certain on historiographical grounds).

Brown's second argument against birth in Bethlehem as historical fact is the evidence for Nazareth and Galilee being Jesus' hometown or native region. But, again, this is no argument. Nazareth was indeed Jesus' hometown. It had always been held that Jesus grew up there. The fact that he was born in Bethlehem and that his family moved to Nazareth would not incline people to think of Bethlehem as his home or native region. Mark 6:14 indicates Nazareth and Galilee as his home and Mark shows no knowledge of a birth at Bethlehem. True, but Mark was not interested in the infancy and childhood of Jesus. Brown writes, "It is possible that the original idea was that the *patris* of Nazareth and Galilee was where Jesus was born" (515). It is true that this is possible. But it is also purely speculative. The

would have influenced Jewish Christians. Brown concludes, "The scientifically controllable biblical evidence leaves the question of the historicity of the virginal coneption unresolved."[100] Again, this does not mean that it was not therefore historical, but rather that it is not historiographically determinable. One can see different levels of determinable historicity from a scientifically historiographical point of view.

2. A common theological point in the two prologues is the sonship of Jesus from the moment of his conception, a christology for which the virginal conception is important, one that is neither adoptionist nor incarnational.

At first, the resurrection was the time after which Jesus' identity was revealed and with which his divine sonship was associated. (It may well have been that there was an even earlier christology focused simply on the parousia.) A

evidence points toward being *born* in Bethlehem and *growing up* in Nazareth. Brown also writes, "Certainly, in the dialogue of Mark 6:2-3, none of Jesus' neighbors betrays any knowledge that Jesus had an auspicious beginning by being born in the Davidic city of Bethlehem" (515). But why would they? Brown already indicated earlier that we cannot assume a widespread belief within Judaism that the Messiah would be born in Bethlehem. Why then would being born in Bethlehem be so auspicious? The silence about Jesus' birthplace does not indicate an ignorance of it. People simply considered him as from Nazareth because that is where he was from, where he grew up. That was his home, even if his parents had originally come from Judaea.

There is no other way to account adequately for the tradition of birth at Bethlehem. Jerome Murphy-O'Connor's statement makes the most sense:

Mary and Joseph were natives of Bethlehem, and only moved to Nazareth because of the atmosphere of insecurity generated by the Herodian dynasty (Mt. 2); their long residence in Galilee gave Luke the impression that they had always lived there and he had to find a reason which would place them in Bethlehem at the moment of the birth of Jesus (Lk. 2:1-7). The Greek underlying the phrase, 'she laid him in a manger because there was no room for them in the inn' (Lk. 2:7) can also be rendered, 'she laid him in a manger because they had no space in the room.' (*The Holy Land, An Archaeological Guide from Earliest Times to 1700* [Oxford University Press, 1980], 147; or Second Edition, 1986, p. 166.)

[99]Brown, *The Birth of the Messiah*, 517-33. Also see Fitzmyer, *Luke I-IX*, 341-50. Also, Brown, "Gospel Infancy Narrative Research From 1976 to 1986: Part II (Luke)," 662, 675-80.

[100]Brown, *The Birth of the Messiah*, 527. Also see Raymond Brown, *The Virginal Conception and Bodily Resurrection of Jesus* (New York: Paulist Press, 1973), 21-68.

resurrection christology is found in Acts (2:32, 36; 5:32; 13:32-33) and Paul (Rom 1:3-4; Phil 2:8-9). It is through the resurrection that the disciples came to know Jesus more fully and they associated this moment of revelation with his becoming God's Son.

Further reflection, however, led to the expanded awareness that Jesus had already been Messiah and Son during his ministry. The resurrection had revealed who Jesus already was. Jesus was what he was before the disciples knew it. This awareness had already developed by the time the Gospels were written and it is reflected in Mark. For Mark, although the disciples never recognized Jesus (and Jesus never disclosed his full identity to them), Jesus already was Messiah and Son from the time of his baptism (1:11).

Just as there is development between the christologies reflected in Paul and Acts and that of Mark, so there is continuing development after Mark. Eventually the time of Jesus' becoming God's Son is perceived to be even earlier. It is important to distinguish the christological moment of his becoming Messiah and the moment of the recognition of this by others. In a resurrection christology these moments are the same. In Mark they are distinguishable. Jesus became God's Son at the baptism but the disciples do not recognize this Sonship until after the resurrection. In Matthew even the moment of recognition gets moved up to Jesus' lifetime, but the moment of his becoming God's Son gets moved even earlier, to the moment of conception. In the infancy narratives, Jesus was who he was from the moment of his conception, although recognition of this did not take place until during his ministry. At this point we are saying nothing of Jesus' self-recognition but of his recognition by others. (Another example of this may be found in the Prologue of the Fourth Gospel where the moment of becoming Son is pushed back prior to his conception, even prior to creation. He was before anything else came to be. He was with God in the beginning. His pre-existence becomes a part of christological understanding.) The infancy narratives manifest then a christological understanding all their own.

3. Different theological emphases reflect the two different

settings of Matthew's and Luke's Gospels. Matthew's community reflects mixed Jewish Christian and Gentile Christian membership; Luke's reflects a primarily Gentile Christian setting. Thus Jesus has a mission both to Jews and to Gentiles for Matthew. Luke sees Jesus as primarily a light to the Gentiles. For Matthew, Jesus is the Christ, son of David, son of Abraham, Son of God, Emmanuel, and the new Moses. For Luke, Jesus is primarily son of Adam and Son of God.

Although the tradition of virginal conception assists both writers in sustaining a christology from the moment of Jesus' conception, it serves a different function in both Gospels. For Matthew, the virginal conception helps to establish the how of divine sonship and Davidic descent. For Luke it points to the superiority of Jesus over John. In Matthew, Joseph's accepting Jesus draws Jesus into Jewish history, and in Luke Mary plays an important role as Jesus' disciple in establishing continuity between Israel and Christianity. Luke gives much attention to Jesus being greater than John, a motif not present in Matthew. Both, but especially Matthew, construct their prologues to show that Jesus is the fulfillment of the Hebrew Scriptures and history. Matthew shows this genealogically, geographically, and through his use of biblical citations. Luke does so in his linking Jesus, through Gabriel, to the prophecy of Daniel, and through the numbered pattern in Daniel's theology of history.

One Jesus, Many Christologies

Although there is and was but one Jesus of Nazareth, we are more than aware today that there are many interpretations of his life and mission. This was already eminently true in the New Testament period. There never was only one christology, nor even only one valid christology. Diversification accompanied the proclamation as far back as we can go historiographically. This does not mean that the diverse New Testament christologies were all incompatible, or even conflictual. Nor does it mean that they can be harmonized.

They are distinctive and remain so.

We have primarily concerned ourselves with Synoptic materials thus far, although Pauline and Johannine materials have been essential for interpreting the death and resurrection event. If we were to look at all the New Testament material more closely, which is not our purpose here, we would see much diversity. In Galatians Paul speaks of his own gospel for the Gentiles as well as the gospel for the Jews (2:7). The most Jewish of the early Christian writings, Matthew and James, could hardly be acceptable in their entirety to Paul. The two christologies of the two infancy narratives are quite compatible, but both are clearly distinct from that of the prologue to the Fourth Gospel. The theology of the Johannine community has a history and a character all its own.

All of the kerygmata and confessional formulae in the New Testament have at least this much in common: their focus is on Jesus. But that focus can vary from Jesus, a new Adam, for Paul, to Jesus as Son of God for Luke, to Jesus as the pre-existent Son for John. That Jesus was the Christ was the earliest confession of faith among the Jews, that Jesus was Lord was the primary confession of the Pauline churches. But even the central christological titles are quite flexible or wide ranging in meaning.

This New Testament diversity, however, does not imply that there is no common christological core. James D. G. Dunn concludes that there is, although this core never existed as such in the concrete, historical situations of the first-century churches.[101] In the concrete one has only the varying christologies from which one can abstract a common element. The common core or unifying element in the diverse first-century christologies was the affirmation of the

---

[101] James D.G. Dunn, *Unity and Diversity in the New Testament* (Philadelphia: The Westminster Press, 1977). Although one might not accept all of Dunn's conclusions in this earlier work of his, it is a wide ranging treatment of important materials on an important theme. Also see Joseph Fitzmyer, *A Christological Catechism*, 62-67; Jerome H. Neyrey, *Christ Is Community, The Christologies of the New Testament* (Wilmington, Del.: Michael Glazier, 1985).

identity of the man Jesus with the risen Lord,[102] between the exalted Christ and the earthly Jesus, that Jesus and the Christ are one and the same person; namely, that he who was, is—or he who is, was—an understanding of Jesus in two stages. It is Jesus that all the christologies proclaim, but this Jesus lives. All the christologies proclaim the resurrection of Jesus and invite us to believe in him.

The common element, however, is not the core emphasis of each of the christologies; it is simply common to them. The primary emphasis may be Jesus saves (as in Paul) or Jesus will come again (as in Mark). Although christology affirms the resurrection of Jesus, christologies understand the implications of that differently. The earliest christologies seem barely distinguishable from eschatology. Later eschatology is hardly distinguishable from christology. A christology which primarily asserts, "Jesus will come again" is still an eschatology. The resurrection had primarily eschatological implications.

Christianity moved from being an eschatological expectation and sect to a developing understanding of the person of Christ. This shift does not imply decades of theology. Indeed, it may have taken place with the earliest preaching. But it does manifest a shift from a future, eschatological understanding of the Christ event to the present activity of the Risen Lord.

The development of christology involved a shifting of the "christological moment" from an eschatologically oriented resurrection back to Jesus' being anointed with the Spirit on the occasion of his baptism, which is characteristic of Mark's christology, and even further back to the moment of conception, as is the case in the infancy narratives of Matthew and Luke. The concepts of pre-existence and incarnation may reflect the last stage in such a growth of insight.

---

[102]Dunn, *Unity and Diversity in the New Testament,* 29-32, 56-59, 199-205, 226-31, 369.

In the first century there was no one christology nor one normative expression of Christianity. Yet the diverse christological traditions had at least one thing in common: the humanity of a man Jesus who was one and the same person as the Risen Lord; the Jesus whom we knew had been raised from the dead and still lives. The story of Jesus was a story with two major stages to it.

The Synoptic accounts have given us a life of Jesus, not in any historiographical or biographical sense, but more in the sense of a theological interpretation which understands Jesus to be still alive, thus an interpreted life of Jesus in two stages. We learn that there are in fact two stages in the life of this one person, a pre-death-resurrection stage and a post-death-resurrection stage (which is true of us as well). Thus the very early christologies, albeit varied, were two-stage christologies. They affirmed both that there was more to the life of Jesus than his earthly existence and also that the Risen Lord of their present experience was that selfsame Jesus of Nazareth who had been crucified. Jesus is one person whose life had been experienced in two ways which revealed two stages in that life.

Although other events or moments in the life of the earthly Jesus would acquire interpreted significance (the transfiguration, Caesarea Philippi, the baptism, the Temple at the age of twelve, the conception), none of these would acquire greater significance than the resurrection—the moment or period of greatest revelatory character for the disciples as well as the moment of being transformed into a new and eschatological mode of existence for Jesus himself. The two stages are there both from the perspective of the church's experience and understanding as well as from the perspective of the life of Jesus itself. It was an event which happened both to Jesus and to the disciples. Jesus was raised and made his ongoing presence known to them. As they came to understand more fully, they began to see that Jesus was who he was before they knew it or before they truly recognized it. They could now begin to *see* in the earthly life of Jesus what they had at first seen only after the resurrection. Already on earth Jesus had been God's Son. But this sonship had been lived out in an earthly mode as it was now being exercised in a heavenly way. This Jesus was made Son of God not only with his resurrection but had been so while he was still on earth—although we failed to recognize him fully. There are a variety of two-stage christologies (Jesus becoming God's Son at the moment of resurrection, or baptism, or conception), but all affirm that Jesus and the Risen Lord are one and the same Jesus Christ and that this Jesus cannot be understood in terms of one stage only. Before long, however, there would be another distinctive christology in the church which would interpret the life of Jesus in three stages.

In Conclusion

Both historiographically objective scientific knowledge and a personal experiential faith are necessary if we are to understand Jesus of Nazareth, the earthly Jesus, the Jesus of history. The personal experiences in which the first disciples experienced Jesus as raised from the dead, or the personal experiences by which women and men through the centuries have experienced the Risen Lord, are constitutive of our knowledge of who Jesus is. Apart from faith, apart from the personal knowledge or conviction that Jesus was raised from the dead and revealed as having been from God, one would not know Jesus any better than his disciples who had daily contact with him understood. It took another kind of experience, the resurrection and appearance-experiences, before they recognized who he truly was. But faith, which reveals Jesus to us as alive, raised from the dead, and sent by God, cannot be a substitute for the historiographical knowledge of Jesus as a prophet to Israel, a sage, and servant of the Lord. For Jesus was a person on earth in whom heaven and history met. The earliest written accounts we have, the Scriptures, which give us historical data about Jesus, at which we can arrive by historiographical, scientific, and critical methods, are all primarily confessions of faith. Both history and faith, events and interpretations, historiography and theology are woven together in all four of the Gospels in order to convey something of who Jesus is—a response to which requires both kinds of knowledge. Both the nature of the event (both historical and meta-historiographical) and the possibilities for interpretation permitted a diversity of faith expressions, but all focused on the one Jesus. Thus the Gospels, and the written tradition as a whole, give us access both to the Jesus of historiography and the Jesus of faith, both pre-resurrection Jesus material and post-resurrection oral tradition, both the Jesus of history and the faith of the first-century church.

Although the expressions of that faith are diverse, the whole of the New Testament gives witness to the Risen Lord as the selfsame Jesus of Nazareth whom many had known. Jesus is from God. And this Jesus, baptized by John, an eschatologically and socially conscious prophet to Israel, preacher, healer, and teacher, who so authoritatively proclaimed God's presence to the people, unrecognized by many as God's true and faithful servant, was crucified and put to death as a socio-economic, political, and religious threat. God raised up this Jesus and proclaimed him as his own eschatological messenger for Gentiles as well as for Jews. Understanding Jesus requires theology. Historiography by itself alone is insufficient. Only an historically sensitive theology of Jesus can do justice to Jesus who even on earth and most clearly in his resurrection was both "of history" and "from above," both historical and meta-historiographical.

Soon another theology, that of the Johannine community, would contribute its understanding of Jesus as well. It too will see Jesus as both "from heaven" and "of earth," but that is the beginning of the next volume.

Suggested Readings

The following is neither an exhaustive bibliography nor a list of sources cited, but rather what it says—a list of suggested further readings, combining some introductory and some specialized works. Additional bibliography on particular questions can readily be found in the notes, and most of the works cited in the notes as well as the references below contain ample bibliography themselves.

I have subdivided this list of readings into three categories which may at times overlap, but consider the subdivisions still to be of more help than one lengthy alphabetical listing. Within each of the three subdivisions, I list the entries alphabetically, but for a particular author I list them chronologically. At times I have included a few annotations that may be of further help.

I. The Crucifixion, Death, and Servanthood of Jesus

Bammel, Ernst, ed. *The Trial of Jesus.* Studies in Biblical Theology, Second Series, 13. Naperville: Alec R. Allenson, 1970.

Bammel, Ernst and C.F.D. Moule, editors. *Jesus and the Politics of His Day.* Cambridge: Cambridge University Press, 1984.

Blinzler, J. *The Trial of Jesus.* Westminster, Md.: Newman, 1959.

Catchpole, David R. *The Trial of Jesus, A Study in the Gospels and Jewish Historiography from 1770 to the Present Day.* London: E.J. Brill, 1971. A study of Jewish approaches to the death of Jesus.

Clifford, Richard J. *Fair Spoken and Persuading, An Interpretation of Second Isaiah.* New York: Paulist Press, 1984.

Hengel, Martin. *Crucifixion.* Trans. John Bowden. Philadelphia: Fortress Press, 1977.

Hooker, Morna. *Jesus and the Servant, The Influence of the Servant Concept of Deutero-Isaiah in the New Testament.* London: SPCK, 1959.

Kelber, Werner H., ed. *The Passion in Mark.* Philadelphia: Fortress Press, 1976.

Lindblom, John. *The Servant Songs in Deutero-Isaiah.* Lund: C.W.K. Gleerup, 1951.

McKenzie, John L. *Second Isaiah,* Anchor Bible, vol. 20. Garden City, N.Y.: Doubleday and Co., 1968.

Mettinger, Tryggve N.D. *A Farewell to the Servant Songs, A Critical Examination of an Exegetical Axiom.* Trans. Frederick H. Cryer. Scripta Minora: Regiae societatis humaniorum litterarum lundensis. Lund: C.W.K. Gleerup, 1983.

Mowinckel, Sigmund. *He That Cometh, The Messiah Concept in the Old Testament and Later Judaism.* Trans. G.W. Anderson. Nashville: Abingdon Press, 1954. Pp. 187-257.

North, Christopher. *The Suffering Servant in Deutero-Isaiah.* London: Oxford University Press, 1956. Provides an excellent summary of the history of interpretation of the servant songs.

O'Neill, J.C. "Did Jesus Teach That His Death Would Be Vicarious As Well As Typical?" In *Suffering and Martyrdom in the New Testament, Studies Presented to G.M. Styler*, 9-27. Eds., W Horbury and B. McNeil. Cambridge: Cambridge University Press, 1981.

Rivkin, Ellis. *What Crucified Jesus?* Nashville: Abingdon Press, 1984.

Rowley, H.H. "The Servant of the Lord in the Light of Three Decades of Criticism." In *The Servant of the Lord*, 1-60. Oxford: Basil Blackwell, 1965. An excellent, concise and thorough essay.

Senior, Donald. *The Passion of Jesus in the Gospel of Matthew* and *The Passion of Jesus in the Gospel of Mark*. Vols. 1 and 2 in a series of four. Wilmington, Del.: Michael Glazier, 1985 and 1984.

Sherwin-White, A.N. "The Trial of Christ." In *Historicity and Chronology in the New Testament*, 97-116. Theological Collections 6. London: SPCK, 1965.

Sloyan, Gerard S. *Jesus on Trial, The Development of the Passion Narratives and Their Historical and Ecumenical Implications*. Philadelphia: Fortress Press, 1973. A good introduction to the sources, issues, and bibliography.

Sobosan, J. "The Trial of Jesus." *Journal of Ecumenical Studies* 10 (1973): 70-91.

von Rad, Gerhard. *Old Testament Theology*, vol. 2. Trans. D.M.G. Stalker. New York: Harper and Row, 1965. Pp. 238-62.

Wilson, W.R. *The Execution of Jesus*. New York: Charles Scribner's Sons, 1970. A readable study sensitive to complex issues.

Winter, Paul. *On the Trial of Jesus*. Berlin: Walter de Gruyter and Co., 1961. From the perspective of Jewish historiography.

Zimmerli, W. and Joachim Jeremias. *The Servant of God*. Naperville: Alec Allenson, 1957. Covers the servant concept in general, the four Deutero-Isaian songs in particular, as well as the meaning and use of the expression in early Judaism and the New Testament.

II. The Resurrection, Exaltation, and Lordship of Jesus

Benoit, Pierre. *The Passion and Resurrection of Jesus Christ*. Trans. Benet Weatherhead. New York: Herder and Herder, 1970.

Benoit, Pierre, and Roland Murphy, editors. *Immortality and Resurrection*. Concilium, 60. New York: Herder and Herder, 1970.

Brown, Raymond. *The Virginal Conception and Bodily Resurrection of Jesus*. New York: Paulist Press, 1973. A good introduction to the critical issues.

Cavallin, Hans Clemens Caesarius. *Life After Death, Paul's Argument for the Resurrection of the Dead in 1 Cor. 15, Part I, An Enquiry into the Jewish Background*. Lund, Sweden: C.W.K. Gleerup, 1974. An important study of the Jewish background to the doctrine of resurrection. Disproves that there was one Jewish conception of life after death.

Charles, R.H. *Eschatology, the Doctrine of a Future Life in Israel, Judaism, and Christianity*. New York: Schocken Books, (1899/1913) 1963. The work was first published in 1899; there was a second edition in 1913 which has been reprinted. Charles was a noted master of Jewish apocalyptic literature. Given the developments in this field as well as the discoveries in the Judaean desert, this work is now dated in some areas. Yet it still serves as a worthy introduction to Jewish eschatology.

Dahl, Murdoch E. *The Resurrection of the Body, A Study of 1 Corinthians 15*. Studies in Biblical Theology, 36. Naperville, Ill.: Alec Allenson, 1962.

Davies, W.D. *Paul and Rabbinic Judaism.* New York: Harper and Row, 1948.

DeLubac, Henri. *The Religion of Teilhard de Chardin.* Trans. René Hague. New York: Desclée, 1967.

Derrett, J. Duncan M. *The Anastasis: The Resurrection of Jesus as an Historical Event.* Shipston-on-Stour, Warwickshire, England: P. Drinkwater, 1982. See n. 28 of chapter four.

Dunn, James D.G. *Jesus and the Spirit, A Study of the Religious and Charismatic Experience of Jesus and the First Christians as Reflected in the New Testament.* London: SCM Press, 1975. Pages 95-156.

Durrwell, F.X. *The Resurrection.* Trans. Rosemary Sheed. New York: Sheed and Ward, 1960.

Evans, C.F. *Resurrection and the New Testament.* Studies in Bibilical Theology, Second Series, 12. London: SCM Press, 1970.

Fiorenza, Francis Schüssler. *Foundational Theology, Jesus and the Church.* New York: Crossroad, 1984. Pages 1-56.

Fitzmyer, Joseph. "The Semitic Background of the NT *Kyrios*-Title," In *A Wandering Aramean, Collected Aramaic Essays*, 115-42. Missoula, Montana: Scholars Press, 1979.

_____ "The Ascension of Christ and Pentecost." *Theological Studies* 45 (1984): 409-40.

Fuller, Reginald H. *The Formation of the Resurrection Narratives.* New York: The Macmillan Co., 1971. Perhaps the best introduction to a study of the resurrection narratives themselves.

Furnish, Victor Paul. *Two Corinthians.* Anchor Bible 32A. Garden City, New York: Doubleday and Co., 1984.

Galvin, John P. "The Resurrection of Jesus in Contemporary

Catholic Systematics." *Heythrop Journal* 20 (1979): 123-45.

Gillman, John. *Transformation into the Future Life: A Study of 1 Corinthians 15, Its Context and Related Passages.* Doctoral Dissertation. Catholic University of Louvain, 1980.

Gundry, Robert H. *Soma in Biblical Theology, with Emphasis on Pauline Anthropology.* Cambridge: Cambridge University Press, 1976.

Hick, John H. *Death and Eternal Life.* New York: Harper and Row, 1976. An excellent contemporary, interculturally conscious effort to construct a viable eschatology and theology of life after death.

Jewett, Robert. *Paul's Anthropological Terms, A Study of Their Use in Conflict Settings.* Leiden: E.J. Brill, 1971.

Küng, Hans. *Eternal Life?* Trans. Edward Quinn. Garden City, N.Y.: Doubleday and Co., 1984.

Künneth, Walter. *The Theology of the Resurrection.* Trans. James W. Leitch. St. Louis, Missouri: Concordia Pub. House, (1951) 1965.

Lambrecht, J. "Paul's Christological Use of Scripture in 1 Cor 15, 20-28." *New Testament Studies* 28 (1982): 502-27.

Léon-Dufour, Xavier. *Resurrection and the Message of Easter.* Trans. R.N. Wilson. New York: Holt, Rinehart and Winston, 1974.

Marxsen, Willi. *The Resurrection of Jesus of Nazareth.* Trans. Margaret Kohl. Philadelphia: Fortress Press, 1970.

Moltmann, Jürgen. "Resurrection as Hope." *Harvard Theological Review* 61 (1968): 129-47.

Murphy-O'Connor, Jerome. "Recognizing the Risen Lord,

The Historical Genesis of Belief in the Resurrection."
Kansas City, Missouri: NCR Cassettes, 1978.

_____. "Tradition and Redaction in 1 Cor 15:3-7."
Catholic Biblical Quarterly 43 (1981), 582-89.

Nickelsburg, George W.E. *Resurrection, Immortality, and
Eternal Life in Intertestamental Judaism.* Cambridge:
Harvard University Press, 1972.

O'Collins, Gerald. "Is the Resurrection an Historical Event?"
Heythrop Journal 8 (1967), 381-87.

_____. *The Resurrection of Jesus Christ.* Valley
Forge, Penn.: Judson Press, 1973.

_____. *What Are They Saying about the Resurrec-
tion?* New York: Paulist Press, 1978.

Ogden, Schubert. *Christ Without Myth.* New York: Harper
and Row, Pub., 1961.

Pannenberg, Wolfhart. *Jesus—God and Man.* Trans. Lewis
L. Wilkins and Duane A. Priebe. Philadelphia:
Westminster Press, 1968. Pp. 53-114.

_____. "Did Jesus Really Rise from the Dead?" *Dialog*
4 (1965): 128-35.

Perkins, Pheme. *Resurrection, New Testament Witness and
Contemporary Reflection.* Garden City, N.Y.: Doubleday and Co., Inc., 1984. Contains an extended
listing of further works to consult.

Perrin, Norman. *The Resurrection according to Matthew,
Mark, and Luke.* Philadelphia: Fortress Press, 1977.

Robinson, J.A.T. *The Body, A Study in Pauline Theology.*
London: SCM Press, 1963.

Schillebeeckx, Edward. *Jesus, An Experiment in Christology.* Trans. Hubert Hoskins. New York: Crossroad,
1979. Pp. 399-571.

Stendahl, Krister, ed. *Immortality and Resurrection.* New

York: Macmillan Co., 1965. Contains essays by Cadbury, Cullmann, Jaeger, and Wolfson.

Vermes, Geza. *Jesus the Jew, A Historian's Reading of the Gospels*. Philadelphia: Fortress Press, 1973. Pp. 103-28 on the title "Lord." See n. 22 of chapter five.

III. History, Historiography, Faith, and the Formation of the Christian Scriptures

Anderson, Charles C. *The Historical Jesus: A Continuing Quest*. Grand Rapids, Mich.: William B. Eerdmans, 1972.

Aulen, Gustaf. *Jesus in Contemporary Historical Research*. Trans. Ingabill H. Hjelm. Philadelphia: Fortress Press, 1973.

Boring, M. Eugene. *Sayings of the Risen Jesus, Christian Prophecy in the Synoptic Tradition*. Cambridge: Cambridge University Press, 1982.

Brown, Raymond. *The Birth of the Messiah*. Garden City, N.Y.: Doubleday and Co., 1977.

——————. "Gospel Infancy Narrative Research From 1976 to 1986." *Catholic Biblical Quarterly* 48 (1986): 468-83, 660-80.

Bultmann, Rudolf. *Jesus and the Word*. Trans. Louise Pettibone Smith and Erminie Huntress Lantera. New York: Charles Scribner's Sons, (1934) 1958.

——————. "New Testament and Mythology." In *Kerygma and Myth, A Theological Debate*, vol. 1, 1-44. Ed. Hans Werner Bartsch. Trans. Reginald Fuller. New York: Harper and Row, 1953. Bultmann's initial statement on demythologizing.

——————. *History and Eschatology, The Presence of Eternity*. New York: Harper and Row, 1957.

——————. *Jesus Christ and Mythology*. New York:

Charles Scribner's Sons, 1958. A later discussion of demythologizing.

_____. "The Primitive Christian Kerygma and the Historical Jesus." In *The Historical Jesus and the Kerygmatic Christ*, 15-42. Ed. C.E. Braaten and R.A. Harrisville. New York: Abingdon Press, 1964. Bultmann's definitive statement of his views on the relationship between the historical Jesus and the Christ of faith.

Burkitt, F.C. *The Gospel History and Its Transmission* . Third Edition. Edinburgh: T. and T. Clark, 1911.

Calvert, D.G.A. "An Examination of the Criteria for Distinguishing the Authentic Words of Jesus." *New Testament Studies* 18 (1971-72): 209-19.

Collingwood, R.G. *The Idea of History*. Oxford: Oxford University Press, (1946) 1967.

Dunn, James D.G. *Unity and Diversity in the New Testament*. Philadelphia: The Westmister Press, 1977.

Edwards, Richard A. *A Theology of Q: Eschatology, Prophecy, and Wisdom*. Philadelphia: Fortress Press, 1976.

Fitzmyer, Joseph A. "The Biblical Commission's Instruction on the Historical Truth of the Gospels," *Theological Studies* 25 (1964): 386-408. Reprinted in *A Christological Catechism*, 97-140. New York: Paulist Press, 1982.

_____. "The Biblical Commission and Christology," *Theological Studies* 46 (1985): 407-79.

Fuchs, Ernst. "The Quest of the Historical Jesus." In his *Studies of the Historical Jesus*, 11-31. Studies in Biblical Theology, 42. London: SCM Press, (1956) 1964.

Gelwick, Richard. *The Way of Discovery, An Introduction to the Thought of Michael Polanyi*. New York: Oxford University Press, 1977.

Gilson, Etienne. *Reason and Revelation in the Middle Ages.* New York: Charles Scribner's Sons, (1938) 1966.

Harvey, Van A. *The Historian and the Believer, The Morality of Historical Knowledge and Christian Belief.* Philadelphia: The Westminster Press, 1966. An excellent study of the challenges of historical inquiry for Christian faith.

Havener, Ivan. *Q, The Sayings of Jesus.* With a reconstruction of Q by Athanasius Polag. Wilmington, Del.: Michael Glazier, 1987.

Hendrickx, Herman. *The Infancy Narratives.* Revised Edition. London: Geoffrey Chapman, 1984.

Hooke, S.H. *The Resurrection of Christ, as History and Experience.* London: Darton, Longman & Todd, 1967.

Johnson, Elizabeth A. "The Theological Relevance of the Historical Jesus: A Debate and A Thesis." *The Thomist* 48 (1984): 1-43.

Kähler, Martin. *The So-Called Historical Jesus and the Historic Biblical Christ.* Trans. Carl Braaten. Philadelphia: Fortress Press, (1896) 1964.

Käsemann, Ernst. "The Problem of the Historical Jesus." In his *Essays on New Testamemt Themes,* 15-47. SBT 41. London: SCM Press, (1954) 1964.

Kealy, Sean. *Mark's Gospel, A History of Its Interpretation.* New York: Paulist Press, 1982.

Keck, Leander. *A Future for the Historical Jesus.* Nashville: Abingdon Press, 1971.

Kee, Howard Clark. *Community of the New Age: Studies in Mark's Gospel.* New York: Harcourt Brace Jovanovich, Inc., 1977.

Kegley, Charles W., ed. *The Theology of Rudolf Bultmann.* New York: Harper and Row, 1966.

Kelber, Werner H. *The Oral and the Written Gospel.* Philadelphia: Fortress Press, 1983.

Kingsbury, Jack Dean. *The Christology of Mark's Gospel.* Philadelphia: Fortress Press, 1983.

Küng, Hans. *On Being A Christian.* Trans. Edward Quinn. Garden City, N.Y.: Doubleday and Co., 1976. Pages 119-65.

Lonergan, Bernard. *Method in Theology.* New York: Herder and Herder, 1972. Pages 175-234.

Macquarrie, John. *An Existentialist Theology, A Comparison of Heidegger and Bultmann.* New York: Harper and Row, (1955) 1965.

_____. *The Scope of Demythologizing, Bultmann and His Critics.* New York: Harper and Row, (1960) 1966.

Mann, C.S. "The Historicity of the Birth Narratives." In *Historicity and Chronology in the New Testament,* 46-58. Theological Collections 6. London: SPCK, 1965.

Marxsen, Willi. *Mark the Evangelist.* Nashville: Abingdon Press, 1969.

McArthur, Harvey K. "From the Historical Jesus to Christology." *Interpretation* 23 (1969): 190-206.

Moule, C.F.D. *The Origin of Christology.* Cambridge: Cambridge University Press, 1977.

Neill, Stephen. *Jesus Through Many Eyes.* Philadelphia: Fortress Press, 1976.

Neyrey, Jerome H. *Christ Is Community, The Christologies of the New Testament.* Wilmington, Del.: Michael Glazier, 1985.

Niebuhr, Richard R. *Resurrection and Historical Reason, A Study of Theological Method.* New York: Charles Scribner's Sons, 1957.

O'Meara, Thomas F. and Donald M. Weisser, editors. *Rudolf Bultmann in Catholic Thought.* New York: Herder and Herder, 1968.

Perrin, Norman. *Rediscovering the Teaching of Jesus.* New York: Harper and Row, 1967. Excellent for its annotated bibliography, 249-66.

——————. "The Christology of Mark: A Study in Methodology." *Journal of Religion* 51 (1971): 173-87.

Polanyi, Michael. *The Study of Man.* Chicago: University of Chicago Press, 1959.

——————. *Personal Knowledge, Towards a Post-Critical Philosophy.* New York: Harper and Row, 1964.

Ramsey, A.M. *The Resurrection of Christ, An Essay in Biblical Theology.* London: Geoffrey Bles, 1945.

Reimarus, Hermann. *Fragments.* Trans. R.S. Fraser. Ed. C.H. Talbert. Lives of Jesus Series. Philadelphia: Fortress Press, 1970.

The Resurrection and Modern Biblical Thought. Trans. Charles Underhill Quinn. New York: Corpus Books, 1970. A collection of five essays by P. Grelot, M. Carrez, A. George, J. Delorme, and X. Léon-Dufour.

Roberts, T.A. *History and Christian Apologetics.* London: S P C K , 1960.

Robinson, James. *A New Quest of the Historical Jesus.* Trans. W. Montgomery. New York: Macmillan Co. (1906) 1961.

Strauss, David Friedrich. *The Life of Jesus Critically Examined.* Trans. George Eliot. Ed. P.C. Hodgson. Lives of Jesus Series. Philadelphia: Fortress Press (1835) 1972.

Weiss, Johannes. *Jesus' Proclamation of the Kingdom of God.* Trans. and ed. R.H. Hiers and D.L. Holland. Lives of Jesus Series. Philadelphia: Fortress Press (1892) 1971.

Wilder, Amos. *Early Christian Rhetoric, The Language of the Gospel.* Cambridge: Harvard University Press, 1971.

Wright, A.G. "The Literary Genre Midrash." *Catholic Biblical Quarterly* 28 (1966): 105-38, 417-57. Also as *The Literary Genre Midrash.* Staten Island, New York: Alba House, 1967.

Indices

Index of Authors

280   *Index of Authors*

Index of Biblical Citations